ACTION AND IMAGE
Dramatic structure in cinema

Roy Armes

Manchester University Press
Manchester and New York

Distributed exclusively in the USA and Canada by St. Martin's Press

Published by Manchester University Press
Oxford Road, Manchester M13 9PL, UK
and Room 400, 175 Fifth Avenue, New York, NY 10010, USA

Distributed exclusively in the USA and Canada
by St. Martin's Press, Inc., 175 Fifth Avenue, New York,
NY 10010, USA

British Library Cataloguing-in-Publication Data
A catalogue record for this book is available from the British Library

Library of Congress Cataloging-in-Publication Data
Armes, Roy.
  Action and image: dramatic structure in cinema/Roy Armes.
    p. cm.
  Includes bibliographical references.
  ISBN 0-7190-3554-6. -- ISBN 0-7190-3555-4 (pbk.)
    1. Motion pictures--Aesthetics.   2. Motion picture plays--History and
criticism.   3. Motion pictures--Plots, themes, etc.   4. Narration
(Rhetoric)   I. Title.
PN1995.A748   1994
791.43'015--dc20   93-10963
                                                            CIP

ISBN 0 7190 3554 6 *hardback*
     0 7190 3555 4 *paperback*

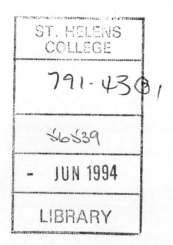

Printed in Great Britain
by Biddles Ltd, Guildford and King's Lynn

12.99

Action and image

Th'

The cinema, even the kind which doesn't seem at the outset to be commercial, is a discourse in which the story, the anecdote, the plot (with its major consequence, *suspense*) are never absent.

ROLAND BARTHES (1985)

Contents

For Annie. Always

Preface

> The film is in one way a single recorded performance, but in another way, and more significantly, it is in itself the dramatic production: the actual shaping of the work.

RAYMOND WILLIAMS (1991)

The aim of this book is to look at a variety of issues and films from a perspective not usually adopted in film theory. As Dudley Andrew has noted, film theory has been dominated by a succession of visual metaphors: first those of the frame, or the window, or some combination of the two, and, more recently – since the coming of psychoanalysis – that of the mirror (1984: 12–13). Film theory has placed particular emphasis on the visual aspects of film – camera placement, point-of-view structures, editing patterns – to which a quite unwarranted power to dupe and deceive is commonly attributed (see Carroll, 1988b, for an impassioned critique of this approach). This concentration on the visual, explored by means of concepts derived largely from literary theory and psychoanalysis, has led to a great many unnecessary confusions. Particularly damaging has been the continuing disregard of the dramatic structure of fictional films. Yet if we look at films as examples of drama and explore them with the concepts currently being developed in the theorisation of drama and theatrical performance, a radically new view of film's generation of meaning and of its relationship to its audience emerges. In particular, the current obsession with narration – with the question of who 'tells' the film – can be seen to be as fallacious in the questions it poses, as it is obscurantist in the terminology it adopts.

This book is not intended as a theoretical polemic, but rather as a guide to practice. Twenty years of involvement in teaching media production courses have convinced me that an understanding of overall structure is one of the key requirements both for the successful shooting of dramatic films or tapes and the scripting of them. The key to such understanding lies in an acknowledgement that film shares with the stage play a dual identity, as drama text and performance text. It is only when one appreciates the role of the writer in shaping the action, prior to the realisation of the film, that one can understand fully the role of the director in making the specific choices, in terms of the organisation of sounds and images, necessary for the production of that action on screen.

Part One of this present volume looks at some of the general implications of an approach which stresses the similarities, as well as the dissimilarities, linking film and stage drama. The traditional theoretical reluctance to link film and theatre is explored briefly in chapter 1, and it is argued that the dramatic structure of a film, as well as its overt content or purely visual organisation, is a prime element in the creation of meaning. The fact that film and theatre share with written forms of narrative the double structure most usually defined as the distinction between plot and story, does not mean that films or plays are narrated. In chapter 2, a variety of models of communication are examined, and the relevance to cinema of modes of analysis devised for the novel – for which the concept of narration is crucial – is questioned. Chapter 3 explores the implications of the key distinction between novels and all forms of drama (including film), namely, that the latter have a dual identity, as both text and performance. chapter 4 looks in greater detail at the comparison between screen and stage drama, arguing that the development of film's narrative style can be best understood in terms of strategies devised to match stage drama's impact in the creation of emotion, despite the lack of that most powerful of all theatrical attributes, the presence of the living actor.

Parts Two and Three apply the insights offered by an approach to film as drama so as to provide detailed analysis of a variety of films. The closely interrelated notions of plot and protagonist are successively explored, firstly, as they have been developed in Hollywood and then in various examples, drawn from the European art film and from non-Western cinema, which adopt other approaches. Each of these chapters includes a detailed discussion of the implications of one key issue related to dramatic structure in terms of a single film, analysed on the basis of a detailed shot breakdown of its whole dramatic structure. This is a somewhat cumbersome procedure, but a necessary one if we are to grasp the way the action of a film is shaped. While it may be possible to base a valid literary analysis of very simple printed stories on a synopsis – as Tzvetan Todorov (1969) attempts to do in his treatment of Boccaccio – it is certainly not possible to use a brief verbal account as the basis for the satisfactory analysis of the audio-visual complexities of a film. Ian Jarvie demonstrates this with regard to *Casablanca*, when he considers in turn eight different paraphrases of the action and is forced to reject them all – his own included – as being fundamentally inadequate as a basis for analysis (1987: 9–10). If a synopsis is unsatisfactory as a means of dealing with as traditional and unambiguous a film as *Casablanca*, it is clearly totally inadequate when one is confronted with as complex a narrative structure as that in *L'année dernière à Marienbad* or *Pierrot le fou*.

It must be admitted that the breakdown of the action into scenes, sequences or acts is to some extent a matter of interpretation. In the case of Hollywood films, the problem is whether to rely on the continuities of time or those of space. The opening of *The Big Sleep*, for example, follows Marlowe as he meets first Carmen Sternwood in the hallway, then General Sternwood in his greenhouse, and subsequently the second daughter, Vivian Rutledge, in her bedroom. Since there is a single general location – the Sternwood mansion – and a continuous time scheme, I have treated it as a single three-part scene. But a good case could be made for an analysis in terms of three separate, if related, scenes. Bresson's *Un condamné à mort s'est échappé* presents somewhat different problems, since the various sequences are clearly marked off by fades to black. But most of these sequences break with the Hollywood conventions in that they contain sharp discontinuities of time and space fused into a single flow by means of the constant use of dissolves. In *L'année dernière à Marienbad* the images unfold in a continuous but constantly shifting stream and in themselves offer no basis for a division into sequences. Here I have used the stages of the voice-over, the verbal persuasion, as a way of establishing the symmetrical patterning which becomes intuitively apparent after a number of viewings of the film (and which can be confirmed by comparison with the other films made in the 1960s and 1970s by the writer-turned-director, Alain Robbe-Grillet).

These distinctions in the method of arriving at a coherent ordering of the shot breakdown might seem to indicate a lack of theoretical rigour, in comparison with the precise taxonomies proposed by such French theorists as Metz (1974a) and Percheron (in Collet *et al.*, 1977). But their advantage is that they underline one of the points I am most keen to establish here, namely, the specificity of each of the films I consider in terms of its own structuring of the interplay of action and image, both in the overall shaping of the dramatic narrative and in the detail of the scene construction. The choice of this format of detailed discussion of a handful of films, rather than a wider-ranging general discussion of the issues using a mass of examples, I owe to the planned five-volume *Fischer Filmgeschichte*, edited by Werner Faulstich and Helmut Korte. The first three volumes of this historical study appeared in 1990–2, and I found its pattern of illustrating issues in film history through the choice of individual films, analysed in great detail, as the basis for discussion particularly illuminating. I have deliberately taken my own examples from classics likely to be widely known and readily available on video. The shot breakdowns given here have been established in a video editing suite, so any timings are given in terms of television length (i.e. at twenty-five rather than twenty-four frames per second).

I am indebted to Heather Stewart, Head of BFI Film and Video Distribution, for access to a copy of *Ceddo*.

Part one   FILM AS DRAMA

To look at the whole 'field of drama' seems to be a useful undertaking, precisely because only by starting from an overview of all the aspects of dramatic performance can we arrive at a clear differentiation of those features that each of the separate media – stage, film and television – can claim as specifically their own, as against the much larger number of aspects they have in common.

MARTIN ESSLIN (1987)

1 Readings and viewings

> Every reception of a work of art is both an *interpretation* and a
> *performance* of it, because in every reception the work takes on a fresh
> perspective for itself.
>
> UMBERTO ECO (1989)

At the most basic level of storytelling there are common factors which
unite all forms of narrative, whether spoken or written, mimed or
acted. The basic structural characteristics of a story – the features
which differentiate it from lived experience and which give it its
universally recognised coherence – are the same everywhere, as are the
activities demanded of the recipient of a story. The fundamental
interplay of story and plot, for example, is as much a feature of
drama as it is of oral or written tales. The fictional feature film has
its place in the spectrum of dramatic media, as a form of enacted
storytelling. Film theory, however, has always questioned, and at
times even denied, that film is a form of drama, and it is a brief look
at the reasons for this which forms our starting point here.

Film theory and ideology

To those unfamiliar with film theory it might seem obvious that,
though there are marked differences between them, film and stage
drama have much in common and might be used to illuminate each
other. But in fact, film theory has always been hostile to the
definition of any link with the stage. For the pioneer theorists of the
silent era, 'theatrical', as V. F. Perkins notes, 'became, and has
remained, the most contemptuous adjective in the theorist's vocabulary':

> The danger was that if the movie were not shown to be an extension of
> visual art, it would be seen as a corruption of drama. It would be exposed
> as 'canned theatre', drama without the power of speech and thus deprived

of its most powerful resource. The cinema would rightly be despised as a
mere dumb-show (1972: 16).

A typical attitude is that of Ernest Lindgren who praises the director
who seeks to impose his creative vision through the use of editing
techniques, adding that 'if he lacks this compulsion, he will fall back
on glib, superficial, and essentially non-filmic methods, such as
relying on his actors and using cinematography simply to record their
performance' (1963: 167).

The early theorists' decision to take fine art as their model resulted,
in Perkins' view, in 'an inability to find the recorded action a place in
the critical scheme or to allow it any artistic status. The object in
front of the camera was simply reality' (1972: 17). Though the model
currently adopted in film theory is now literature – and more
specifically the novel – an examination of much contemporary film
theory shows a similar weakness, attributing to camerawork and
editing those powers to capture and hold our imagination which in
fact belong to the dramatic action.

André Bazin, for all his opposition to many of the tenets of the
pioneer film theorists, shared their doubts about drama. In his article
'In Defence of Mixed Cinema' he describes the theatre as 'a false
friend', which set the cinema 'en route to a dead end, luring it on to
the slippery slope of the merely facile' (1967: 55). Noting that 'it has
always been a temptation to the film maker to film theatre since it is
already spectacle', his conclusion is none the less harsh: 'We all know
what comes of it. And it is with good reason that the term "filmed
theatre" has become a commonplace of critical opprobrium' (1967:
54). Elsewhere, in his two-part article on 'Theatre and Cinema',
Bazin shows a characteristically appreciative response to certain
contemporary films adapted from plays, singling out *The Little
Foxes*, *Henry V* and *Les parents terribles* for particular praise. But
always it is the problem of adaptation that concerns him, not the
notion that film and stage drama could be used to illuminate each
other, since, as parallel examples of spectacle, they have so much in
common.

The particular turning taken by film theory, especially in the pages
of *Screen* in the 1970s, did little to remedy matters. The crucial shift
was perhaps Christian Metz's move from his early phenomenological
approach to film to his attempts to apply linguistic and semiological
concepts, which is reflected in two books translated into English in

the mid-1970s, *Film Language* (1974a) and *Language and Cinema* (1974b). In the latter, Metz explicitly claims that the only principle of pertinence now capable of defining the semiology of film is 'the will to treat films as *texts*, as units of discourse' (1974b: 21). From films as texts, it was but a small step to convert spectators into readers, as in James Monaco's volume, *How to Read a Film* (1977), or John Izod's *Reading the Screen* (1984). Monaco, moreover, posits a totally untheorised and unproven identity between 'films as texts' and 'novels as texts', by arguing that film 'has developed its strongest bond with the novel, not with painting, nor even with drama' (1977: 29). In his defence it has to be admitted that there is in fact a lengthy tradition, on the part of philosophers and literary theorists, of treating films as novels. Avrom Fleishman, for example, quotes both Suzanne Langer ('The structure of a motion picture is not that of drama, and indeed lies closer to narrative than to drama') and Käte Hamburger ('When we see a film we are viewing narrated material, a novel') (1992: 205).

The move to treat films as texts on a par with novels might have provided valuable insights if the full complexities of the author/text/ reader model, as elaborated by Seymour Chatman and others, had been adhered to and developed. Instead, particularly in the pages of *Screen*, the crucial distinctions in the levels of the narrative are blurred. Moreover, in what is clearly an exaggeration of Bertolt Brecht's critique of illusionism, the actual spectator of a film is denied any sort of autonomous response or even social existence. Brecht's own position was quite explicit concerning where what he termed 'bourgeois classical theatre' was located. It was 'happily situated half-way along the road to naturalistic illusionism, at a point where the stage machinery provided enough elements of illusion to improve the representation of some aspects of reality, but not so much as to make the audience feel that it was no longer in a theatre – i.e. stopping short of the point where art comes to mean obliterating all the clues that show art to be involved' (1964: 218). But for film theorists, cinema – and the whole 'bourgeois' tradition of represen- tation, for that matter – was suspect in the allegedly total illusionistic hold it exercised over the spectator.

As a spectator, one is *bound* into place by perspective-system images (Heath, 1976: 99), as the film becomes 'not a static and isolated object but a series of relations with the spectator it imagines, plays and sets as subject in its movement' (Heath, 1976). As subject

one is *fixed* in a point of view from which everything
Cabe, 1974: 16), *held* in a shifting and placing of
ontradiction (Heath, 1976: 99) and defined as no
fect of the structure (the subject is simply the sum of
propositions allocated to it)' (MacCabe, 1976: 25). Eventually all
autonomy is denied, as the very categories themselves are negated:
'Traditional criticism holds text and author/reader separate, with the
author able to inject meaning which is then passed on to the
reader. . . . But the text has no such separate existence. . . . It is
impossible to hold text and reader (or author as first reader) separate'
(MacCabe, 1976: 25). This heady stuff shaped a decade or more of
thinking about film as a narrative medium, and in so doing destroyed
any sense of film as drama, so that one can only echo Avrom
Fleishman, when he notes that 'witnessing shifts from one predomi-
nant and largely unquestioned metaphoric usage to another, we may
suspect that the terms primarily reflect the discourse economy of an
interpretive community, rather than referring to a set of commu-
nicative events in cinema' (1992: 8).

Many of the problems encountered in semiological approaches to
film stem from the extended application of linguistic procedures
developed to deal with purely verbal texts (such as novels) to audio-
visual communication systems, thereby reversing Ferdinand de
Saussure's clear realisation that 'linguistics is only a part of the
general science of semiology' (1974: 16). A striking recent example is
André Gaudreault and François Jost's *Le récit cinématographique*.
This takes as its starting point the moment in *Citizen Kane* when the
voice reciting the text of Thatcher's memoirs – 'I first encountered
Mr Kane in 1871. . .' – fades, and there is a dissolve from the
manuscript page to an enactment of the recorded events. For the
authors, this sequence raises what they see as the key issues of film
narratology:

> The problems of *film narrative* (how does the cinema tell a story?), of
> *narration* (who tells the story? who speaks?), of the *relations between
> words and images* and, more broadly, of audio-visual relations in general
> (how does the transition from written narrative to audio-visual narrative
> work?) and, finally, of the *point of view* on the narrated events (1990:
> 10).

These are questions very relevant to a theorisation of the novel (from which the authors have clearly derived them), but I shall argue that it is by no means self-evident that they are the fundamental issues raised by film narrative.

Ironically, the text by Roland Barthes on which the opening of *Le récit cinématographique* is clearly based (so closely indeed as to constitute almost a parody of it), is 'The Death of the Author'. In one of the most eloquent denials of the validity of seeking an answer to the question, 'Who speaks in a literary text?', Barthes here quotes a passage from Honoré de Balzac's story *Sarrasine*, describing a castrato disguised as a woman and asks who is speaking – the hero? Balzac the individual? Balzac the author? universal wisdom? romantic psychology? – only to conclude: 'We shall never know, for the good reason that writing is the destruction of every voice, of every point of origin' (1977: 142). Barthes was a major influence of 1970s film theorists and this essay first appeared in 1968. In one sense – though drama is never explicitly mentioned – it constitutes an application and extension to the novel of conventional theoretical wisdom about the playwright, namely, that the author of a play is never explicitly present in his own voice, but has to be sought in the polyphony of the play's dialogue (Page, 1992: 1).

Yet even in the 1980s and early 1990s, the search for authors and narrators in film has continued. Seymour Chatman, for example, continues to assert, quite fallaciously, that all narratives 'must be *told* by a human narrator' (1990: 114). But though he struggles to hold this position, he is forced on the very next page to admit that 'human personality is not a sine qua non for narratorhood' (1990: 115), then that the human narrator can be reduced to a potentially non-human 'agency' and the act of narration to the more neutral 'presentation', so that his original proposition has to be weakly reformulated: 'The agent of presentation need not be human to merit the name "narrator"' (1990: 116). Chatman's problems stem from his creation of a hierarchy with 'narrative', in the sense of story*telling*, at its peak. Had he chosen a more neutral term, such as 'story', or defined the activity in potentially non-verbal terms as, say, story *making*, his system could still function, without prompting the need to seek non-existent narrators in mimetic forms such as plays or films. The crucial flaw, however, does not lie in the creation of such mythic entities as non-human narrators, though such a position can, in film theory, slip all too easily into the absurd notion that 'the camera tells the story'. Rather it is the fact that it leads to the neglect of such very real entities as the performers who enact the text of a play or film. In Chatman's increasingly abstract narrative universe, actors, directors, composers and crew members have no place (since they do not qualify as 'narrating agents'), though clearly they have a key role to play in the way a film story is conveyed to an audience.

Even David Bordwell, in his study of *Narration in the Fiction Film*, has to admit to being baffled at discovering that most films 'do not provide anything like such a definable narrator, and there is no reason to expect they will'. His response is to argue that 'on the principle that we ought not to proliferate theoretical entities without need, there is no point in positing communication as the fundamental process of all narration, only to grant that most films 'efface' or 'conceal' this process'. But instead of seeking an alternative model – in, say, the theory of drama – Bordwell proposes instead that we simply turn the conventional literary model of one-way communication between author and reader on its head. In his view, it is better 'to give the narrational process the power to signal under certain circumstances that the spectator should construct a narrator'. This narrator, however, is a distinctly odd entity, since he or she 'does not create the narration, the narration, appealing to historical norms of viewing, creates the narrator' (1985: 62).

Part of the problem stems from the use of the term 'narration' itself, since it is capable of such a wide range of interpretations. For Robert Scholes, for example, 'narration' is a basic and banal feature of all our normal lives, 'a process of enactment or recounting that is a common feature of our cultural experience. We all do some of it every day' (1982: 60). For David Bordwell, on the other hand, the same term is an *artistic* process, 'the activity of selecting, arranging, and rendering story material in order to achieve specific time-bound effects on a perceiver' (1985: xi). Whereas 'enactment' correctly implies, for cinema, an actor and hence a performance behind which lies a text, 'narration' – as the work of André Gaudreault and François Jost shows – leads almost inevitably in the direction of a search for abstract, arguably non-existent, entities who 'narrate' the film. It is far better to follow the example of Avrom Fleishman, who offers an admirable and detailed critique of these positions, and to use the term 'narration' only in its literal sense, applying it strictly to those moments when, in some films, we hear (and perhaps also see) someone telling a story (1992: 9).

Frustrated in its attempt to find authors and narrators, much film theory for two decades or more has come to regard the concealed author as part of some ideological conspiracy. Instead of recognising that an effaced author has been a feature of Western dramatic art since the time of the Greeks, film theorists have used the 'absence' as a reason to dispute the validity of what they designate the 'classic realist text'. Since this term is used so broadly that it embraces virtually all non-self-conscious narrative, we have the paradoxical situation of film theorists, who are evidently film enthusiasts, rejecting as ideologically suspect not only all Hollywood movies, but even work with dissimilar aims, such as the basically neo-realist vein of film making that stretches from *Bicycle Thieves* to *Charulata* and beyond. This is clearly an absurdity. Hollywood movies carry important ideological meanings in their structures as much as in their content, but, as we shall see from the examination of specific films, quite small structural variations – of a kind possible within the commercial organisation of Hollywood or any major production industry – can convey quite other meanings.

It is quite reasonable to assert in general terms that the structures of the conventional Hollywood movie carry the implications that the world is legible, stable, knowable, coherent, continuous, that is, that it constitutes a very different world from that described to us by modern science. A Hollywood movie implies that the world depicted in the cinema can be deciphered directly and unproblematically: all we need to do is watch the screen and we shall understand fully (though not until the end of the movie) the meaning of the events depicted. Yet with comparatively small structural changes to the Hollywood pattern, Michelangelo Antonioni's films of the 1960s can convey a world of human uncertainty and alienation in which human actions do not constitute a neat causal chain.

Many Hollywood movies imply that being in the world means operating in an environment that makes sense, where time is sequential, causality is absolute and life moves towards a goal that can be seen clearly and unequivocally. We are constantly shown that though an event involving chance, coincidence, or irrationality – such as falling in love at first sight – may occur, the consequences following from such an event will be logical and fully understandable. How a particular person responds will determine outcomes, and the circumstances will always ultimately allow a clear decision, after which well-directed human action will suffice. Yet, with only a few modifications to the conventional pattern of the prison escape movie

– by particular forms of sequence structure and camera placement –
Robert Bresson can transform a prison escape celebrating human
ingenuity into a demonstration of the hand of God guiding human
endeavour.

The world of the Hollywood movie is the perfect illustration of
that memorable phrase by Margaret Thatcher (whom one would not
have taken for a film fan) that 'there is no such thing as society'. In
the Hollywood movie there are only individuals who make choices
and act upon them. These choices and actions have consequences
which flow logically from them and, in essence, a human being is a
sum of his or her individual choices and actions. But as many African
films, such as those of Sembene Ousmane, show clearly, it is perfectly
possible to construct dramatic structures which, though still broadly
within the vein of realism, demonstrate the workings of social groups
and forces against which the will of the individual is powerless.

Story making

If we are to make a fresh beginning, one obvious starting point is to
look at the nature of the creation and conveying of stories. Storytelling is a universal feature of human culture, indeed, as Umberto Eco
observes, 'man is a storytelling animal by nature' (1985: 13). All
societies known to anthropologists create and consume stories of
various kinds. All of us know how to tell a story – even if few of us
do it well – and this ability is acquired quite early in childhood.
Similarly we are all able – intuitively at least – to distinguish between
stories and non-stories. Moreover we all have a basic comprehension
of a story when we are confronted with one. As John Peter argues,
'All narratives can be understood. We may protest that they are
illogical, improbable, ridiculous or confusing – but we can understand them' (1987: 3). There is no sign that our consumption of
stories is declining in modern industrial societies. No seaside holiday
is complete without a weighty novel (a Jeffrey Archer perhaps) to
help while away the time as we acquire our suntan. Similarly the
telling of bedtime stories continues to form an essential part of family
bonding between parents and children (*see*, for example, Bettelheim,
1978), and the transmission of stories (particularly dramatic stories)
forms a key part of the marketing and audience-building strategies of
our newest mass medium, television. The tightly-wrought structure

of the Hollywood movie – perhaps the dominant dramatic form of our century, in the West at least – remains virtually unchanged over sixty years or more and clearly constitutes one of the major cultural artifacts of our age.

Though a story is a commonplace notion which we all understand, it is extremely difficult to generalise about how stories are communicated. Stories can be 'told', for example, with words or without them (in ballet or mime, for example), and if words are used, they may be written or spoken, enunciated by just one person or by several. Stories can use words alone, or actions alone, or if a mixture of words and actions is employed, the weight given to each of these two elements may well vary from form to form. Some stories may be improvised on the spur of the moment, while others are recounted or enacted with a solemnity and formal precision that underlines their ritual importance. An added complexity is that the story medium does not in itself define the story as such: the same story may be told as a novel or enacted as a play, as a mime performance or as a ballet, it may be read aloud, recounted or dramatised, it may be seen performed live or recorded on film or tape.

But whatever the story medium, we recognise that the characters and events presented are separate from our immediate, lived present, that they belong to a remembered past perhaps, or an imagined future, or even happen in a purely imaginary world. The actions and events of the story occur in their own coherent time and space, which allows them to be shaped and patterned, so offering us a sense of unity and completion. Stories work with material which we can relate to our own lives, but which is given distance and form, so as to offer the joys of pattern and rhythm in addition to the satisfaction of insight and meaning. Above all, their structures are shaped by what Frank Kermode has termed our need for 'the sense of an ending'. Kermode is surely right to argue that the multiple retarding devices which characterise complex fictions, such as novels, plays or films, are effective only because of our confidence of the end: 'the interest of having our expectations falsified is obviously related to our wish to reach the discovery or recognition by an unexpected and instructive route' (1967: 18).

The diversity of forms of story making is matched by the variety of the terminology used by critics and theorists to discuss them. There is a clear distinction in rhetoric between *mimesis* (the imitation of an action) and *diegesis* (the recounting of an action or the verbal statement of a case), yet the conventional term used in film theory for the enacted fictional world of a film is 'diegesis'. In a similarly misleading fashion, Erich Auerbach gives his admirable study of the representation of reality in written fiction the title *Mimesis*. Basic terms such as 'story', 'plot' and 'narrative' are used in so many ways as to make any definition of their precise usage problematic. For example, Robert Scholes makes a seemingly useful distinction between narrative and story, arguing that when narration is 'sufficiently coherent and developed to detach itself from the flux of cultural interchange, we perceive it as a *narrative*. As a perceived narrative begins to imply a special kind of pointedness or teleology, we recognise that it is a *story*' (1982: 60). But making the same kind of distinction in terms of complexity, though in a more down-to-ɔ arth way, E. M. Forster uses 'story' for narrative and 'plot' for story. Both a story and a plot, he says, can be defined as 'a narrative of events', but "The king died and then the queen died" is a story. "The king died, and then the queen died of grief", is a plot. The time-sequence is preserved, but the sense of causality overshadows it' (1962: 93-4). Clearly terminological difficulties are to be anticipated whenever we deal analytically with narratives of any kind.

Story structure

One useful way of generalising about stories is to look at their structure. Theorists are able to give us a very clear idea of what the internal structure of a story involves. Gerald Prince, for example, offers a precise definition of the constituents of the basic narrative unit, the 'minimal story'. This consists of three linked events, of which the first and third are states, while the second is an action. The three events are linked in time, with the first event preceding the second in time and the second event preceding the third. There is also a causal link: though event one does not cause event two, event two must cause event three. Finally, event three must in some sense be the inverse of event one (1973: 31). This ties in perfectly with our common-sense notion of a story as having a beginning, a middle and an end (though in the telling these elements may not appear in their logical order).

    Some theorists have followed E. M. Forster in querying the need for causality, Shlomith Rimmon-Kenan, for example, arguing that 'temporal succession is sufficient as a *minimal* requirement for a group of events to form a story'. But though he argues this line very forcefully, even he is compelled to admit that 'causality and closure (i.e. a sense of completion) may be the most interesting features of stories, and the features on which their quality as stories is most often judged' (1983: 18). Certainly a *sense* of causality is a key element in our appreciation of any successful story, and Roland Barthes may well be right to argue that 'the mainspring of narrative activity is the very confusion between consecutiveness and consequence, what comes *afterwards* being read in the text as *caused by*' (1977: 94). Moreover, the tradition of Western drama has always afforded a key significance to those moments which involve causality to back up a twist in the plot. Aristotle, for example, maintains that:

> A complex action is one in which the change is accompanied by a discovery or reversal, or both. These should develop out of the very structure of the plot, so that they are the inevitable or probable consequences of what has gone before, for there is a big difference between what happens as a result of something else and what merely happens after it (1965: 45).

But again is it difficult to generalise, since certain modern forms of storytelling are specifically shaped to frustrate our attempts to find causal links within a seemingly random series of events.

What the notion of a story as a patterned structure implies is perhaps most clearly demonstrated if we consider first a very basic form of story: the joke or visual gag. Jerry Palmer argues in his study of visual comedy that any gag consists of two successive strands of development leading out of an initially stable situation. The first development is a preparatory stage of some kind, the second is the 'turning' of this in the moment of comic shock or 'punch-line'. Basically we have the fundamental, three-part narrative pattern: an initial (non-comic) situation, a development or action of some kind (setting the joke in motion) and a moment of surprise reversal (the realisation of the joke). What Palmer makes clear is that this latter is not some random or quirky occurrence, but the rigorous bringing together of two separate lines of logic. The first – the logic of everyday life as we experience it – says that the outcome of this particular development is implausible. The second is a false reasoning of some kind, but one which is imbued with a certain level of plausibility, which we are happy to accept in a storytelling situation. This says that there *is* indeed a logic involved, even if this is the logic of the pun, the double-meaning, the visual ambiguity. What is crucial is the balance between the two logics:

> We know that what we see on the screen is funny in so far as it is simultaneously plausible and implausible, but more implausible than it is plausible, absurd, in short; it is precisely because it is absurd, more implausible than plausible, that we 'don't take it seriously', that we have the emotional security that all will be well immediately after (Palmer, 1987: 56).

Palmer uses as his initial film example a moment from a Laurel and Hardy comedy, *Liberty*. The pair are located on the top of the scaffolding surrounding a half-built skyscraper. Inadvertently they have showered a policeman down below with various objects from their lofty perch (the non-comic beginning of the joke). They decide to descend by the builder's lift at exactly the same moment that the policeman decides to take shelter in the lift shaft, so that the lift crushes the policeman (the middle stage: preparation of the gag – the double action that sets it in motion). But when the lift rises again, a midget in policeman's uniform emerges (the comic reversal of the gag). As Palmer points out, this climax of the gag involves a clash of two logics. Against the (non-humorous) conventional logic of our everyday lives (being crushed by a lift means death) is set an alternative logic (being crushed means being made smaller), which has validity in some situations but obviously not when applied to human beings. Knowing we are in a storytelling (joke-making) context, we can accept the latter logic and respond with laughter to the shock image of the midget.

The logic of the absurd, which Palmer sees as underlying all comedy, has many implications for cinema, but what is most important for an understanding of storytelling in general is the demonstration of how pattern and meaning are linked. Any successful narrative that involves or entertains us is structured to combine logic and surprise. We reach a point which is surprising (either we had not anticipated this development at all or, if we had indeed anticipated it, we did not see how it could possibly be reached). At the same time, when we reach this point, we are able to look back and say that the development does indeed have a logic to it and *could* therefore have been anticipated (had we been ingenious enough). The logic in the way that events unfold needs to satisfy no more than the minimal requirements of a drama, a fiction, a make-believe, but it must be present. The patterned combination of logic and surprise is crucial to the meaning generated by any form of successful storytelling.

Plot and action

Fundamental to an understanding of the role of either the reader or the spectator is a distinction which is characteristic of all forms of narrative, that between the story or action on the one hand, and plot on the other. However close to real life a related or enacted story may be, there is one crucial difference: a story always offers us the promise of meaning. When the tale comes to an end, we shall – potentially – understand everything that has gone before. When we are confronted with a story and wish to enjoy to the full the pleasure it offers, we have no alternative, as readers or viewers, than to search out this meaning. To understand how this occurs we need to explore the conventional distinction – common to drama theory as much as to literary theory – between story and plot. Since the principles are common to all forms of narrative, we can examine the issue in terms of film itself, without in any way limiting the argument.

The basic distinction is very straightforward, but despite this film theorists have tended to cloud the issue. David Bordwell, for example, oddly refuses to translate the terms 'fabula' and 'syuzhet' which he has derived from Russian formalist theory. Bordwell's *fabula*, what most literary theorists term the story, 'embodies the action as a chronological, cause-and-effect chain of events occurring within a given duration and a spatial field'. In his view, the recovery of the story – crucial to an understanding of what the film is about – is one of the principal activities of the spectator: our understanding at the end of the work depends on our ability to put all the parts together properly 'into a single pattern of time, space and causality'. Yet though the story is, in this sense, what the author of a play or film has conveyed to his or her audience, it has no tangible existence as such and 'is never materially present on the screen or soundtrack' (1985: 49). It is not an element of reality (even if it is a 'real-life' story), but a construct, pieced together by the spectator. But equally it is arguably not art, since the whole art of narrative is inseparable from *how* a story is told, that is, the precise ordering of events in a specific telling or enactment. The story may well not have existed explicitly in its 'pure' form even for the original scriptwriter, since for a writer a tale is inseparable from the way of telling it.

By contrast, the plot, in the sense that the term is used here (Bordwell's *syuzhet*), is the precise structuring of a particular story as it literally unfolds on the screen. It is 'not the text in toto. It is a more abstract construct, the patterning of the story as a blow-by-blow recounting of the film would render it' (Bordwell, 1985: 50). The plot contains all the specific devices which generate our interest: the blocks and merely partial views of the action, the ellipses and retardations, the elements of suspense and surprise, the clues and the red herrings, and so on. The plot – the ultimate outcome of the efforts of writer, director, actors and crew to enact the story in the most effective way possible – is what immediately confronts us when we begin to analyse a film as drama. It is what principally concerns us when we investigate dramatic structure in cinema, since it is in the shaping of the plot that the artistry of the enacted storytelling is most apparent. It is the plot – the unique, once-and-for-all enactment of events – that constitutes one of the immediate sources of aesthetic pleasure in a film.

Bordwell's analysis is always insightful, despite his predilection for obscurantist terminology. Within his self-imposed limits, his work is admirably precise, rigorous and detailed. But just as his inability to break free of literary theory (rooted in the analysis of prose fiction) left him floundering when confronted with the question, 'Who narrates?', so too the literary models he chooses preclude him from capturing fully the excitement which watching drama provides. The 'fabula', in his technical sense, is paradoxically that least interesting of entities: a story told from the point-of-view of the ideally placed spectator from whom nothing is concealed and who already knows both the beginning and the end. Bordwell offers no hint as to why the spectator should undertake the arduous task of constructing such an entity, and significantly the examples he chooses in this part of his study – a thriller, two detective stories and a melodrama – are the sorts of films which do not raise the question of the spectator's motivation.

All drama, in which a story is enacted, not told, has indeed a double identity, in terms of plot (the outer arrangement of events) and action (the inner sense of coherent time, space and meaning). But because a drama offers its action without authorial explanation or comment, the action is always rich (ambiguous even) in meaning and implication. Umberto Eco captures this well in a discussion of that most Aristotelian of tragedies, *Oedipus Rex*:

> Oedipus investigates the causes of the plague and, upon discovering that he has murdered his father and married his mother, blinds himself: this is the plot of *Oedipus Rex*. But the tragic action lies at a yet deeper level, where the complex relationship between deed and guilt unfolds according to immutable laws, steeped in existential angst. The plot is absolutely univocal, but the action is fraught with ambiguity, open to a thousand possible interpretations (1989: 114).

This is the case too in all classic cinema – such as the Hollywood movie – which concerns itself with the construction of a strongly plotted storyline: the action is potentially richer in meaning and ambiguity than the plot, exquisitely crafted and aesthetically satisfying though this latter may be. But before we explore this seeming paradox, we need to look more closely at the distinction between narrated and enacted stories which has been touched on above.

2 Showing and telling

People have tried for centuries to use drama to change people's lives, to influence, to comment, to express themselves. It doesn't work. It might be nice if it worked, but it doesn't. The only thing dramatic form is good for is telling a story.

DAVID MAMET (1992)

In addition to the universal identity of all storytelling, or story making, at the level of the distinction between action or story and plot, there is also the fact – underlined by most literary and dramatic theory – that the communication of virtually any story involves some combination of showing and telling. There are very wide variations in the balance of these two elements and, in view of the confusions wrought by film theory, a clear definition of film's particular identity within the spectrum of narrative communication is needed. Here a whole range of aspects of the communication process are examined: the medium and its physical form, the role of the reader or spectator, the status of the author, the existence or absence of a narrator, and the interaction of the work with the reader or spectator. The ensuing differences will allow us to distinguish clearly between the four basic and separate forms of storytelling considered here: prose fiction, as exemplified by the novel; oral literature, frequent in traditional societies and still finding some echo in modern literate societies; the situation that arose when silent cinema first became a narrative form; and contemporary drama which, at this level of generality, can embrace both stage and screen drama.

The novel

The novel is the prime example of indirectly narrated fiction. The author does not meet his or her readers, but communicates with them solely through words on a page. In prose fiction the narrative exists in a single form, as a written text. This text must be fixed, tangible and (ultimately) marketable, but though the novel as a literary genre is very much a product of the era of printing, the actual physical form of the book is irrelevant to our enjoyment. It may be printed and published as an expensive hardback or as a cheap paperback, it may be produced on a word-processor, typed or handwritten, it may be pirated on a photocopier; but if the words are the same (and the punctuation etc. is adequately represented), the novel remains essentially unchanged. In other words, the novel has an abstract identity as a written text, free from the constraints of its material circumstances. If we wish to analyse such a text, precisely the same methods can be applied whatever physical form it takes. The novel is a product of the age of mass reproduction, but has a complete existence as soon as a single version of the words is complete in any written form whatsoever, so that any subsequent replication or transmission of copies is, by definition, secondary.

What is also crucial to the form of the novel is the reader's freedom to control the story flow. He or she has the possibility of random access, the liberty to choose his or her own time and place for reading, to read in instalments, returning to the text at leisure, with lengthy pauses in between, or indeed to read the text out of order (looking at the final pages to anticipate the ending, for example). The commercialisation of prose fiction is based on the purchase of a copy of the text in book or magazine form. Purchase gives us complete rights of ownership (subject to copyright limitations): we can treat the book as we wish and, when we have finished with it, we can resell it, or give it to a friend, or simply throw it away.

In order to hold the reader's attention, the author of a novel must use the words of the text both to advance the story by giving significant actions and events and, at the same time, to establish a coherent and credible world in the minds of readers through the description of people, places and objects. Words are well suited to advance the story through the narration of action and event, but efforts to achieve this are always at odds with the equally pressing need to offer description, which will always slow or even stop the action. Everett Knight bases his definition of the classical novel on a distinction between showing and telling, representation and narration: 'We have seen that the novel must be about the real and that it must say something of consequence. To put this more succinctly: *the novel must simultaneously show and tell*. But how? The more accurately the real is shown, the less sense it will make, the less one can "tell"' (1969: 61).

When we read a novel, we usually get a sense of the author's presence, through the way that words are used and events are shaped. It can be argued that we are personally conducted through the novel, with the author as our guide (Willis and D'Arienzo, 1981: 183). But demands are still made upon us, since our role as readers is essentially to bring our powers of visualisation to the action. Indeed Robert Scholes notes that 'readers who are feeble at such visualising often fail to realise important aspects of fictional texts' (1982: 61). One test of the skill of an author is his or her ability to enable the reader to create a coherent fictional world out of the words offered on the page. To quote Scholes once more, 'literature, beginning in language, must exert extraordinary pains to achieve some impression of the real. For this reason written fiction has almost always used some notion of realism or verisimilitude as an evaluative standard' (1982: 72). This is a sentiment echoed by the novelist-turned-film maker Alain Robbe-Grillet, in an essay entitled 'From Realism to Reality':

> Every writer thinks he is a realist. No writer ever calls himself abstract, an illusionist, a visionary, a fantast, a falsifier. . . . Realism is not a clearly defined theory by reference to which we can classify some writers as being opposed to others; on the contrary, it is the flag flown by the immense majority – if not the sum total – of present-day novelists. . . . Realism is the ideology each one throws in his neighbours's face, the quality each thinks he is the only one to possess (1965: 153).

Clearly the author of a novel may put into any given work ideas and opinions which he or she does not personally hold. Similarly other works by the same author may reflect quite different belief systems. But in any particular novel (or other work of prose fiction) there will be a definable and unified narrating presence, what literary theory calls the 'implied author'. Seymour Chatman offers an excellent definition:

> He is 'implied', that is, reconstructed by the reader from the narrative. He is not the narrator, but rather the principle that invented the narrator, along with everything else in the narrative, that stacked the cards in this particular way, had these things happen to these characters, in these words or images (1978: 148).

As Chatman's definition makes clear, the 'implied author' of a novel is a product of what binds the text together, gives it its coherence. In the words of another theorist, Shlomith Rimmon-Kenan, the 'implied author' is 'a stable entity, ideally consistent with itself within the work' (Rimmon-Kenan, 1983: 87).

Any analysis of a written fictional prose text, such as a novel, needs to take into account the careful balancing of levels of discourse and the precise delineation of the various narrating voices – separating out real author, implied author and narrator. To these categories correspond the various classes of reception or readership which literary theory has defined: real reader, implied reader and narratee. The correspondence of the two sets of roles is crucial, since fiction, as conceived by most contemporary literary theory, is a system whereby a real author communicates, via a complexly structured text, to a real reader. Though this basic structure needs to be elaborated to cover the full complexities of narration in prose fiction, it fits the conventional sociological model of one-way communication. As in Seymour Chatman's graphic version, the links take the form of arrows pointing in a single direction, with no possibility of significant feedback:

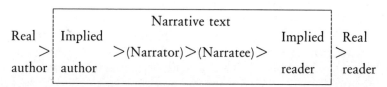

Source: Chatman, 1978: 151

I have begun this chapter with a consideration of the novel, because for Chatman, and indeed for most theorists of narratology, the structures and procedures of the novel form the starting point for an investigation and definition of narrative itself, and hence the key to an understanding of narrative structure in film. Yet, when we think of the role which stories play in our lives – as a way of making sense of our own everyday experiences and communicating these to others (everyday vernacular tales), as a means of sharing experience and emotion with our children (bedtime stories), as a method of understanding complex physical or mental phenomena (case studies in medicine and psychiatry), or as a form of domestic relaxation, which can also be used as a basis for discussion of personal, family issues (soap operas on television) – the novel can be seen as a very particular mode, extremely literary, not only verbal but exclusively written, abstract and normally consumed in solitude, with none of the personal interaction which characterises most story situations. The novel is less a starting point for insight into the nature of other narrative forms, than an artistically successful but highly individual end-product. For a fundamental understanding of the basics of narrative we need to follow such theorists as Vladimir Propp, Tzvetan Todorov, Claude Brémond, Gerald Prince and A. J. Greimas and return to oral storytelling (Maclean, 1988: 1).

Oral literature

In even the most basic form of direct storytelling – oral narration to an audience – the system of communication is very different from that which we find in the novel. To begin with, the story is personally narrated, even perhaps partially enacted. While a key part of the storytelling process is contained in the spoken words, other elements too are involved: gesture, costume, diction, tone, intonation, etc. Moreover, the moment of telling is crucial: the tale exists only there and then, when it is told. Each enactment is both unique and indispensable: the story has none of the abstract existence possessed by a written text, which can be copied (published in a new edition, for example) without being essentially changed. In the case of oral literature, a new telling on another occasion – with another speaker or another audience – results in an essentially different storytelling situation. As Ruth Finnegan has pointed out, the first and most basic characteristic of oral literature is not the verbal text, which can be written down, published and consumed as fiction (as in published anthologies collecting traditional African tales). The key element is the actual presentation, 'dependent on a performer who formulates it in words on a specific occasion – there is no other way in which it can be realised as a literary product' (1976: 2). As early as 1927 – before the general availability of the sound film – one researcher into African oral narratives noted that simply copying down the words was not enough, 'to reproduce such stories with any measure of success, a gramophone record together with a cinematograph picture would be necessary. The story suffers from being put into cold print' (quoted in Finnegan, 1976: 383).

The key distinction lies in the fact that what, in literate societies, 'must be written, explicitly or implicitly, into the text' can, in orally delivered forms, 'be conveyed by more visible means – by the speaker's gestures, expression, and mimicry' (Finnegan, 1976: 5). As a result, the verbal – the sole resource of prose fiction – becomes just one element in the overall performance, alongside gesture, music and dance (in much the same way that the written text of a play or film script is transformed when it is realised in performance). Finnegan gives a vivid picture of oral storytelling in the traditional African context:

> A particular atmosphere – whether of dignity for a king's official poet, light-hearted enjoyment for an evening storyteller, grief for a woman dirge singer – can be conveyed not only by a verbal evocation of mood, but also by the dress accoutrements, or observed bearing of the performer. This visual aspect is sometimes taken even further than gesture and dramatic bodily movement and is expressed in the form of dance, often joined by members of the audience (or chorus) (1976: 5).

Participation in an oral storytelling event does not give members of the audience the freedom and control over the story enjoyed by purchasers of a novel. Each performance is unique, the order and elements of the story are fixed (often derived from tradition and handed down from generation to generation) and repeatable (though with variations for each new presentation to each new audience). Oral storytelling is a powerful form, since the teller is able to back up the words with at least partial enactment through the mimicking of the voices and gestures of the characters. Yet the listener has a key part to play too, since participation in the moment of telling implies being able to influence the teller, who combines the roles of author and narrator. There is direct address by a real storyteller to a real listener, and a direct interaction – mostly from teller to listener, but with a real possibility of interplay and feedback from the listener to the teller, who is likely to respond in some immediate way to the reactions of the audience.

Though we tend to associate oral literature exclusively with preliterate cultures, something of the same effect may be achieved in literate societies through public renderings of works not originally conceived for the stage. Martin Esslin chooses as examples Dickens giving readings from his novels, and solo performances by star actors based on a writer's diaries and/or letters (1987: 24–5). These are written prose texts, but they become drama as soon as they are enacted on the stage. The key transformation which occurs when this happens is that the past of the written prose narrative (the recounting of events which have happened – in reality or imagination – and can therefore now be recorded in writing) becomes the present of an enacted performance (the unfolding of events seemingly as they occur, in their present-tense form). Esslin, along with most theorists of drama, regards this time-shift as one of the key distinctions between prose fiction and drama as a whole (1987: 25).

Similarities can be established linking some forms of oral literature to the structures of popular cinema. If we follow Bruno Bettelheim's admonition that fairy-tales are stories that should be told, not read, to children (1978: 150), we can find a number of fascinating parallels to film in both the structure and the reception of the fairy story. Bettelheim sees a crucial distinction between a fable, which explicitly states a moral truth, and a fairy-tale, which, like a film or any other form of drama, 'leaves all decisions up to us, including whether we wish to make any at all' (1978: 43). A fairy-tale, like a film, is often compared to a dream, but though it 'may contain many dreamlike features, its great advantage over a dream is that the fairy-tale has a consistent structure with a definite beginning and a plot that moves toward a satisfying solution which is reached at the end' (1978: 57). The trajectory of the fairy-tale, from 'its mundane and simple beginning', through fantastic events and detours, to a final return to reality 'in a most reassuring manner' (1978: 63), has clear parallels with popular cinema. So too has its meaning, in so far as a fairy-tale leaves no doubt that 'the pain must be endured and the risky chances taken, since one must achieve one's personal identity; and, despite all anxieties, there is no question about the happy ending' (1978: 79). Fairy-tales, like films, 'describe inner states of the mind by means of images and actions' (1978: 155), giving an active role to the listener which parallels the active role of the film spectator.

In the case of oral storytelling in general we have a model of communication which is in many ways more complex than is the case with the novel, since it contains the physical presence of the storyteller, multi-channel communication, direct address to an audience and the possibility of significant feedback. In the case of oral literature, therefore, one might set out the situation schematically thus:

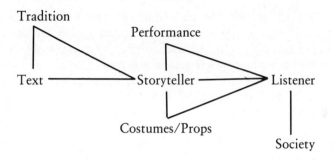

If we look at the novel from the standpoint of earlier forms of oral literature, it is apparent, as Marie Maclean observes, that writing enabled narrative 'to emancipate itself from the limitations of spatial presentation and from the time limitations oral performance placed on absorption' (1988: 9). One way forward involved the creation of a form of purely written (and printed) prose fiction – the novel – in which the key features of the oral storytelling event find themselves reflected in the complex internalised system of implied author/ narrator and implied reader/narratee: 'The printed text is a representation of the act of telling itself, and so the actual narration becomes part of the fictional world' (1988: 10). This is, however, only one of the possibilities for which oral storytelling opened the way. The second was dramatic enactment, in which the notion of a written text is not lost, but is supplemented by a further level, that of performance, and in which the single voice of the author/narrator becomes lost within the multiple voices of the dialogue. The ways in which film, a medium with unforeseen narrative potential, was first presented to audiences allows us to see clearly what is involved in this transition.

Historical interlude: the beginnings of cinema

Both the public presentation of an oral tale and the stage enactment of the presence of the author as character are clearly hybrid forms, as is the method of presentation used when film was first introduced as a storytelling medium in the late 1890s. The situation at the birth of cinema is a fascinating one, in that it shows both an intuitive awareness of the commercial attractions of using film as a story medium and a profound uncertainty about the extent to which film could be made to fill this role. Film, as Christian Metz has aptly observed, had not been invented to tell stories, and in the late 1890s critics, journalists and pioneer cinematographers 'disagreed considerably among themselves as to the *social function* that they attributed to, or predicted for, the new machine'. Most felt that it likely that film would fill the same sort of functions as still photography – identification and analysis on the one hand, and the preservation of memories on the other. That, 'above these possibilities, the cinema could evolve into a machine for telling stories had never been really considered' (Metz, 1974a: 93). As a mere extension of still photography, film was seen as able to do no more than *illustrate*, through its silent images, a story which would need to be told in words. Two live elements were deemed necessary for a successful presentation: a presenter who would tell the story verbally as the images unfolded and performers whose musical accompaniment would 'flesh out' the images. This mode of presentation vanished fairly quickly in the West, where increasing emphasis was laid on internalising the storytelling within the images, but it persisted elsewhere, in Japan (Anderson and Richie, 1959: 23–6) and in India (Baskaran, 1981: 81), for example.

While this mode of presentation clearly draws on a tradition of public storytelling, it presents some significant divergences from the oral literature model which stem from the involvement of a machine, the film projector, in the performance. Because the images unfolded at a more or less constant speed (small variations deriving from the fact that film projectors were hand-cranked at this time), the freedom of the presenter to change the pace and rhythm of his storytelling in response to audience reaction was limited. Moreover, since the cinema was from the start a commercial entertainment, for which the audience paid, there was a real need for the performance to be repeatable, so that each show on a given day or in a given week resembled its predecessor precisely (until the films themselves were changed). The story was initially told in words, but at least in the West, with its traditions of theatrical illusionism, the focus soon switched to the images, which, gradually if unevenly, took on a power and flexibility which no doubt surprised the pioneers. The images ceased to be mere props – an adjunct to the presentation – and developed a life of their own, transforming the audience from listeners to spectators avid for fresh images.

Given a different theatrical history in Europe, however, this shift might never have happened, as is shown by the situation during the silent era in Japan, where the presenter (or *benshi*) achieved great popularity. In Japan, as Noël Burch points out, presentations 'weren't really *film* performances at all, since often the *benshi* was felt to be the *centre of interest*'. As a result:

> . . . the Japanese silent film was the most silent of all, if by silence we mean, as most people do when they talk about that film era, the absence of speech. Speech was indeed explicitly absent, since it was *removed*, put to one side; the voice was there, but detached from the images themselves, images in which the actors were thereby all the more mute and were confined, moreover, in many instances, to remarkably static renderings of the scenes unfolding through the *voice*, much like the dolls or, to a lesser extent, the kabuki actors of the Edo stage (1979: 78).

During the brief period in which this mode of presentation was in vogue in the West, the members of the audience found themselves in a complex and to some extent divided situation: listening to the words telling the story, but increasingly watching – and making their own sense of – the images on the screen. The music added yet another dimension, helping to shape the audience response, but from its own location within the film theatre and deriving directly neither from the presenter nor from the images. The three channels of communication – words, images, music – might complement each other, but they still remained separate, each addressing the spectator by its own means. To fuse the performance into a single entity there were, however, elements shared with traditional oral storytelling performances: direct address to the spectator's ear and eye, together with the possibility of some interaction with the presenter (though not, of course, with the images as they unfolded on the screen). The moment of presentation was again a crucial unifying factor, but now this had become the uniform performance time of a commercial entertainment. A graphic representation of this situation is therefore:

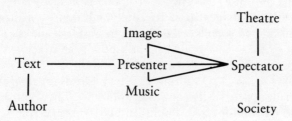

In the West, the development of silent cinema can be seen as an erratic and fumbling progress towards a form of enacted story which, aided by verbal intertitles, would allow the audience's attention to be captured and held for an hour or two. The narrative function performed by the live presenter was internalised within the organisation of the action captured by the images, and eventually, with the coming of synchronous sound at the end of the 1920s, an enormously powerful audio-visual narrative form evolved. Yet interestingly the cinema never fully discarded the two elements seen as necessary adjuncts to the very first film presentations: the spoken words of a narrator and a musical accompaniment. Though the use of a spoken commentary and a musical accompaniment is just as feasible in the theatre, stage drama makes comparatively little use of such resources. By contrast, the inclusion of extra-dramatic sound – that is, sound which has no visible origin on-screen and which cannot be heard by the characters – continues to be a marked feature of the fictional feature film. Despite the power which many theorists attribute to the screen image and the devices of film editing, most film makers continue to find the need to employ a musical score to shape the audience's emotional response, and a surprising number make at least some limited use of a narrating voice to guide the viewer's comprehension of the action.

Stage and screen drama

Though there are important differences between stage and screen drama (w ich will be considered later), the two forms share enough in common for them to be treated together here in contrast to the novel. Dramas of any kind are representations of an action and derive their name, according to Aristotle, 'from their representing men doing things' (1965: 34). The essence of drama is in many ways its set of interlocking dual identities. Its total multidimensionality involves both images and sounds – an address to both eye and ear – in direct contrast to the single strand of words on a page which is the novel's sole resource. There is also an ontological difference, since virtually any drama exists in two forms, as a text (words on a page) and as a performance (enacted live on stage, transmitted live by television, or recorded on film or tape). Published play texts and film scripts – as written, verbal structures – can share many of the characteristics of novels and short stories. But plays and scripts are not complete in themselves: the ways in which they are shaped and structured imply performance, enactment. As Raymond Williams has observed, the distinguishing characteristic of a dramatist is that he is not writing a story which may be adapted for performance: 'he is writing a literary work in such a manner that it can be directly performed' (1991: 159).

Drama's time scheme is complex and very different from that of a novel. A drama unfolds in a real-time duration, which matches the real time of the audience attending the performance and which is repeatable, whether at the next evening's performance on stage or when the film is screened at the second showing of the day. This time-span of performance constrains us, as spectators, since we acquire no rights of ownership when we pay to attend a play or film. Instead, we buy the 'right to view' on one single occasion. If we walk out in the middle, we cannot expect to be allowed to see the rest of the performance without paying a second entrance fee. But at the same time any drama has its own internal time scheme which relates to this real-life time span, but is not identical with it, even in the case of a work like the film *High Noon*, in which the time of the action ostensibly matches the duration of the screening.

The demands made by drama on its spectators are in many ways the very opposite of those made by a novel on its readers. Richard Dyer makes an interesting comparison between the performance of Montgomery Clift in *The Heiress* and the depiction of the character he plays, Maurice, in the Henry James novel on which the film was based, *Washington Square*:

> In the latter, we are clearly told from the word go that Maurice is deceitful. In the film, however, we are in the same position as Catherine (Olivia de Havilland) in this regard; we have to work out from our observation of him whether he is sincere or not. . . . In these ways, film and especially performance in film fabricates a relationship to, rather than a telling about, the characters (1979: 152).

Because of its multidimensionality, dramatic action does not need to strive for the realism and verisimilitude which are the common concerns of novelists. The represented scene on stage or screen is full of richness of detail at any given moment. To take a very basic example, when we read a play, we are aware only of the speaker's words. As Benjamin Bennett appositely observes, in scene two of

Hamlet, 'for the reader of the text . . . Hamlet is in effect simply *not* there until, in due course, his name and the first words he speaks are arrived at' (1990: 66). When the drama is enacted on stage, however, we are all the time aware not only of the words and intonations of the speaker, but equally of the responses of the person to whom the words are addressed, though the latter may not yet have spoken.

Moreover the detail of any particular scene is constantly shifting throughout the period during which the action unfolds. Far from being able to be passively consumed, drama on stage or screen demands an active participation from its audience (a point to which I shall return). Indeed the situation is particularly acute in cinema, because, as Robert Scholes has noted, the scope and precision of its photographic images and recorded sounds make it 'closest to actuality, to undifferentiated experience'. Crucially the film image does not *name* what it shows, and hence lacks the element of distance and generalisation which the word offers in a novel. As a result, the film spectator, instead of seeking to provide the visualisation required of the reader of a novel, must instead supply 'a more categorical and abstract narrativity', which will allow the film to achieve 'some level of reflection, of conceptualisation' (1982: 67).

As cinema's narrative potential has been developed, it has attracted the attention of novelists (just as the stage proved such a magnet for novelists in the nineteenth century). Those who have worked most successfully in the two media have been those who have understood the fundamental differences between novel and film, and sought not realism but multidimensionality. Alain Robbe-Grillet, who from the early 1960s onwards combined work as a novelist with film making, has defined the particular attraction of cinema for novelists of his generation:

> It is not the camera's objectivity that fascinates them, but its subjective and imaginative possibilities. They don't think of cinema as a means of expression, but of research, and the thing that interests them most is, quite naturally, the thing they found the least possible to render in their writing: not so much the image, that is to say, as the sound track – voices, noises, different effects, different kinds of music – and above all, the possibility of playing on two senses at the same time, the eye and the ear (1965: 146).

The public presentation of an oral tale, the stage enactment of the presence of the author as character, and the verbal presentation of a silent film to an audience are clearly hybrid forms, though they contain many of the key features of drama, such as the element of performance, the wealth and multiplicity of aural and visual signs needing to be deciphered, and the sense of events happening here and now, all of which are absent from written prose fiction. But a further step beyond these forms is needed for a realisation of drama's full potential. This concerns the particular role of the author in drama.

Drama theory has no need of a construct such as an implied author: indeed such a concept is quite contrary to the manner in which drama operates. Peter Szondi is adamant that in post-Renaissance European drama, the dramatist is absent. For Szondi, the dramatist 'does not speak; he institutes discussion' and the lines spoken are 'spoken in context and remain there. They should in no way be perceived as coming from the author' (1987: 8). Similarly, in J. L. Styan's broader-based theorisation of drama, the author does not figure as one of the three key elements of 'the irreducible theatre event', which are script, actor and audience (1975: 6). The reasons for this are clear. The creator of a play does not speak directly to the audience: the words are mediated through one or more actors. He or she may have strongly held opinions, but is nevertheless denied the opportunity to express any moral or political views directly. In drama, the author disappears within the dialogue and conflict of the characters, none of whom can be taken as representing the author's personal viewpoint. Henrik Ibsen put this view very forcefully in response to criticism of the text of his play *Ghosts*: 'They endeavour to make me responsible for the opinions which certain of the personages of any drama express. And yet there is not in the whole book a single opinion which can be laid to the account of the author' (quoted in Pfister, 1988: 297). Any intended authorial viewpoint embodied in a dramatic work is not to be found in the consistencies of a narrating presence (an 'implied author'), but instead emerges from the clash of views and debate about values among the characters. In Martin Esslin's felicitous phrase, 'it should emerge from the very polyphony of its conflicts' (1987: 161).

J. L. Styan's full diagrammatic representation of the performance situation is inevitably more complex than any offered by theorists of the novel. In place of Seymour Chatman's one-way communication situation, we find a network of reciprocal interactions, which Styan insists must be seen as situated precisely in time – caught in an unfolding present, held between past and future:

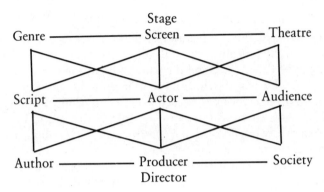

Source: adapted from Styan 1975: 14

It is clear that there is an alternative to the dominant, literary-based theory of film, which derives its concepts from the theorisation of the novel. Fundamental differences can be established between prose fiction and drama, stemming from the differing balance of telling and showing, and from the different demands made on the spectator, as opposed to the reader. Differences exist indeed at every level: in the physical identity of each medium and the way in which it is marketed and consumed, as well as in each medium's mode of production and its pattern of reception. To get a fuller understanding of drama itself, we need now to look more closely at a point touched on above: the dual identity of any drama, as drama text (or script) and as performance text (or realisation).

3 Text and performance

The word *drama* is used in two main ways: first, to describe a literary work, the text of a play; and, second, to describe the performance of this work, its production.

RAYMOND WILLIAMS (1991)

One of the conclusions which follows from the distinctions we have been making between prose fiction and drama, in terms of telling and showing, is that a novel, whatever its complexity, has only one form of existence: as a text to be read. If it is read aloud on stage, it ceases to be a novel. The situation with regard to drama is very different and a useful starting point is to follow conventional theatre studies in recognising that, as examples of drama, both plays and films have what Egil Törnqvist calls 'a double or hybrid existence' (1991: 3). They both customarily exist, physically and tangibly, in two distinct but intimately related forms: a written form and an audio-visual form.

Drama's dual identity

The spontaneously improvised play or the totally unscripted film may, of course, exist, but the lack of a predefined written text is comparatively rare. Jean-Luc Godard may, on occasion in the 1960s, have jotted down his actors' dialogue on the morning of the shoot, and Mike Leigh may improvise freely with his actors for weeks on end, but usually the improvisation is completed and a definitive text is agreed by all participants before the production stage begins. Certainly, if we look at most conventionally funded areas of production, we can say that a play text is as vital to obtaining backing for a stage production, as is a script for getting the production finance to realise a film. The contracts entered into by director, actors and crew specify the production of a particular text (though there may, of course, be considerable changes to this text before the realisation is complete). If there is no text, the whole theatrical experience is different, since there is no repeatability. As Peter Brook writes of his improvised spectacle on the Vietnam war, *US*, 'had we shaped a text, we could have played in other places, without one we were like a happening – and in the event we all felt that something was lost in playing it even through a London season of five months. One performance would have been the true culmination' (1972: 27).

Though both stage and screen make use of a text as the basis for performance, a very different weight is attached to it in the two media, and this, in turn, reflects the different importance given to dialogue and action, word and image. A play text is always seen as, at least potentially, literature. Its prestige stems from the fact that in traditional Western drama, with its focus on the interpersonal, the writer's work in shaping the dialogue can be seen to contain the essence of the work. As Peter Szondi argues, 'every line of dramatic dialogue is irrevocable and full of consequence. As a causal series, it constitutes its own time and, thus, lifts itself out of the temporal flow. This is what engenders the absoluteness of Drama' (1987: 53). If the realm of traditional Western theatre is, in this sense, the spoken word, then the realm of conventional cinema is the action. But of course such distinctions can never be absolutely clear-cut. Much modern theatrical practice departs from such a definition of the authority of the text, with Peter Brook, for example, arguing that 'it does not seem that the word is the same tool for dramatics that it once was' (1972: 54). Nowadays anything – certainly a mere alphabetical listing of names, perhaps, as Patrice Pavis suggests (1987: 389), even the telephone directory – can become the text of a performance. Yet the tradition of buying, reading and studying play texts persists.

Cinema has no such established tradition. Indeed, Jean-Claude Carrière, who has written scripts for Luis Buñuel, Jean-Luc Godard, Miloš Forman and Andrzej Wajda among others, begins his book of advice for potential scriptwriters by observing that 'usually, at the end of the shoot, scenarios are thrown into the studio dustbin. They are torn, crumpled, dirtied, abandoned. Very few people keep a copy, and even fewer still have them bound, or collect them' (1990: 11). Certainly this is what traditionally happened to film scripts – reflecting both the low esteem in which writers were held in the studio system and the view that since the essence of film is action not words, the text as such has little intrinsic value. But nowadays a script has a prestige virtually akin to that of a play, and many film scripts are published. At the time of writing, the French *L'avant-scène du cinéma* series has published well over 400 scripts – including several by Jean-Claude Carrière – and all Harold Pinter's screenplays have appeared in print alongside his plays, either in the neat blue format put out by Methuen or, more recently, in the black-covered imprint of Faber & Faber. A film script may be published even if it cannot actually be realised in performance: Pinter's *The Proust Screenplay*, for which he and Joseph Losey were never able to obtain production finance, is a good example of this. In its published form, Pinter's text offers us not only an imagined film but also a literary text: a reading of the theme of time in Marcel Proust's *A la recherche du temps perdu* which is as perceptive as that contained in any recent volume of explicit critical analysis.

The relations between the two manifestations of drama – text and performance – and between their respective modes of consumption are complex. The written form (drama text or script of a film) is initially designed to be read by a very few people – its potential producer, director, cast and crew – and to serve as a guide and stimulus to production. The text is a paradoxical object in that, on the one hand, it contains the performance – in Carrière's phrase, 'a scenario is already the film' (1990: 12) – yet, on the other, it is, in an equally real sense, incomplete if it is not performed. In this respect, film shares the fundamental paradox of theatre, in that performance or realisation 'contributes to *constituting* the very object (the work) of which it is an interpretation' (Bennett, 1990: 67). This is a view supported by the literary critic Terry Eagleton who writes that 'a dramatic production does not "express", "reflect" or "reproduce" the dramatic text on which it is based; it "produces" the text, transforming it into a unique and irreducible entity' (1976: 64). This is an approach broadly endorsed, from the standpoint of theatrical semiotics, by Patrice Pavis, for whom any approach which 'presupposes that the dramatic text has an innate theatricality, a matrix for production or even a score which must be extracted at all costs and expressed on stage' is simply 'begging the question' (1992: 26). For Pavis, the relationship of text and performance must be seen not as 'the translation or reduplication of the former by the latter', but as 'a transfer or a confrontation of the fictional universe structured by the text and the fictional universe produced by the stage' (1992: 28).

The implications of this combination of identity and opposition between text and performance are crucial for the analysis of all forms of drama, including film drama. In its purely verbal form of words on a page, the text of a play or film has its own distinctive style of marketability and, if published, can be acquired by ordinary readers who buy or borrow a copy. Like all written texts, it can then be read in whatever manner the reader finds most appropriate or convenient. For those who have seen the play or film, it can serve as a source of recollection (like a set of snapshots); for others, who have only this written text for reference, it can be a powerful stimulus for imaginative visualisation (like a novel). In terms of critical discussion, play and film texts can be 'read' as examples of a particular literary genre, using the models of literary analysis devised by Seymour Chatman and others. But this does not mean that this is the sole means of analysis, or that the same frame of analysis is appropriate for performance texts. Though we can speak meaningfully of stage performances and films as 'enactments' of the text, this metaphor of enactment, as Terry Eagleton notes, can be misleading, in so far as it implies that the text determines the production. In fact, the relationship is one of mutual interaction and determination since 'the theatrical mode of production in no sense merely "mediates" the text; on the contrary, its practices and conventions "operate" the textual materials according to an internal logic of their own' (1976: 66). Patrice Pavis even goes so far as to see the notion of fidelity as valid in both directions. Just as we can ask 'whether the *mise en scène* is faithful to the text', so too we have a right to ask 'whether the dramatic text is faithful to its *mise en scène* , whether it corresponds to what is seen on stage' (1992: 27).

The audio-visual form (performance text of a play or production of a film script) is a specific realisation of a text (perhaps with modifications) by a particular producer, director, cast and crew – designed to be received by paying spectators during a prearranged performance of a specifically predetermined duration in a theatre or cinema. It may be argued that, in the case of cinema, this involves such a transformation of the written text that to talk of mere realisation is inadequate: meanings are clearly added which are not accessible to the ordinary reader, as the action envisaged in the text is realised with the full power of the filmic image. But, as Benjamin

Bennett points out, the same is precisely true of much theatrically self-conscious modern drama (his chosen examples are Pirandello, Beckett and Ionesco): 'Since the performance generates meanings that belong to the work but *are not there* for the reader . . ., we are compelled to recognise that true understanding occurs *only* via performance, whereas the situation of the reader makes available, at best, a defective, verbally conditioned *selection* of meanings' (1990: 76). Stage and screen provide in many ways analogous situations since both involve theatrical presentation. Even when the performance is transmitted live from the stage via television to the home, many of the particular qualities of the theatrical situation are preserved, though the reception of the performance text is strongly influenced by the domestic viewing situation. It is only when video tape is used, either as a medium to record broadcast output or as the form in which a film is bought or hired, that the immediacy of performance is lost, as the spectator recovers a control over duration and linearity akin to that possessed by the reader of a written text.

The written form of the drama is in some ways easier to consume, since it consists simply of a single level of information (words on a page), whereas in any production of a play or film a wealth of complex and constantly shifting audio-visual information will be directed at the spectator. The writer's script of a film will be set out in a stylised form but it will invariably offer both the words of the dialogue, which may be cut or altered in the finished film, and a precise and evocative account of the action, which the reader, whether or not he or she is a potential director, must visualise. The text of a play will have a similar dual pattern, offering both the dialogue, generally seen as the immutable essence of the play, and the stage directions, which prompt the reader to visualise a performance of the text. Just as a film director will feel free to alter the dialogue, so too a stage producer may disregard the stage directions. A playwright such as Eugène Ionesco may protest, 'my text is not only the dialogue, but also the "stage directions". These stage directions are to be respected as much as the text: they are necessary' (1962: 185), but such sentiments are likely to have little impact thirty or forty years later, if the play is restaged. In any case, the written form throws up a vast range of potential interpretations for its readers, since each will visualise the text in his or her own personal manner, in much the same way that he or she will approach a novel.

The realisation of the text

Whether publication occurs or not, there is normally a recognised definitive written version of the drama text or film script (the final rewrite, the writer's last word, as it were), before the first stage of realisation of the performance text or film begins. At this point another version – the specific blueprint for a particular production – begins to be created, often by another hand, as when the stage director marks up his text as a guide for himself and his actors, or a film director creates his shooting script or shot list. In cinema, because of the emphasis on action rather than dialogue, considerable weight is attached to this stage of the overall production process. Often it is this version of the shooting script (or a post-production transcript or adaptation of it) which is published as a record of the film, and some directors give themselves a screen credit accordingly (Marcel Carné, for example, customarily included a credit to himself for the 'découpage technique' of his films).

Any given production of a play (the creation of a specific performance text) is as much the fixing of one possible performance among many, and the closing-down of other potential versions, as is the recording of a film production. The spectator loses the reader's control over pace and rhythm, but, at the same time, there is a reduction of ambiguity and a real degree of closure. Performance lacks the multivalence of a written text, since the words of dialogue, for example, will now be recited by a specific actor dressed in a particular costume, in a precise tone of voice, with a particular accent, creating a distinctive rhythm etc.

The distinction between the single text of the novelist and the dual system of drama text and performance text is very apparent if we consider, for example, how the key characteristics of a character are conveyed to the spectator by a novelist as opposed to a dramatist or screenwriter. The author of a novel uses all the resources of words on a page (including, of course, such devices as metaphors and similes) to convey the particular qualities of a fictional character directly to the reader's imagination. The text of a novel is a complete entity in itself, the sole resource offered to the reader. But the text of a playwright or film scriptwriter is designed to serve as stimulus to actors who, under the guidance of a director, offer a personal interpretation of each character. The drama text, if it is evocative, may be said to contain its potential performance, yet it is complete only when it receives such realisation. The performance which reaches the spectator is therefore not merely one version of the author's text (a particular fixing or closing of it by the producer), but also one which has added elements, since it now involves the contribution of another equally key contributor to any dramatic performance: the actor. The latter will bring to the part not merely his or her own reading of the character (translated into a particular set of mannerisms, vocal effects, etc.), distinguishable elements of his or her own real person (real-life physique, appearance, voice and habitual gestures), but also – if he or she is a star or well-known player – a persona established in the audience's mind by previous performances. The creation of the character is therefore a complex process, in which text and performance, author's intention, director's interpretation and actor's contribution, are inextricably mixed.

In studies designed to draw out the contrast between theatre and film, much is made of the distinction between the variety of actual productions of a successful play text and the single realisation of a film script, which will be distributed and shown worldwide (remakes will almost always be made from a new script). Yet at its premiere, when it receives the maximum critical attention and its commercial value is normally determined, a play customarily exists as performance text in just this one interpretation (provided by a single producer, director, cast and crew), very much as a film does. Patrice Pavis even goes so far as to argue that 'different *mises en scène* of a common text, particularly those produced at very different moments in history, do not provide readings of the same text. The letter of the text remains of course unchanged, but the spirit varies considerably' (1992: 27). The paradox is that explored by Jorge Luis Borges in his story of Pierre Menard, the turn-of-the-century French poet whose partially achieved ambition was to compose, not another *Don Quixote* – 'which would have been easy – but *the Don Quixote*' (1962: 48). The work of Menard, a nineteenth century French poet writing in a foreign language, is inevitably quite distinct from that of Cervantes, a seventeenth century Spanish novelist working in the vernacular language of his day, so that Borges can convincingly argue that 'the text of Cervantes and that of Menard are verbally identical, but the second is almost infinitely richer' (1962: 52).

The performance text of a play may have been developed and changed during rehearsal (just as a film script may be modified during shooting), but during the run of the play it will be a fixed entity, with the pattern of its speeches, actions, entrances and exits clearly worked out and rigidly adhered to. Its duration, as determined by the director during rehearsal, will also be rigorously adhered to (again giving a fixity akin to that in a film). Often – as with the Methuen and Faber & Faber editions of plays – the details of this first presentation will be included when the text is published. Obviously, with the passage of time, a drama text may be given a performance quite literally unimaginable to its author, but nevertheless the historical study of drama lays much emphasis on the nature of the original performance, with J. L. Styan arguing forcefully that 'the discipline of studying a play is absolutely subject to understanding its original conditions of performance' (1975: 108).

In contemporary theatre, the success of the first production normally determines whether a new play will receive a diversity of further productions and perhaps translation into other languages. Yet a play performed just once (i.e. for which only one performance text exists) is no less a play than one which subsequently receives dozens of separate stagings. A film script will normally receive only the one realisation as performance text (which the techniques of mechanical reproduction allow to be marketed worldwide, in a way that a stage production can never be). But there is no way in which the text can be said to determine this realisation totally, so that text and performance have to be seen as one and indistinguishable. During the period of production the multivalence of the written text may well lead to a variety of differing interpretations among those involved. This, in turn, may cause tension and dispute between producer, director, star and writer, so that the resultant film is no more than one interpretation among a number of potential versions that could be made at this point (a situation which becomes very clear when the producer replaces one director with another in mid-production).

The place of the camera

Much writing on the theory of drama which concentrates on the written text and ignores this shared dual identity in terms of text and performance shows a marked hostility, or at best indifference, to film. Typical in this respect is Manfred Pfister, whose book, *The Theory and Analysis of Drama*, devotes less than two pages out of a total 339 to a section entitled 'Drama and Film: Some Observations'.

While conceding that drama and film can be regarded as 'structurally closely related variants of the same authorial method', Pfister is quick to emphasise those differences which align film, in his view, with prose narrative, particularly the role of the camera, which he sees as constituting a 'mediating communication system' and as 'corresponding to the fictional narrator . . . in narrative texts' (1988: 24–5). This is clearly a misreading. Though films certainly contain the potential space for a narrator, this space can only be occupied by one of the characters or another of the author's surrogates. There are indeed innumerable films which contain 'invisible storytellers' whose voice-over narrations shape our approach to a story but who, at least in conventional film making, lose their privileged status as narrators, and revert to being characters on the same level as all the others, in the scenes which enact the narrated verbal text (*see* Kozloff, 1988; Fleishman, 1992).

It is sometimes argued that the camera occupies a position akin to that of the implied author in a novel, with Benjamin Bennett, for example, drawing attention to 'the camera as a controlling presence of roughly the same sort as the controlling authorial presence that we cannot help inferring when we read a text' (1990: 66). But the correspondence is limited. If we apply the distinction between text and performance, and take into account the writer's script that precedes and underpins a film's realisation, it is clear that the camera does not create the drama text, which any concept of authorship would clearly imply. Long before the camera begins to roll, the dramatic structure already exists in the scriptwriter's words which set out the action and dialogue, usually with no more recourse to the technical vocabulary of direction than is customary in any contemporary theatrical drama text. The role of the camera is in the realisation of the performance text. There it is used to create, through the sequence of shots and the use of close-up and long shot, the filmic version of that shifting distance between intimacy and detachment which Peter Brook, for example, regards as the basis of all drama in performance:

> The true theatrical relationship is like most human relationships between two people: the degree of involvement is always varying. This is why theatre permits one to experience something in an incredibly powerful way, and at the same time to retain a certain freedom. This double illusion is the very foundation both of the theatre experience and of dramatic form (1988: 190).

Recognition of the proper status of the camera in the creation of meaning is crucial to the understanding of dramatic structure in cinema. Though the basic minimal unit into which a film can be divided is generally agreed to be the shot (with its accompanying sound), the next highest unit of analysis – the scene or sequence – is not simply a patterned collection of shots as such. In any well-made film a pattern will be there within the visual organisation of the scene, but that is not what defines the scene as such. A scene is in fact a link in the overall dramatic development of a film, what Raymond Bellour describes as 'a moment in the filmic chain which is delimited both by an elusive but powerful sense of dramatic or fictional unity, and by the more rigorous notion of identity of setting and characters of the narrative' (1974–5: 7). What creates the unity of a scene is not the pattern of its shots, but the shaped succession of its 'beats' – the single units of behaviour that make up its dramatic action. These beats are, of course, the product, not of the positioning of the camera, but of the screenwriter's imagination. Indeed they exist prior to the realisation of the film, being already contained in the script.

In film, as in stage drama, the beats take the form of action and response – a question and an answer, an exchange of looks, an insult and a retaliatory blow, for example. A key aspect of the writer's work in scripting a drama is to establish, structure and pattern these beats, both at a literal level (making clear exactly what happens) and in terms of the sub-text (communicating what this literal action implies in terms of the interrelationship of the characters). In any dramatic form, the beats of the action will themselves form larger patterns: a simple crescendo of personal interaction leading, say, to a kiss, or an apparently harmless symmetry resulting in a sudden and unexpected pay-off, as in a comic gag. Only in the very dullest drama are the literal text and the sub-text identical. Making sense of a play or a film, as a spectator, depends to a great extent on judging the implications of such interplay – much as we appraise the actions of the people around us in our everyday lives, while bearing in mind the conventions that go to make up performance in the theatre or cinema. The writer's words and the director's visual interpretation will help us, of course, but ultimately, as in all drama, we must make up our own minds.

In film there is obviously a close relationship between the dramatic interplay apparent in the writer's text and the individual shots and sounds chosen by the director in order to realise it on film. Certain actions, for example, will seem to demand to be seen in close-up. But just as a writer's skill can be seen in the relationship of text and sub-text, so too that of a director is most apparent in the relation between the dramatic action on the one hand and the shot patterning and handling of sound on the other. The power of film as a dramatic medium stems in part from the fact that the pattern of the shots does not have simply to echo or mimic the dramatic build-up. The shots edited together and overlaid with sounds have, in any successful film, their own precise rhythm and pattern, which is a second and equal contributor (along with the text itself) to both the aesthetic pleasure and the generation of meaning. Though spectators often talk about films as if the key to our enjoyment was simply their performers or their subject matter, and much film theory seems to assume that films are no more than sequences of shots and sounds, it is clear that, as in any form of drama, it is the structured relationship which links all levels of text and performance that is crucial to both pleasure and the creation of meaning. Martin Esslin makes this point well: 'Dramatic structure, analogous to musical structure, depends on the interaction, in sequence, and contrapuntally, at any given moment, of melodic and rhythmic elements that are established, varied, juxtaposed, combined and recombined' (1987: 119).

The director and the spectator

Theatre studies setting out to distinguish between stage and screen drama also tend to undervalue the role of the director in theatre. Aston and Savona, for example, call attention to the camera's role in 'directing the meaning-creating processes' and argue that 'in theatre, there is no such mediating device. Everything is put before us and we have a panoramic as opposed to a partial and preselected view of the stage' (1991: 101). Much film theory suffers from the same defect, since it too assumes that because the theatre lacks the specific rhetorical devices of cinema's *mise en scène* (camera angles, montage, close-ups, etc.), watching a play somehow equates with ordinary everyday looking. Gaudreault and Jost, for example, take the commonplace recognition that the camera 'can intervene and *modify* the spectators' perception of the actors' performance' (1990: 26) as being enough to set cinema totally apart from the theatre. Yet this is to ignore the fact that the very term *mise en scène* is a theatrical one, whose usage, Patrice Pavis points out, dates from the latter half of the nineteenth century, when stage production was transformed by mechanisation and the introduction of electric lighting (1987: 244–5).

In fact, a consideration of the role of the stage director, as it emerged in the latter part of the nineteenth century can give insight into what a director does and does not contribute to a film, and what role the camera occupies in the realisation of the action. In this connection, a perceptive essay by Martin Esslin on Max Reinhardt, who was, in the eyes of his contemporaries, 'something of a magician because he was among the first to employ the whole gamut of the new technical means at the disposal of the theatre', is of particular interest. Esslin shows how the rise of the director can be closely linked to technological developments in both society and the theatre itself: 'tradition and the stereotyped ways of producing plays by drawing on stock scenery, primitive lighting and conventional costume succumbed to the speed and scope of technical innovation. New complexities made a coordinating and commanding mind essential' (1983: 10). Thus the rise of the theatre director prefigures precisely the emergence of direction as the key specialist role in the early film industry.

Modern theatrical practice – from the visions of Antonin Artaud and the theorisations of Bertolt Brecht to the contemporary innovations of, say, Ariane Mnouchkine or Peter Brook – is very much concerned with the imposition of a particular director's view on the theatre audience. But any study of drama in performance will show that the responses of spectators in a theatre are as shaped as those of film viewers (though, of course, by other technical means from those used in cinema). J. L. Styan even goes so far as to use an allusion to cinema to make clear how the interaction of spectator and stage occurs, positing that the spectator 'scans the picture as if he were many cameras with many lenses'. The generalised impressions offered by the stage in terms of voice, posture, costume and the physical bonds between characters prepare the spectator for the 'specific and incisive focus of the words', so that the study of drama is 'the study of how the stage compels its audience to be involved in its actual processes' (1975: 4).

Part of the problem created by 1970s film theory is the fact that it blurs the key distinction between text and performance by its misleading use of metaphor, whereby the phrase 'reading the text' is applied not to considering a film script, but to the very different activity of viewing a film. Though the techniques employed by film theory are largely derived from literary theory (where they have appropriately been developed to deal with novels, i.e. texts which exist only in a written form), the very existence of a written text of the film has been almost universally ignored by film theorists. The processes involved in the film makers' actual reading of the written text, and the decisions leading to the choice of the particular forms of fixity and closure involved in the realisation of it, have seldom been investigated outside the largely untheorised world of film directing manuals and journalistic accounts of the making of a particular film. Moreover the image of the 'reader' of a film given in film theory is often that of the passive dupe of a powerfully illusionist medium, whereas theatre studies give us a much more active view of the spectator and his or her role, which is as true of cinema as it is of the stage.

Regardless of the nature of the production itself – whether, for example, it has a 'closed' or an 'open' structure – the role of the spectator, as the person to whom the story is addressed, has a dual identity, well characterised by Umberto Eco. Eco's argument is couched in general terms, posited as applicable to the reception of all forms of art, but it has particular relevance to the reception of drama, whether on stage or screen. On one level, 'the addressee is bound to enter into an interplay of stimulus and response which depends on his unique capacity for sensitive reception of the piece. In this sense the author presents a finished product with the intention that this particular composition should be appreciated and received in the same form as he devised it' (1989: 3). At a second level of reaction to the play of stimuli and personal response to their patterning, 'the individual addressee is bound to supply his own existential credentials, the sense of conditioning which is peculiarly his own, a defined culture, a set of tastes, personal inclinations, and prejudices' (1989). Reception thus involves both submission to the pattern of the work and a creative critical response to it, or in Eco's terms, it is both an *interpretation* and a *performance*.

Because of the complexity of the situation in which the spectator finds him- or herself, viewing either a film or a play is by no means a passive activity. As Martin Esslin emphasises, just as, in real life, all of us must arrive at our own assessment of events, spectators of drama are compelled to extract their own value judgement, their own sense of what it ultimately 'means' from what they have perceived in the course of the performance (1987: 161). This implies a very active role for the spectator, ordering events and examining their causes. As John Peter notes, 'in performance, the economy of dramatic construction demands that we perceive these causes swiftly; we need to be alert, logical, questioning' (1987: 256). Some theorists go even further in the role they attribute to the spectator, and Patrice Pavis quotes with approval an argument advanced by Danièle Sallenave:

> The actor *plays his role* in the play, but the spectator *plays the game*. In order for the spectator to play the game, somebody had to set up the game: this somebody is the director. But when the spectator plays the game, he does not play with the director, or even with the actor, but with the text, with the idea of the text' (1992: 44).

Though some drama theorists, such as Benjamin Bennett (1990: 73), wish to limit simply to the theatre the distinction between reading a play and watching a performance, this is in fact another characteristic shared by stage and screen. It is a part of the normal activity of any spectator in a theatre or cinema to look beyond the specificities of the particular realisation so as to experience the text which lies behind it. This is particularly clear when one mentally compares a particular new production of a classic play with others which one may have seen before, or weighs the screen adaptation of a favourite novel against one's memory of the experience of reading the original. But even if the actual play text or a film script is not available to the spectator, he or she will normally construct an imagined text or script against which the actual production can meaningfully be measured. This allows us to say, for example, that an original play or film is ill-written but well-directed – even if we have not seen the script in question – that it is badly cast, that the star's performance is excellent in capturing the essence of the leading character, and so on. In the words of Patrice Pavis, *mise en scène* 'exists only when the spectator appropriates it, when it becomes the creative projection of the spectator' (1992: 34). Any analysis of plays or films as drama must constantly take into account their inextricable dual identity as both drama text (known or imagined) and performance text (single or multiple).

4 Stage and screen

There is no point in defining theatre as 'pure art', or in outlining a theatre theory that does not take into account media practices that border on and often penetrate contemporary work on stage.

PATRICE PAVIS (1992)

In the two previous chapters the concern has been to establish some basic distinctions between drama and prose fiction in terms of the difference between telling and showing and the dual identity (as text and performance) which sets film and stage drama apart from the novel. At this point it is necessary to discuss in greater detail some of the common factors linking film and stage and enabling us to talk meaningfully of them as parallel examples of enacted stories, that is, as drama. Differences will predominate if the discussion is kept on the level of literal, physical characteristics treated in isolation. Then we will put all the stress on the presence of the live performer on stage or, conversely, on the sheer size of the image on a traditional cinema screen which gives it an enormous power, 'so great that it engulfs one' (Brook, 1988: 190). But it will be argued here that the overlaps and similarities are equally significant. There are differences in the particular methods and techniques which are employed to arouse emotion and hold the audience's attention, but the basic system of drama is common to both media.

The frame

The procedures of both stage drama and film involve a framed action and this has important consequences. In each case, the placing of events and actions, people and objects into a frame adds an interest and significance which would otherwise be lacking. As David Mamet notes, 'If the overriding idea is that *a play is taking place*, then we will form the images that we see between the time the curtain goes up and the time the curtain goes down *into* a play whether or not they have been structured as one. Just so with the movie'. (1992: 61). The space of the action – stage or screen – is marked off as a special area where the spectator is confronted not by the 'real', the everyday, but by a symbolic representation which reveals the dramatic truth through the use of elements variously drawn from the real.

There are theoretical accounts of cinema which take to extremes Bertolt Brecht's critique of illusionism in the theatre and posit that the spectator is somehow duped or deceived by conventional realist cinema. This is clearly an absurdity: knowledge that we are watching a play or film is fundamental to our aesthetic experience, and the only plausible reason to explain, for example, our failure to intervene in the action – to save a child from threat, for example, or to avert a disaster of which the characters are still unaware. Jean-Luc Godard is perhaps the most Brechtian of film makers. In *Les carabiniers*, Michel-Ange (Albert Juross) visits a cinema to watch *Le bain de la femme du monde* and clambers up the screen to get a clearer look at the naked woman. The whole point of the joke is that only someone immensely naive would mistake filmic images for reality and behave in this way to get a better view. Even the classic instance of spectators' mistaking film images for reality, cited by most film histories – the spectators diving under their seats at an early screening of Louis Lumière's *L'arrivée d'un train à la gare de La Ciotat* – is apocryphal.

When we watch a film, we make a conscious decision to enter a world of fiction and make-believe; in Robert Scholes's words we express 'our desire to abandon certain dimensions of existence, certain quotian responsibilities, and place ourselves under the illusory guidance of a maker of narratives' (1982: 64). We are not duped or deceived in the sense that we believe we are still in the world of everyday reality, but we do desire to have our emotions aroused and our thoughts provoked by a 'maker of stories' whose skill in plot construction and manipulation is greater than our own. It is not simply that we are held, like children, by the question of what will happen next. Even when we know the outcome (and outcomes are very predictable in much popular cinema) we can still be entranced by the skill with which the suspense is created: a second viewing can be even more pleasurable than the first, since we are now in a better position to admire the dexterity of the enactment of the story. What we admire are the games with temporality and causality, the play with structures of time and logic, which we must unravel in order to comprehend fully the richness of the action.

In this context, Brecht's advocacy of 'alienation' has to be seen as a polemical stance, representing one possible development from the situation prevalent in the German theatre of his time, as is clear if we consider what he actually wrote in 'The Mother Courage Model':

> Restoring the theatre's reality as theatre is now a precondition for any possibility of arriving at realistic images of human social life. *Too much* heightening of the illusion in the setting, together with a 'magnetic' way of acting that gives the spectator the illusion of being present at a fleeting, accidental, 'real' event, create such an impression of naturalness that one can no longer interpose one's judgment, imagination or reactions, and must simply conform by sharing in the experience and becoming one of 'nature's' objects. The illusion created by the theatre must be a partial one, in order that it may always be recognised as an illusion (1964: 219, *my emphasis*).

Peter Brook, for whom alienation is 'the possible device of a dynamic theatre in a changing world' (1972: 82), puts it well: 'It was out of respect for the audience that Brecht introduced the idea of alienation, for alienation is a call to halt: alienation is cutting, interrupting, holding something up to the light, making us look at it again. Alienation is above all an appeal to the spectator to work for himself. . .' (1972: 81).

Our awareness that we are in a theatre or cinema shapes the way we look and respond to what we see and hear. This is a fact ignored by those, like Christian Metz, who argue that the crucial distinction between theatre and cinema is that the actors and objects are there, to be seen by us, in the theatre, whereas a film offers only shadows or reflections of people and things which are absent (1982: 44). Even the most real element in a stage performance – the human being, the actor – is, at the same time, a sign for a human being (Esslin, 1987: 56). Conventional Western drama is based on acceptance by actors and spectators of their separate places inside and outside the frame. Much is made, in studies setting out differences between stage and screen, of the fact that the human performer on stage has the possibility to cross the footlights – whereas a screen actor clearly cannot (except in Woody Allen's *The Purple Rose of Cairo*) descend from the screen. But as soon as a stage performer exercises this option and steps across into the spectators' physical space – and hence out of the frame – the conventions of drama are broken and we are in the domain of the 'happening', rather than that of drama itself.

The performer

The presence – here and now – of the living performer is the key distinguishing element of stage drama, and this creates an important gulf between stage and screen performance. But it is vital to recall that the stage/film dichotomy is not simply a matter of setting a real presence against a photographic image. Crucial to our appreciation of dramatic action on both stage and screen is the dual identity of the performer. An actor on stage is not simply himself (with his own personal physique, gestures and voice), but also the character – Othello, say, or Lear – that he is playing, with all the transformations of his speech patterns and appearance which he has chosen to bring to the role. If the actor is also a star – famous, say, for his role in a long-running television series – then memories of other appearances will add yet another dimension. It is not sufficient to say that the actor on stage is a real human being, he is also simultaneously and unavoidably an imaginary being.

In a similar way, in Alfred Hitchcock's film *Suspicion*, we do not see simply a photographic representation of a character called John Aysgarth (who will never be incarnated by anyone else and hence, in a sense, has no other identity). We are simultaneously aware of the presence and personality of the star playing the role, Cary Grant, who is familiar to us from a host of other roles. Indeed, in Hollywood, the awareness that audiences would bring to a film their knowledge of the screen persona of favourite star performers was such that producers would not allow a star to act against type. In the particular instance of *Suspicion*, the whole narrative strength of the novel on which the film is based lies in the fact that a woman realises that her husband is slowly killing her, but, because of her love for him, she is unable to confront him with this fact and goes passively to her death. But when Hitchcock set out to make the film, he was confronted by the producers with a simple fact that rendered this particular plot line impossible: 'Cary Grant could not be a murderer' (Truffaut, 1968: 49). The result is the awkwardly shot and psychologically unsatisfactory ending of the film, in which the wife's suspicions are shown to be baseless.

In terms of the conventional classification of signs derived from Charles S. Peirce, the actor on stage is an iconic sign, a sign which represents its object mainly by its similarity to it. It is, of course, through the iconicity of its signs that cinema achieves much of its power. Indeed, if film is able to match stage drama's powerfully direct representation of reality (deriving from the use of real human beings and, to some extent, real objects), it is to a large extent by exploiting the strong impression of reality given by photographic reproduction. Stanley Cavell observes that a photograph is not simply a likeness, a replica, a facsimile; nor is it a relic, a shadow, an apparition. There is a particularly close link between the photograph itself and the reality it represents that makes us want to say that it presents us 'with the things themselves' (1971: 17).

Our verbal confusions – we can hold up a photograph of Garbo and say with equal conviction 'This is Garbo' and 'This is not Garbo' – point, in Cavell's view, to the fact that 'we do not know what a photograph is; we do not know how to place it ontologically' (1971: 17–8). Susan Sontag concurs with this view of the photograph as a very special object, pointing out that we experience a photograph 'not only as an image (as a painting is an image), an interpretation of the real', but also as 'a trace, something directly stencilled off the real, like a footprint or a death mask' (1978: 15). To this sense of the real in still photography's reproduction of the appearance of forms, film adds two further powerful realistic elements: the convincing reproduction of movement and (since the late 1920s) the synchronis-ation of speech and sound with the image. The effect is an immensely powerful impression of reality, and since we are happy to accept the truthfulness of still photography for identification purposes in our real lives, we have little difficulty in accepting the image of reality (of people, places, things) given us in the make-believe world of screen drama.

Dramatic experience of any kind – the power which captures and holds the attention of an audience – invariably involves a dynamic combination of involvement and separation. In the theatre, stage drama offers its audience a uniquely direct contact with the actors in a shared space and time (that of the performance). Yet the stage itself is marked off as a special kind of space, inviolable and quite separate from the auditorium, and the actors on the other side of the footlights are not just ordinary people, but performers embodying beings we know to be imaginary. In the case of cinema, there is a radical separation – in time, space and level of reality – between the audience and the actors captured by the images on the screen. Yet the images have the power to draw us into the world they portray through the combination of their strong impression of reality (deriving from their photographic origins) and the fact that we still perceive them as images (we are not duped when we watch a film). Indeed, it is possible to turn the argument about the film image's lack of reality on its head, as when Christian Metz, for example, argues that it is 'because the art of theatre is based on means that are too real that the belief in the reality of the diegesis finds itself compromised', whereas the 'total unreality of the filmic means' allows a film's fictional world to assume reality (1974a: 13).

Metz's argument is ingenious, though it underestimates the power of performance. But this concentration on the reality (or lack of reality) in the forms of dramatic presentation risks obscuring the other crucial aspect of our relation to the fictional world of the drama. However our relationship with actors on stage and actors on screen is construed – and clearly there are significant differences – our relationship to the fictional characters they portray is structured in an identical way: we have access to these characters only through the actor's performance. In terms of Metz's notion of a play of presence and absence, the procedures of stage and screen are arguably alike, since, as Noël Carroll points out, 'in both fictional film and theatrical fiction, the characters are absent from the continuum of our world in the same way' (1988: 38). Laurence Olivier may have been present on stage in the same time and space as his audience, but how far is it meaningful to say that King Lear was there too? Lear belongs to a different plane – the domain of fiction – accessible only through Olivier's performance, in exactly the same way that John Aysgarth in *Suspicion* is reachable only through Cary Grant's playing of the role.

A number of film theorists have wrestled with the problem of the audience's relationship with the performers on screen, and how this relates to the experience of live theatre. Stanley Cavell explores the shared quality of presence/absence: on both stage and screen, the actors are present to us, while we are absent to them (mechanically so in the case of the cinema). Cavell tries out a number of intriguing propositions: 'In a play the character is present, whereas in a film the actor is', or 'For the stage, an actor works himself into a role; for the screen, a performer takes the role onto himself' (1971: 27). But he finds any kind of conclusion difficult. Confronting the 'incontestable fact that in a motion picture no live human being is up there', he can only respond, 'but a human *something* is, and something unlike anything else we know' (1971: 26). Leo Braudy adds a few further paradoxes, derived from the idea that 'the line between film actor and part is much more difficult to draw than that between stage actor and role, and the social dimension of "role" contrasts appropriately with the personal dimension of "part"' (1977: 193). This leads Braudy too to deny the greater reality of the stage performer, as he argues that the inability of the film actor to 'get over the footlights' does not make him less real, but rather 'makes his relation to the character he plays much more real'. For Braudy, the balance shifts in the direction of the film performer:

> The stage actor is performing a role: he may be the best, one of the best, the only, or one of many to play that role. But the role and its potential will exist long after he has ceased to play it, to be interested in it, to be alive. The film actor does not so much perform a role as he creates a kind of life, playing between his characterisation in a film and his potential escape from that character outside the film and perhaps into other films (1977: 194).

These kinds of arguments about absence and presence, parts and roles, come close to constituting mere games with words. We may be 'absent' to the film actor, in the sense that the performance gives no acknowledgement that we are watching. But at the moment of filming, the actor was most certainly aware of the camera and knew that, if the shots were retained at the editing, the performance would be projected for an audience. The fact that the character shows no awareness of being a character in a fiction is no more than a stylistic feature of mainstream Western drama – exactly akin to the way in which, on a theatrical stage, Lear addresses the Fool, as if the two were alone. Equally, rather than making semantically dubious distinctions between 'parts' and 'roles', we need instead to explore the shared elements in the actor-spectator relationship in all forms of drama, captured in all their paradoxical richness by Peter Brook:

> It is hard to understand the true function of spectator, there and not there, ignored and yet needed. The actor's work is never for an audience, yet always is for one. The onlooker is a partner who must be forgotten and still constantly kept in mind: a gesture is statement, expression, communication and a private manifestation of loneliness (1972: 57).

There is, however, no denying the unique quality of a live stage performance, and if film had remained a mere recording medium, capturing the action with a static camera placed at some equivalent to the best seat in the stalls, it would never have developed a dramatic power to match that of the stage. But as film and story were welded together during the development of the feature film in the period preceding World War I, a whole range of technical devices were evolved which served to enhance the dramatic power of film. From the perspective of a theorist of drama, Peter Szondi picks out three discoveries in particular – the mobility of the camera, the close-up, and montage – arguing that with their application the motion picture 'ceases to be filmed theatre and becomes an independent pictorial narrative' (1987: 68). As far as the foregrounding of the actor is concerned, the key device is, of course, the close-up, which works to create a direct link between film actor and spectator. Its operation has been well defined by Richard Dyer, who places particular stress on those close-ups which are not part of the interaction of a scene (another character's point-of-view, for example) but are seen only by the audience 'disclosing for us the star's face, the intimate, transparent window to the soul' (1987: 11). Certainly when one considers film stars, there is nothing paradoxical in talking of 'screen presence'. What Martin Esslin calls 'the profoundly *erotic* nature of drama', deriving from the 'sheer magnetism of human personality', is as much a feature of screen as of stage drama, and hence a powerful generator of meaning in both forms (1987: 60).

Space

The concrete depiction of space is one of the features that separate both stage and screen from the novel, where space is presented 'in a verbally encoded and abstract form only' (Pfister, 1988: 246). Stage and screen – for all their numerous differences, share a double, overlapping, system of spatial representation. At the first level, there is the physical space that is shown – the actual space of the stage or that captured on screen in the film images – what can be termed the scenic space. While there may be real objects on the stage, and the actual, authentic, locations may be used for a film, these become no less representations of the drama's setting than painted backdrops or studio-designed sets. Like the performer on stage or screen they take on a dual identity – as themselves and at the same time as representational signs – when they are caught within the framed action of the drama.

Beyond the frame there is an implied extension of this physical space, indicated by the entrances and exits of the characters and, particularly in film, by sounds 'off'. This space may be all the more menacingly threatening or tantalisingly luring for being unseen, and therefore unreachable by the characters, and perhaps for dramatic purposes it will remain unseen. Equally it may be not shown because it is of no dramatic interest – the hotel corridor from which a character enters the bedroom where the key confrontation is to occur, for example. In stage drama – the space unseen in one act may take on a new importance and concreteness by being used as the setting for a subsequent scene or act. In the cinema the use of space is much more fluid – with changes coming from shot to shot rather than between one scene and the next – but the same spatial system is in operation.

All this scenic space, which – whether shown or implied – is marked by constant movement as the characters act and react, needs to be distinguished from the dramatic space itself, the imagined space in which the action unfolds. The dramatic space can be constructed mentally by any reader from indications given in the drama text (stage directions, movements and gestures implied by the dialogue) or from the more cryptic annotations of a conventional film script (INT. ADRIENNE'S BEDROOM. NIGHT). The director's physical realisation of the performance text (or actual film) is the concretisation of one of the possibilities inherent in the written text. Another director staging the same play or directing the same film, or the reader of a play text or film script who has not seen an actual production, may well come up with an equally satisfactory but quite different construction of the dramatic space (Pavis, 1987: 147). When we talk of the spectator's double role in both interpreting and realising the film, we are talking in part of the creation of this dramatic space. Just as the spectator must construct the action, which is not literally shown, by sorting out the true chronology and pattern of cause and effect from the clues given by the plot, so too he or she must create a coherent dramatic space for the action from the fragmentary glimpses of the scenic space which the drama furnishes.

Interestingly, in its use of sound, film makes use of a third space which is potentially there for stage drama but is only infrequently employed in the theatre. This is what one might term the extra-dramatic space, a realm of sound which exists outside the dramatic space (it is inaudible to the characters) but nevertheless helps to shape the audience's reaction. Here, as a kind of aural frame for the action, we find two types of sound – the musical score used in most fictional films and the voice-over narration common in documentaries and used too in a significant number of fictional films. Music in particular is used to convey the inner life of the characters. In the case of cinema, both these elements formed part of the presentational style thought necessary for the very first film shows, when the verbal narration and the musical accompaniment were produced live in the actual acoustic space of the audience. It tells us something about the limitations as well as the frequently remarked power of the image track that these two features have been preserved even in the era of the synchronous sound film. This third spatial category, like the other two, is marked by great fluidity as far as the identity of the sound is concerned. The categories of scenic, dramatic and extra-dramatic space are not watertight compartments: occasionally music initially experienced as extra-dramatic turns out to have a source within the images and, in comedy, we occasionally find a character directly addressed by (and responding to) a voice-over narration which, logically, the character should not be able to hear.

The particular utilisation of spatial features in any given play or film is very dependent on the nature of the chosen dramatic structure. Conventional, plot-based, plays and films subordinate space to the presence and actions of the performers, often reducing elements of the spatial organisation to mere 'props' to be used by the ever-present characters and then discarded from the action. Certainly, in classic Hollywood cinema one can talk meaningfully of space being 'used up' by the film's action. In extreme cases – a James Bond action film, for example – a plot which does not need to pause for interiority, characterisation or reflection will use up (even literally destroy) its settings at an alarming rate.

At the other extreme, on both stage and screen, space can take on a life of its own. Manfred Pfister, in his attempt to separate film and stage drama, takes the example of the extended period when the stage is empty between scenes 14 and 15 in Act IV of Chekhov's *The Seagull* to argue that film has no equivalent to such a moment when emptiness is 'not simply a descriptive section inserted for its own sake' because 'all that this emptiness emphasises is the absence of people' (1988: 25). Yet certain 'open' film structures work in precisely the same way, the most striking example being the last seven minutes (fifty-eight shots) of Michelangelo Antonioni's *L'eclisse*. These shots depict aspects of life around a street corner where the protagonists, Piero and Vittoria, have arranged to meet. Neither comes to the meeting, and the succession of empty images reinforces the isolation and anguished solitude which characterise Antonioni's vision in the film. Such drama as there is involves their non-appearance: several times we think we see them, and each time we are disappointed.

Time

There are parallel links between stage production and film in their treatment of certain key aspects of time. As the action of a play unfolds, the actors and the audience share a span of present time – the time taken by the performance. As spectators in the theatre, our sense of unity with the actors is strengthened by the fact that the actions of the characters in a play appear to occur in this present time which we share with the performers. This though is an illusion, since the unfolding present of a drama obeys quite different laws from those of the present which we inhabit. The present of a stage action is a constructed present. For some, this sets the theatre apart from the cinema. Peter Brook, for example, argues that 'there is only one interesting difference between the cinema and the theatre. The cinema flashes on to a screen images from the past' (1972: 111). But while it is true that film images must by definition be images of the past, since they have been photographed, processed and edited, the fact of projection onto a screen totally changes their temporality in comparison to, say, still photographs.

The relationship of still photography to time has been eloquently discussed by Roland Barthes, who notes that photography cannot be confused with reality – which he defines as the *here-and-now* – since, even with a Polaroid camera, there is always a gap between the moment of shooting and the moment of seeing the photograph. What photography offers is – in Barthes's view – something quite unique – 'a new category in space-time . . . an illogical conjunction between *here* and *then*'. Photography's key feature is its special way of preserving the past: 'in every photograph there is the stupefying evidence of *this-is-what-happened-and-how*'. Hence its use in our society for information and identification purposes and for the

preservation of memories (1977: 45–6). But the addition of movement to still photography – which the development of cinema
involves – does much more than create an added dimension of
realism. It changes the nature of our whole response to the depicted
world, since, as Christian Metz has noted, movement is not simply
reproduced in cinema, rather it is re-produced time and again – in the
present– each time the film is projected (1974a: 9). It may be illusory,
but our experience of cinema is of a *here-and-now*. As we view a film,
it unfolds in time, recreating the present of the recorded action. There
is none of the distancing occasioned by the linguistic past tense of
prose fiction or by the paradoxical *here-and-then* of a photograph. In
cinema, everything appears to happen as we watch – in Barthes's
terms, the *has-been-there* of the photograph vanishes into the *being-
there* of the film – creating an illusory time scheme precisely
equivalent to that which links spectators and actors during a stage
performance. We experience a film in the same way as a play, as an
'event', as 'a unique kind of narrative because it is a story which tells
itself *by taking place*' (Peter, 1987: 252)

In a manner distinctly reminiscent of the pioneer film theorists,
who wanted to affirm a unique identity for film through concentration on the powers of editing, while ignoring the particular
qualities of the dramatic action in film, John Ellis has underlined the
transformation which occurs when still images are projected at
twenty-four or twenty-five frames per second, designating it as one of
the (highly suspect) illusionary techniques specific to film: 'The
cinema image is marked by a particular half-magic feat in that it
makes present something that is absent. The moment shown on the
screen is passed and gone when it is called back into being as an
illusion' (1982: 58). This leads Ellis to a complex and paradoxical
definition of film's uniqueness: 'Cinema is present absence: it says
"This is was"' (1982: 59). Yet, though unanticipated before the
projection of the first moving pictures, this transformation of the past
(photographic image) into an unfolding present (the projected film) is
in no way remarkable in the context of drama. Precisely the same
effect occurs whenever a written text (recording events which, real or
imaginary, must be complete and, in that sense past, or they could not
be written) is transformed in performance (an enactment which
unfolds in an apparent – but highly constructed – present before an
audience). Far from being a uniquely illusory aspect of cinematic
practice, needing 'the voyeuristic attention of the cinema viewer' and

'concentrating the gaze upon illusion' (1982: 61), this transformation
is a commonplace of the make-believe world of all drama.

It is important to realise too that the relation of simultaneity
between spectator and performer, which exists phenomenologically in
stage drama and which is convincingly reproduced in the cinema, is
only part of the organisation of time in a dramatic performance.
Because everything is enacted in an apparent present, both stage
dramatists and screenwriters are to a large extent limited to what can
plausibly happen in the real time devoted to any given scene. Yet in
fact the time *within* a play as a whole is as structured as the time
within a film: in neither case does it equate with the actual unfolding
time of the performance. A play, like a film, deals freely with the
flow of time inside its own boundaries: events may be compressed or
expanded, speeded up or slowed down, jumbled in order or even
reversed from their normal logic. Even in a work where the
performance time is ostensibly the same as the time in which the
action unfolds – such as the film, *High Noon* – there are enormous
discrepancies when one looks at the work in detail. In this particular
example, the duration of the film is 85 minutes, while the screen
action it depicts begins at 10.40 and ends shortly after noon – an
apparent equivalence. Yet there are huge distortions: on the one hand,
there is a considerable gap in the action, when the time span from
10.47 to 11.03 takes just four minutes of screen-time; on the other, a
significant expansion of time occurs as the clock strikes noon at the
film's climax (Faulstich and Korte, 1990: 197). The organisation of
time in any drama – the time within a given scene or act – remains a
construct, shaped to create the maximum dramatic effect. As a
construct, it is not limited by the vagaries of a particular performance
– it has its own precise duration and precedes at its own pace.

Above all, once the particular time scheme of the work has been
determined by the director, it will be repeatable. This is obvious in
the case of a film, which can only repeat its own sequence of events in
the predetermined order each time it is projected (unless the reels are
jumbled). But – though this fact is usually ignored by theorists intent
on establishing differences between film and drama – the same is true
of stage drama. The events on stage seem to unfold immediately and
spontaneously under the gaze of the spectator, but this spontaneity is
only apparent. The play will be performed again next evening, with
the happenings on stage timed to the same precise second and reaching
the same prescribed end as the performance concludes (at a time

already communicated beforehand in the programme). The particular quality of drama as 'a sequence of moments permanently fixed in a certain order and infinitely repeatable' which is so evident in the case of cinema, is a feature of stage drama too (Esslin, 1987: 41).

Theorists of drama are unanimous in the emphasis they place on the immediacy of stage drama. Peter Szondi, for whom time in drama 'unfolds as an absolute, linear sequence in the present', gives a particularly eloquent definition of the way in which this unfolding occurs: 'the present passes and becomes the past and, as such, can no longer be the present on stage. As the present passes away, it produces change, a new present springs from the antithesis' (1987: 9). This view is echoed by the Russian theorist, D. S. Lixacev, in his response to the question, 'Just what is this theatrical present tense?':

> It is the present tense of the performance taking place before the audience. It is the resurrection of time, events and characters and, moreover, such a resurrection that the audience must forget that they are seeing the past. It is the creation of a genuine illusion of the present in which the actor merges with the character he portrays just as the time shown in the theatre merges with the time of the audience in the auditorium (quoted in Lotman, 1976: 77).

This is precisely what occurs too when a film is projected. Common to both stage and screen drama is the fact that the unfolding action offers no pause for reflection. Therefore the spectator has to offer an active and constant participation in the action as it unfolds, what is seen and heard at any given moment being transformed by recollections of what has already gone before and by anticipations of what is still to come. This combination of immediacy, retrospection and anticipation, which is the key to a spectator's comprehension of the action, has to occur as the play or film continues to move forward. Moreover the precise interpretation of these events – a weighing up of the meaning to be attached to them – also has to be decided personally by each spectator as the present unfolds. Participation as a spectator in a dramatic action is quite the opposite of being duped by an illusion. It is, potentially at least, a profound and all-involving experience.

Part two PLOTS

Naturally, life resembles *Ulysses* more than *The Three Musketeers*, but we prefer to think of it as the other way round.

UMBERTO ECO (1989)

5 The closed plot: *North by Northwest*

> Hitchcock's work shares with the fiction feature genre a dramatic and thematic structure derived from the traditions of nineteenth-century narrative plays and novels.
>
> RAYMOND DURGNAT (1974)

The Hollywood paradigm

The best place to look for examples of film as a 'closed' work is in conventional Hollywood cinema, in the films which for decades have allowed Hollywood to take the major share of cinema world box office receipts (to say nothing of television rights, video sales, merchandising spinoffs, etc). Hollywood movies – as the scriptwriting manuals testify – have an act structure as rigid and as closely adhered to as that governing the organisation of French classical tragedy in the seventeenth century. It is with a consideration of the Hollywood paradigm therefore that we can begin our investigation of dramatic structure in cinema, bearing in mind – as we do so – Umberto Eco's assertion that 'it would be wrong to believe that a poetics of the open work is the only possible contemporary poetics ... A movie as fundamentally Aristotelian as *Stagecoach* is a perfectly valid example of contemporary narrative' (1989: 115).

The Hollywood movie – a form of storytelling able to compete in universality with the fairy-tale or, say, the thrillers of Agatha Christie (five billion world sales) – is a perfect illustration of the emphasis on plot which underlies Aristotle's poetics. Its modus operandi can be taken from *On the Art of Poetry*:

> The plot of a play, being the representation of a single object, must present it as a single whole; and its various incidents must be so arranged that if any one of them is differently placed or taken away the effect of wholeness will be seriously disrupted. For if the presence or absence of something makes no apparent difference, it is no real part of the whole (Aristotle, 1965: 43).

It is not surprising therefore that the Hollywood scriptwriting manuals frequently evoke Greek tragedy. Wells Root recalls that a Greek-American student, with whom he discussed conflict, 'went home that week and dug through his library of Aeschylus, Sophocles and Euripides in native Greek'. When he came back, he was able to tell the class that 'that these conflict principles, which power *M*A*S*H*, *Mutiny on the Bounty*, *Roots*, and *Star Wars*, were present throughout all the great Greek classic dramas' (1979: 44). In similar vein, William Miller argues that 'the narrative film still beguiles us as the dramatic narrative has since the time of Sophocles, Aeschylus and Euripides' (1980: 11), Ben Brady and Lance Lee begin with an excerpt from Aeschylus's *Agamemnon* (1988: 7–8), and Irwin R. Blacker (1986) even goes so far as to include Aristotle – 'first, foremost, and always' – in his acknowledgements.

Much traditional analysis of plot structure in tragedy has made use of three-part models: A. C. Bradley's exposition, conflict and catastrophe (1961: 30), for example, or Francis Fergusson's purpose, passion, perception (1968: 18). In a similar way Joseph Campbell argues that the standard path of the mythological adventure of the hero is 'a magnification of the formula represented in the rites of passage: *separation – initiation – return*' (1975: 31). Some contemporary writing on the semiological study of drama derides this three-stage approach, with Aston and Savona describing it as an 'outmoded form of analysis, which centres on dramatic conflict and opposing forces' (1991: 19). But these categories are crucial to any analysis of popular cinema, since, for over sixty years and regardless of genre, the Hollywood industry has almost invariably used a single story structure comprising a three act pattern. This can be expressed, in terms of plot, as set-up, confrontation, resolution (Field, 1982: 11), set-up, development, resolution (Seger, 1987: 4), conflict, crisis, climax (Brady and Lee, 1988: 55), or establishing, building, resolving (Hauge, 1989: 104). In terms of the protagonist, it can be described as a 'restorative' drama comprising transgression, redemption, restoration (Dancyger and Rush, 1991: 25). It can even be set out, more graphically, as 'get your man up a tree', 'throw stones at him', and 'get him down out of the tree' (Root, 1979: 2). Though the truth is somewhat more complicated, some of the scriptwriting manuals maintain that the three acts of a movie last thirty, sixty and thirty minutes respectively. Certainly the middle act tends to be the longest, and the final act is generally the fastest moving.

In the Hollywood structural pattern, an act is a series of scenes in a strategic sequence, enacting a story, expressing and arousing emotions and conveying a specific view of the world. It is a logical chain of scenes, each of which builds on the scene before. It is also a constantly surprising chain of scenes, with each new scene ideally turning the story in some way or other, so that we reach a point which, though logical, was not foreseen. The overall pattern of an act is one of increasing dramatic tension, building up to a major scene of confrontation, which turns or twists the story into a new act, or – in act three – furnishes a resolution to the action. This climax is logically, dramatically and thematically consistent with the starting point, but could not have been predicted at that point. There is a clear relationship of balance and contrast between the various act climaxes.

As early as the credits, the genre of the film needs to be established and the tone set, partly in order to establish the kind of story logic we will be prepared to accept. The protagonist is normally introduced and established early on, often at the very start of the first scene of act one. There can be only one protagonist. Within five to fifteen minutes of the start of the film there should be an incident, event, action which triggers a major change for the protagonist, that is, an enacted scene which links action and protagonist inextricably together. This triggering incident itself – what Seger calls the 'catalyst' (1987: 12) – can be a chance event or an accident, but everything that follows from it must have at least a story logic. That is to say, the triggering incident did not have to happen, but when it has happened, there are very powerful implications and after-effects. The action of the film is the following through of these implications, until a resolution is reached, whereupon the film ends. In addition to setting the action in motion by posing a question to the protagonist (what to do next?), the triggering incident also indicates the film's central theme and the values with which it deals.

After the triggering incident, the film normally stays with the protagonist as the stakes are progressively raised by new and surprising (but logical) turns of the plot. Normally at this point we share the protagonist's level of knowledge, and we experience the twists of the plot in act one with him or her. The act one climax is a major turning point – a fundamental raising of the stakes – sufficient to propel the action into a new act. In a sense it is a point of no return: nothing can be the same now, until order is finally restored at the very end of the film. The act one climax is usually also a point of major defeat or challenge for the protagonist and puts him or her under the greatest degree of pressure so far, thereby cementing our empathy. We have followed the protagonist since the triggering incident and shared his or her efforts. The climax or turning point shows that these efforts have been misdirected. Order, we both discover, cannot be restored so easily, so that another pathway will be needed.

The first act climax is linked thematically to the rest of the act, relating directly to the initial question raised, illuminating further the underlying theme of the film, and often serving also as a point when our relationship with the protagonist changes. The act one climax often gives us knowledge or information not shared by the protagonist, or insight which he or she refuses to accept. From this point on we are generally ahead of the protagonist, aware that there are dangers or difficulties in the path which he or she has chosen, though we may still be surprised by the actual form these take. But despite what we know or anticipate, it is the protagonist's decision and action that take us on in the narrative, into act two. The path chosen will, conventionally, turn out to be the wrong one – a path that leads only to partial success or even to seeming disaster – but we empathise with the protagonist as he or she pursues it energetically.

The beginning of the second act is usually marked by a major change – such as a shift in location or the introduction of a new major character, or both – motivated by the actions of the protagonist. There is often an initial relaxation of mood, but the tension grows steadily to a point of even greater climax and crisis by the end of the second act. Often the starting point is a point of optimism – the beginning of a new relationship or commitment, for example. The protagonist has an apparent answer (a falsely attractive way of achieving a solution) to the problem posed by the triggering incident and restated in the climax of act one. He or she also has the energy and application to pursue this. Whereas act one sets up the action, act two deals with confrontation and opposition, the progressive complications which stem from the initial disturbance of order.

At the beginning of act two, the protagonist *chooses* a particular line of action (if this had not been chosen, there would be no second act and no drama). We can go along with this choice, even if we have some apprehensions. The second act is generally the longest of the three and, in addition to its climax, it often has a major scene or turning of the plot at its mid-point (the middle of the film). This may well change and complicate all that follows (closing down certain options, placing new emphasis on others). It may also represent a new shift in the relative levels of knowledge of protagonist and spectator. The subsequent climax at the end of act two relates directly to the triggering incident and represents a major reversal of some kind to the act one climax. The act two climax also brings the protagonist to his or her lowest point, to a major crisis. Though the climax (the event) and the crisis (the realisation of its implications) may be in separate scenes, they together serve to focus the action, bringing together (or potentially together) plot and sub-plot. At the end of act two we can normally see no way out of the crisis facing the protagonist (we have no superior knowledge at this point). Therefore we have no alternative but to rely on the decisions and actions of the protagonist, who will drive the action of the film to its final climax and resolution in the following act. The act two climax and crisis present a situation which *has* to be resolved: there is no way that the spectator can be satisfied if the story does not move on to a solution.

Act three begins with a lull in the action. This is necessary to allow the protagonist to take stock of his or her situation. The crisis with which act two ended compels the protagonist to re-evaluate all the efforts made so far. If there is a romance sub-plot, for example, this is a time when a commitment to the relationship must be made (though the expression of this to the partner may come a little later). This decision is one of a series now made by the protagonist as he or she is restored to full potency. At this point the spectator is normally at a loss as to what is to be done next (or how exactly the protagonist can accomplish what obviously has to be done). The crisis and climax of act two have exhausted the spectator's superior knowledge, and much of the satisfaction of the film's resolution stems from the fact that the protagonist now takes over to determine the outcome and thereby surprise us. As soon as the protagonist translates decision into action, the pace of the film increases. More and more obstacles may be placed in the protagonist's way, but they are swept aside because of the protagonist's new clarity of vision and totality of commitment. The protagonist may require help to overcome what is – in the third act climax – the sternest test so far, but essentially the outcome will be the result of his or her own efforts. When the question set by the triggering incident (which has shaped the whole subsequent action of the film) has been answered, order can be restored and a point of stasis reached, so that the film's resolution need be only the briefest of codas, no more than time for the audience to get its breath back or for the curtains to close on the completed action.

North by Northwest

This Hollywood system of plot construction can be clearly seen in action in *North by Northwest*, made by Alfred Hitchcock in 1959 from an original script by Ernest Lehman. The genre is immediately established as that of the comedy thriller by the credits, which feature Saul Bass titles, a score by Bernard Herrman, name Cary Grant as the star, and give us the anticipated personal appearance by Hitchcock himself. The very first scene introduces us to Roger Thornhill (played by Cary Grant) on his way to an appointment in Madison Avenue. He is a man totally in charge of his life and world – suave, assured, and slightly dishonest, telling his secretary that, 'in the world of advertising there is no such thing as a lie, Maggie. Only The Expedient Exaggeration'. But he makes one tiny error: he tells Maggie to phone his mother, forgetting that the latter is playing bridge. His attempt, in scene two at the Plaza Hotel, to put this right by sending a wire to his mother, leads to him being mistaken for a hotel resident called 'Kaplan' by two gunmen ('mere errand boys, carrying concealed weapons') who kidnap him. Like Thornhill, we are totally perplexed, since we know he is not the person the gunmen are seeking. This is the film's triggering incident – the entry of fate, chance, disorder into the protagonist's life – from which will stem all the action of the film. It also defines the central themes which *North by Northwest* will explore: questions of identity, (mis)recognition and – by extension – play-acting.

For the next eight scenes we follow Thornhill and share his growing perplexity. The ride takes him to a surprising location, a mansion in Glen Cove belonging to someone called Townsend. The first major confrontation of the film introduces him to 'Townsend' (in fact, as we later discover, Philip Vandamm). Played by James Mason, 'Townsend' is as suave, attractive and assured as Thornhill himself – a man with whom he would expect to be able to do business. But Thornhill's denials that he is Kaplan are coolly rejected ('I know you are a man of many names') and his offer of proof in the form of his identification papers is declined ('They provide you with such *good* ones'). Instead of being able to resolve the misunderstanding, Thornhill in fact finds himself in real danger, when Vandamm offers him 'the opportunity of surviving the night', in exchange for information which, of course, he does not have. Thornhill's idea of taking a quick trip back to town (he has tickets for the theatre) is turned against him, as Vandamm's henchmen fill him full of bourbon and set him out on the road in a stolen car.

Thornhill, no doubt accustomed to drinking and driving, survives the ordeal and escapes his pursuers by driving into the back of a police car. While the police treat him simply as a drunk talking nonsense, the judge next morning allows him a chance to prove the truth of his seemingly absurd story. But Thornhill's second visit to Glen Cove, this time in the company of county detectives, proves as unhappy as the first. He finds all trace of his earlier presence removed, and when 'Mrs Townsend' enters, she greets him as an old friend who had come to dinner the previous night after having had too much to drink. She caps her performance by telling the detectives that her husband is at the United Nations, addressing the General Assembly. Thornhill has now exhausted the patience of the authorities (police, court, county detectives). He therefore returns to the Plaza Hotel to seek information about Kaplan, taking along his sole ally, his mother (Jessie Royce Landis), and using her to help him get the key to Kaplan's room. At this point, Thornhill, in his quest to prove that he is not Kaplan, has to take on the latter's identity when confronted by the hotel maid and valet. When Vandamm's henchmen ring Kaplan's room and he answers the phone, they are again unimpressed by his protests that he is not Kaplan ('Of course not. You answer his telephone and you live in his room, and yet you are not Mr Kaplan'). They threaten him, but he is able to make his escape, this time to follow up his other main lead, going to see Lester Townsend at the United Nations.

The real Townsend, whom he meets there – after giving his name as Kaplan to the receptionist – seems to know something about Vandamm, whose photograph Thornhill has found in Kaplan's room. But before he can help, Townsend is killed by a knife thrown by one of Vandamm's men. Instinctively pulling the knife out of the dying man's back, Thornhill is photographed by a press man, seemingly brandishing the murder weapon. Though he escapes from the building, he is now in real peril: sought first by Vandamm, who now has additional evidence that indicates that he is indeed Kaplan, and also by the police, who suspect him of murder. The identity which seemed so secure at the outset is now threatened, and several times; in trying to find out who Kaplan is, he has had to use that name himself.

But the final scene of the first act – scene eleven – set in the CIA bureau, has a further twist for the audience. We learn that Kaplan does not exist and is merely a decoy set-up to protect the CIA's real agent, 'working under Vandamm's nose'. While some of the CIA committee members are sympathetic, the decision of the boss, the Professor (Leo G. Carroll), is that they are unable to help Thornhill without endangering their own agent: 'Goodbye Mr Thornhill . . . wherever you are'. This whole first act – eleven scenes, 298 shots, 39.5 minutes – is a perfect example of Hollywood structure: introducing us immediately to the protagonist whose life is promptly turned upside-down, following him in his efforts to put matters right but merely getting ever deeper into trouble. The final scene of the act provides us with information denied to Thornhill, and we are now ahead of him for the very first time. As he plunges forward in act two attempting to recover his identity, we wait for him to find out the crucial fact that has been revealed to us: Kaplan does not exist. As one of the screenwriting manuals puts it, this typical act two situation is as if the character, moving obliviously forward, has a rubber band tied round the waist: 'The character doesn't see the rubber band, but we do. We wait for the band to reach the point of greatest elasticity and snap the character back' (Dancyger and Rush, 1991: 21).

In Hollywood cinema a change of location is customary at the beginning of act two, and accordingly scene twelve opens in Grand Central Station. Symbolically saying goodbye on the telephone to his mother (who does not reappear in the film), Thornhill sets out on the adventure of hunting down Kaplan, who he knows has a room booked at the Ambassador East Hotel in Chicago. Though recognised in the ticket office, he manages to get onto the Twentieth Century express, where he meets a beautiful blonde, Eve (Eva-Marie Saint), who promptly helps him by misdirecting the police. This is the start of the film's romance subplot, which will bear out to the full the Hollywood scripting manuals' definition: romance has nothing to do with sex as such, it is a situation involving a character who offers both support and threat to the protagonist (Hauge, 1989: 59). Later, Eve picks up Thornhill in the dining car and, though she recognises him as the wanted killer, she shows no fear. Instead she invites him back to her compartment and then helps him further when the police threaten. They make love. This first climax of the romance subplot is followed immediately by the first crisis: we (but not Thornhill) see Eve pass a note to Vandamm, who is also on the train: 'What do I do with him in the morning?' While Thornhill continues on his quest, we now know of two key hindrances: Kaplan does not exist and Eve is treacherous.

Arriving in Chicago, Thornhill again evades the police with Eve's help. She even purports to phone Kaplan for him, but in fact the meeting she sets up for him has been devised by Leonard (Martin Landau), Vandamm's secretary. What follows is a classic Hitchcock thriller sequence, in which an innocent man is threatened and almost destroyed, not at night in some dark alleyway, but in broad daylight in an open midwestern cornfield, by a seemingly innocuous crop-dusting plane. This sequence at the midpoint of the film is the action climax – unmatched until the final confrontation on Mount Rushmore at the climax of act three.

Fearing that he was set up, Thornhill goes to the Ambassador East Hotel, where he realises Eve's treachery. She evades him, but he follows her to an auction room. There he abuses Eve and has his second confrontation with 'Townsend', now revealed as Vandamm. Again Thornhill finds himself trapped and under threat, but ingeniously finds a way out, by disrupting the auction, so that the police are called. Instead of arresting him, however, they take him to the airport, where the Professor tells him that Kaplan, whom he has been pursuing so energetically, does not exist but was a decoy to draw attention away from the CIA's real agent, Eve Kendall. This act two climax thus presents Thornhill with the moment of realisation that confronts all protagonists at this point in conventional Hollywood cinema. He now understands that most of his efforts have been misguided and that he has misunderstood the situation to such an extent that he has put the woman he now knows he loves in mortal danger.

Act two ends with a major surprise for the audience as well as for Thornhill, since we had been given no indication that Eve was the CIA agent. But her dual identity does explain her actions to date – why she picked up Thornhill and why she betrayed him after she had seemed to fall in love with him – at least with the degree of logic we demand from a comedy thriller. The levels of knowledge of both audience and protagonist are now equal, but though we know what we want Thornhill to do (defeat Vandamm and win Eve), we are not in a position to see how this can be achieved. Only Thornhill's decision and action – which ironically involves initially becoming Kaplan – can solve the matter. We go into act three following the protagonist, given no prior warning that the meeting with Eve, where he provokes her to such an extent that she shoots him, is a CIA set-up organised by the Professor. The subsequent scene in the woods, when the couple affirm their love for each other is therefore all the more touching. Their mutual questions of love and identity are now clarified, and it seems that the film can find its resolution after just a couple of further scenes. But in fact the Professor has double-crossed Thornhill: Eve is to leave the country with Vandamm and Thornhill's actions, far from saving Eve, have merely placed her in even greater danger by compelling Vandamm to take her along with him when he leaves the country.

Thornhill is therefore now in the classic situation of a protagonist in the last act of a Hollywood drama, compelled to act and confront a powerful adversary alone. But to strengthen him he has his identity restored: he is now Roger Thornhill seeking to rescue the woman he loves and who loves him. He escapes from the Professor and goes directly to Vandamm's house. While outside and unable to contact Eve, he learns that she is indeed in real danger: Leonard has found the gun loaded with blanks and acts out a mock shooting of the startled Vandamm. When Thornhill does get into the house, he reaches Eve, but is trapped when the housekeeper holds him at gunpoint. As Thornhill eventually realises, it is again the gun loaded with blanks (the triple use of this single object is a good indication of the screenwriter Ernest Lehman's structural ingenuity). The couple escape, but are trapped amid the massive stone faces carved into Mount Rushmore. Their fate seems hopeless, but the Professor intervenes, shooting Leonard and provoking Vandamm's final comment, 'Rather unsporting, don't you think . . . using real bullets?'

There is no dramatic logic in the Professor's appearance – though it does complete the pattern already established in the film, that he appears at the end of each act to transform the direction of the plot. But we have no time to query the situation, since, as in a dream and within just two shots, the couple are translated from Mount Rushmore to the express train on which they first met. The pleasure which *North by Northwest* offers its audience is thus very close to the promise which, in Bruno Bettelheim's account, fairy-tales afford a child:

> Fairy tales intimate that a rewarding, good life is within one's reach despite adversity – but only if one does not shy away from the hazardous struggles without which one can never achieve true identity. These stories promise that if a child dares to engage in this fearsome and taxing search, benevolent powers will come to his aid, and he will succeed (1978: 24).

In addition to its clear three-act structure and fairy-tale meaning, *North by Northwest* also shows the way Hollywood creates a hierarchy of plot and subplots, each with its own shape and pattern. The main plot is Thornhill's struggle to recover his identity: he is mistaken for Kaplan, he pursues Kaplan and, eventually, he becomes Kaplan, in order to defeat Vandamm. When he has accomplished this and clarified Eve's feelings and situation – in the scene in the woods near the beginning of act three – he can recover is identity and undertake the final rescue as himself, thereby acquiring a wife (his last words on Mount Rushmore are, 'Come on, Mrs Thornhill'). The second plot strand – the romance with Eve – is structured into three parts, though over only two acts: Eve as lover and helper, Eve as traitor, Eve in danger. A third plot strand – the confrontation with the villain – is more intermittent, but has its pattern too. In act one Vandamm is effortlessly superior, in act two his elaborate execution plans fail, in act three he is duped and finally deprived of his liberty, the microfilm he planned to smuggle out of the country and, of course, Eve. The power of the third act comes partly from the bringing together of the three plot strands as Thornhill – his identity recovered – defeats Vandamm and wins Eve. The role of the Professor would be unacceptable perhaps outside the comedy thriller genre, since he acts as a kind of *deus ex machina*. But each of his appearances is highly structured: at each of the three act climaxes (and also in the scene in the woods) he intervenes to twist the plot in a wholly new direction, though it is only Thornhill's persistent energy and determination that carry the plot forward.

To be as effective as it is, this kind of closed plot needs balance as well as shape. It is crucial that Thornhill and Vandamm, as hero and villain, are well matched, and indeed one can imagine Vandamm being equally successful on Madison Avenue. The key to Vandamm's stature within the plot is that he can delegate the physical activity (kidnapping, killing) to his two heavies and leave the malevolence to Leonard. The way that Eve is caught between Thornhill and Vandamm, and so between good and evil, gives a special poignancy to the film, as, for example at the auction room or in the woods when it emerges that she has agreed to go off with Vandamm. Eve and Thornhill are likewise well matched: attractive, articulate, witty, resourceful. Both have an unhappy past and a complex present, and both have severe identity problems – he as Thornhill/Kaplan, she as lover/spy – which, in the make-believe world of the comedy thriller, can be resolved only in marriage.

The Hollywood movie of the sound era has to a large extent favoured the Broadway plot structure so admirably defined by Walter Kerr: 'A play was held to be something of a machine in those days. . . . It was a machine for surprising and delighting the audience, regularly, logically, insanely, but accountably. A play was like a watch that laughed' (quoted in Kael, 1971: 4). Certainly in this kind of comedy thriller the constant mix of logic and surprise is the immediate key to the film's success, but this does not preclude a thematic richness and unity. In *North by Northwest* the catalyst of misrecognition and loss of identity, of being taken for what one is not, gives rise not only to a highly enjoyable, if totally improbable, plot, but also a whole series of enactments involving play-acting, *mise en scène* and improvisation. Vandamm acts out the role of Townsend, just as his sister plays Mrs Townsend, being later complimented by Vandamm on 'her superb performance'. Thornhill is compelled to act the part of Kaplan with the staff of the hotel and to improvise the role of a drunk at the auction, later earning Vandamm's compliments on his 'colourful exit'. At the time, however, Vandamm is more critical:

> Has anyone ever told you that you overplay your various roles rather severely, Mr Kaplan? First you're the outraged Madison Avenue man who claims he has been mistaken for someone else. Then you play a fugitive from justice, supposedly trying to clear his name of a crime he knows he didn't commit. And now you play the peevish lover, stung by jealousy and betrayal. Seems to me you fellows could stand a little less training from the FBI and a little more from the Actors' Studio (Lehman, 1972: 91).

Just as Vandamm constructs an elaborate *mise en scène* for Thornhill's assassination in the cornfields, so too Thornhill and Eve stage a most convincing shooting incident to deceive Vandamm. His earlier question to Thornhill, 'And now what little drama are we here for today?', does not prevent him from being duped, until Leonard restages the incident by firing blanks at Vandamm. In this morass of deception and play-acting, it is difficult for Thornhill and Eve not to misunderstand each other, until the scene in the woods brings them together for the first time in their true identities. In the final scenes their love is real, though the plot is virtual self parody, so it is appropriate that the film ends with real bullets and a dream resolution.

Shot breakdown

NORTH BY NORTHWEST

(Overall: graphics + 1,321 shots: 130 minutes)
ONE [opening graphics + 315 shots: 39.5 minutes]

	Credits (graphics + 1–8)	8 shots
	Establish the genre: comedy thriller	
1	*Madison Avenue* (9–16)	8 shots
	Introduction to Thornhill	
2	*Plaza Hotel* (17–30)	14 shots
	Thornhill misrecognised	
3	*Taken for a Ride* (31–42)12 shots	
	Thornhill is kidnapped	
4	*Townsend's House* (43–94)	52 shots
	Confrontation with the villain, 'Townsend'	
5	*Night Exterior* (95–161)	66 shots
	Thornhill's escape	
6	*Police Station* (161–8)	7 shots
	Thornhill in safety	
7	*Courtroom* (169–186)	18 shots
	Thornhill given a chance to prove his testimony	
8	*Townsend's House* (187–218)tab 37 shots	
	The tables are turned on Thornhill	
9	*Plaza Hotel* (219–61)39 shots	
	Thornhill is forced to flee	
10	*United Nations Building* (262–98)	37 shots
	The killing of the real Townsend	
11	*CIA* (299–315)	17 shots
	'Goodbye, Mr Thornhill'	

TWO [616 shots, 54.5 minutes]
12 *Grand Central Station* (316–37)   22 shots
      Thornhill makes his escape on the Twentieth Century
13 *On the Train* (338–52)   15 shots
      His first meeting with Eve
14 *The Dining Car* (353–458)   106 shots
      Eve picks him up
15 *Eve's Compartment* (459–93)   35 shots
      The couple evade the police
16 *The Train (Later)* (494–519)   26 shots
      Lovemaking, then betrayal
17 *Chicago Station* (520–75)   56 shots
      Thornhill escapes, but Eve again betrays him
18 *Prairie Stop, Highway 41* (576–708)   133 shots
      The crop dusting sequence
19 *Hotel Ambassador East* (709–70)   62 shots
      Confrontation with Eve
20 *The Auction Room* (771–891)   121 shots
      Confrontation with Vandamm
21 *Police Car* (892–902)   11 shots
      Thornhill taken to the airport, not the police station
22 *Airport* (903–31)   29 shots
      The Professor enrols him to help the CIA

THREE [390 shots, 34 minutes]
23 *Mount Rushmore* (932–82)   51 shots
      Thornhill and Eve fake the shooting
24 *The Forest* (983–1036)   54 shots
      The promise of love, then abrupt separation
25 *The Hospital Room* (1037–49)   13 shots
      Thornhill escapes again
26 *Outside Vandamm's House* (1050–134)   85 shots
      Thornhill tries to reach the endangered Eve
27 *Inside Vandamm's House* (1135–78)   44 shots
      Thornhill trapped and immobile
28 *Outside the House* (1179–222)   44 shots
      Thornhill and Eve make their escape
29 *On Mount Rushmore* (1223–319)   97 shots
      Total disaster threatens
30 *The Miraculous Escape* (1320–21)   2 shots
      The triumph of love

6 The open plot: *L'Avventura*

Antonioni lets his forms express the alienation he wants to communicate
to his public. By choosing to express it in the very structure of his
discourse, he manages to control it while letting it act upon his viewers

UMBERTO ECO (1989)

The open work

Umberto Eco's definition of the novelty of Franz Kafka's work gives
an excellent introduction to the formal and ideological characteristics
of what he terms the 'open' work:

> The work remains inexhaustible in so far as it is 'open', because in it an
> ordered world based on universally acknowledged laws is replaced by a
> world based on ambiguity, both in the negative sense that directional
> centres are missing and in a positive sense, because values and dogma are
> constantly being placed in question (1989: 9).

Eco sees in the poetics of the open work the overtones of trends in
contemporary science, and his consideration of the use of the term
'field of possibilities' is extremely relevant to the work of
Michelangelo Antonioni. In Eco's view it implies 'a revised vision of
the classic relationship posited between cause and effect as a rigid one-
directional system: now a complex interplay of motive forces is
envisaged, a configuration of possible events, a complete dynamism of
structure' (1989: 14). Antonioni himself drew attention to the
dichotomy between science and morality in his presentation of the film
L'avventura at Cannes in 1960, arguing that 'science has never been
more humble and less dogmatic than it is today. Whereas our moral
attitudes are governed by an absolute sense of stultification. . . . The
present moral standards we live by, these myths, these conventions are
old and obsolete' (1989: 178). This presentation set the tone for much
of the discussion of *L'avventura* and the subsequent films of the early
1960s (*La notte* and *L'eclisse* in particular) in terms of such themes as
alienation and lack of communication.

The present analysis looks at the implications of Antonioni's approach for the dramatic structure of *L'avventura*. At Cannes in 1960 the film was very badly received by the audience, no doubt because, as Eco recognises, the public – whether festival goers, ordinary spectators, readers, or television viewers – prefers what one might call a prefabricated view of reality. The public 'not only wants to know what is happening in the world but also expects to hear or see it in the shape of a well-constructed novel, since this is the way it chooses to perceive "real" life – stripped of all chance elements and reconstructed as plot' (1989: 118). This is, of course, also the way in which Hollywood operates.

Throughout most of its history, cinema has been dominated by the tightly plotted 'closed' film, of which *North by Northwest* is a prime example. Until the end of World War II, works which did not fill the requirements of this conventional dramatic structure were isolated films which tended to be marginalised and shown not in commercial cinemas, but only at film societies. Italian neo-realist cinema of the 1940s and early 1950s offered a range of radically new approaches, which implied discarding many of the assumptions of Hollywood: star performances, intricately contrived lighting and camerawork, studio sets, and so on. While an anti-fascist stance is common to the whole neo-realist group, the individual responses of the film makers varied widely. Their great strength was to establish close links with a reality defined in social terms and expressed through the everyday activities of sympathetically drawn characters who were generally helpless to resist the economic pressures to which they were exposed. Within this socially defined framework, the tone was fundamentally optimistic, with the films offering a celebration of human will and an (admittedly muted) hope for the future. In general the neo-realists saw no contradiction in their approach: looking at reality was, in Roberto Rossellini's words, 'an act of humility to life' and, as such, basically unproblematic. Their lack of questioning is perhaps reflected in the fact that collectively they did not seek to adopt a radically new pattern of dramatic narrative. Each film maker chose his own approach: Luchino Visconti favouring an ample storyline of a kind familiar from the nineteenth century novel, Guiseppe De Santis and Alberto Lattuada giving their films a drive that brought them close to melodrama, Roberto Rossellini gravitating towards a loose structure in which the whole weight of the drama was concentrated in a limited number of key extended episodes, while Vittorio De Sica and Cesare Zavattini built their films out of small scenes – often almost gags – arranged in a calculated sequence of dramatic rise and fall (Armes, 1971: 193).

The enormous impact made around 1958–60 by the film makers of the French New Wave, such as Jean-Luc Godard and Alain Resnais, and by such post-neorealist Italian directors as Michelangelo Antonioni and Federico Fellini stems largely from the fact that they offered, for virtually the first time in film history, a rich body of work within the European mainstream which diverged in significant ways from the Hollywood model in terms of dramatic structure as well as content or style. In place of films which relied on the conventions of the closed plot, audiences were now confronted with works based on the premise that, in Umberto Eco's words, 'the world is a web of possibilities' of which the work of art must reproduce the physiognomy (1989: 115).

With the emergence of such a European art cinema, film making was brought at least partially in line with those developments which had been occurring for decades in other art forms, such as music or theatre. With the work of Michelangelo Antonioni, for example, we enter a filmic world in which we find, to quote Eco once more, 'a series of events totally devoid of conventional dramatic connections – stories in which nothing happens, or, rather, where things happen not by narrative necessity but, at least in appearance, by chance' (1989: 115). Many of the familiar landmarks of the Hollywood approach are missing, among them the immediate foregrounding of the protagonist and the clear statement of the focus of the drama, the stereotyped characters with their carefully contrived plot roles, the totally worked-out growth and relaxation of tension and dramatic impact, and the cunningly located plot points which throw the action into a new direction. Yet the vestigial underpinning of a three-act pattern can be uncovered if one looks at the overall dramatic pattern of Antonioni's films.

Antonioni placed a new stress on shooting, on the actual realisation of the film, but the script itself was not discarded, and rejection of so many of the conventions of Hollywood screenwriting did not mean that Antonioni was concerned with any sort of purely improvisatory film making. Introducing a volume containing four of his preproduction scripts, he gives a very clear account of his working methods:

> Rereading these scenes, what I feel most is the memory of moments which inspired me to conceive and write those things. Visits to certain places, conversations with people, time spent at the very spots where the story is said to take place, the gradual unfolding of the picture in its fundamental images, in its tone, in its place: This is very important to me. Perhaps the most important time. The arrangement of scenes is an intermediate phase, a necessary but transitory one. To shoot the film right, in my opinion, I have to reconnect it with that moment, I need to recall that emotion, those feelings, those figurative intuitions, that confidence (1963: xiii).

There are a number of significant changes in the progression from preproduction script to finished film – the Grove Press edition of the post-production script of *L'avventura* lists twenty-two alterations from the earlier published version (1969: 147–81) – but this is merely a continuation of the process of refinement which characterises the stages of the scripting process itself. Tonino Guerra, a script collaborator on *L'avventura* and many other subsequent Antonioni films, makes this clear: 'In the first sketches for the screenplay when we mark out this or that scene everything is entrusted to words. We rework things, change lengthy dialogue scenes and along the way get ourselves accustomed to the way a particular character speaks. Then, very very slowly, the words fall away and gestures begin to take their place, movements of the characters. . . visual marks on which the story of the film more and more begins to rest. Finally, even the most beautiful lines fall away, those that had so charmed us and seemed so necessary' (quoted in Rohdie, 1990: 76). The shooting is crucial for Antonioni, but it remains a time of realisation, not of autonomous creation: 'From the moment the director puts himself behind the camera he opens his eyes to what is the blank page for the writer, the canvas for the painter. . . . At that moment the director is alone, and only he has the chance to create poetry, to translate, let us say it, into poetry, the extremely precious, but nevertheless inert pages of the script' (1990: 81).

Antonioni's roots are in the neo-realist movement – he was shooting his first documentary *Gente del Po* in 1942–3 at the very same time that Luchino Visconti was filming his own first feature, *Ossessione*, elsewhere on the banks of the same river. But from the very beginning, Antonioni stood apart from his contemporaries, because of the way in which, through the rejection of certain neo-realist assumptions, his work opened up new dramatic possibilities. The key stylistic characteristics noted at the time were his distance and austerity: his works were seen as acts of observation, from which moralising is rigorously excluded, rather than emotionally involving dramas. Many of the most obvious features of Antonioni's style are forms of de-dramatisation of some kind. There is a rigid turning away from all aspects of theatricality, a paring-down of dialogue and, eventually, an attenuation of the role of the musical score. The characters are never fully centre-stage. Instead of focusing directly on them, Antonioni probes their *milieux*, the landscapes through which they pass, the spaces between them. Often they are well-educated, affluent individuals, cut off to some extent from their surroundings, articulate about most things, but not about the emotional situations in which they find themselves. The events may lead them to disaster, even to death, but there is no affirmation of value of the kind that we find in Hollywood movies, since in Antonioni's world there is never any real possibility for an individual character to find personal redemption.

Though Antonioni's work was often greeted with hostility by Italian critics, who regarded his departures from neo-realism as a betrayal of the values of that movement, it is in fact far from being a negative style. Sam Rohdie captures the positive, innovative side very well: 'The places are real but unstable. The interest is not with this instability, nor these losses of place, but rather with the productivity of that instability, the new shapes, the new stories, the new temporary subjects which they permit' (1990: 2). The space left by the omission of conventional dramatic climaxes – and the whole series of scenes whose sole function is to build towards a climax – allows space of those purely visual aspects of Antonioni's films which are so captivating: the patterns of figures in a landscape, the play of light and shadow, the gestures and facial expressions of characters caught in privacy or solitude. Far from being empty, the films create a very particular stance that is characteristic of the director. To quote Rohdie once more, the films 'pose a subject (only to compromise it), constitute objects (only to dissolve them), propose stories (only to lose them), but, equally, they turn those compromises and losses back towards another solidity: the new story' (1990: 3). We can see how this works in structural terms if we examine the shape of the film which brought Antonioni his world reputation in 1960: *L'avventura*.

L'avventura

Despite its many formal and structural innovations, *L'avventura*, which runs for some 133 minutes, has, superficially at least, an underlying three-act structure of the conventional kind, with each act given its own specific tone and geographical locale. The long first act (eleven scenes, fifty-five minutes) begins with Anna and Claudia setting out to join a holiday party on Patrizia's yacht, sailing for the island of Lisca Bianca, and ends with the departure of the group from the island after Anna's disappearance. Act two (sixteen scenes and again about fifty-five minutes) takes place in the variety of mainland locations visited by Claudia and Anna's lover, Sandro, as they follow up clues which they hope will lead them to Anna, but without success. The much shorter final act (just six scenes and twenty-three minutes) is set in a single location, the San Domenico Palace Hotel in Taormina, beginning with the couple's arrival and ending with Claudia's discovery of Sandro's betrayal of her.

In conventional terms, the first five scenes of the first act of *L'avventura* establish Anna (Lea Massari) as the protagonist. We first meet her in mid-discussion with her father and then follow her to a meeting with her lover, Sandro (Gabriele Ferzetti), whom she has not seen for a month. In both scenes her friend Claudia (Monica Vitti) is very much a secondary figure, late in joining Anna at the house and subsequently left to wander about in the square while the couple, as she realises, make love above her head. On the yacht, among the members of the lethargic holiday party, Anna is the first to take a decisive action, diving from the boat while it is still moving, to be followed only later by Claudia and Sandro. It is Anna too who becomes the focus of attention when she screams that she is being threatened by a shark, though she subsequently confesses to Claudia, in the privacy of her cabin, that it was all a joke. Later, on the island, she and Sandro, deeper in conversation than any of the other couples, form the focus of attention at the end of the fifth scene.

The dialogue in *L'avventura* is sparse, but there is one theme developed consistently through the opening action: the question of Anna's love for Sandro. Her father annoys her by criticising the relationship ('You know he'll never marry you'), but she shows herself to be uncertain in her conversation with Claudia on the way to visit Sandro ('It's not easy to keep track of things when one person's here and the other far off somewhere'). In their love scene at the flat,

Sandro is relaxed, but she is tense, and her passion has an edge of anger. On the island his firm confidence that they will get married contrasts strongly with her self-doubt ('I'm very unhappy. The thought of losing you makes me want to die. And yet . . . I don't feel you any more'). We are on familiar ground up to this point in the film. The focus is on fundamental aspects of Anna's relationship with Sandro, and this is highlighted by the counter-point of the two other couples on the yacht whose problems exceed theirs: the sarcastic Corrado with his twittering companion of twelve years, Giulia; and the indolent Patrizia, too bored and lethargic even to contemplate being unfaithful to her husband with Raimondo who adores her. We have no way of knowing, at a first viewing, that the key scene here is that between Anna and Claudia in the cabin, where they both take off their swimsuits and seem at moments like mirror images of each other. The crucial transaction comes when Anna gives Claudia one of her blouses – a first visual hint of what the narrative of the film will become: the story of the substitution of Claudia for her friend, both as protagonist and as Sandro's mistress. This first hint of the theme of substitution is backed up, later in the act, when Claudia meets Anna's father and realises to her horror she is wearing the missing Anna's blouse. In retrospect, we know that the substitution of one life for another is one of Antonioni's favourite themes, finding its most forceful and developed expression in *The Passenger* (1974). The disappearance of Anna, which forms the mid-point of the first act has the potential to be a major dramatic scene, since a powerful enigma of the kind that might shape a conventional film narrative has been established. Anna has already talked to Sandro about needing to spend some time on her own, so there is a whole range of possible explanations: has she gone off alone? is this another joke? has she had an accident? Yet in fact very little real drama is generated, the immediate mood among the group being one of uncertainty rather than anxiety. We have here the beginnings of a conventional detective plot, but no sooner have the possibilities been sketched in, than the narrative interest shifts. Though certain draft scenes aiming to offer some explanation were planned before the commencement of shooting, the finished film keeps to Antonioni's initial intention by refusing to offer a solution to the mystery.

During the next five scenes, covering the search of the island, all tension is dissipated, as Anna's friends wander, seemingly aimlessly among the rocks, looking and calling, but finding nothing. The arrival of the police and of Anna's father adds little dynamism, and the act concludes with life resuming its normal pattern – though without Anna – as most of the group resolve to go, as planned, to stay at the Princess Montalto's villa. Claudia feels she must stay to search the islands, and Sandro has to follow up the most tenuous of possible clues, news of the arrest on the mainland of a number of fishermen seen behaving suspiciously. Yet at this point there is nothing driving the plot forward in the conventional Hollywood sense.

In this set of scenes depicting a search which never really becomes one and which peters out even before it has got properly under way, Antonioni's particular modernity, his concern to depict human activity and experience without recourse to ready-made clichés and stock explanations, finds its full expression in the dramatic structure. His interest in margins and transitions, the spaces between actions and between characters, comes to the fore. The effect is tellingly defined by Marie-Claire Ropars-Wuilleumier:

> Through the mobility alone of his camera, which follows the internal itinerary of the characters, through the slow unfolding of places that never appear twice, he succeeds in creating a time dimension which is not that of memory; and if certain images echo the themes from the beginning, they suggest, in the viewer's mind, the present moment and not the past, thus making the viewer aware of time, which passes and modifies human beings though nothing is apparently happening (Antonioni, 1989: 192).

There is a double shift in operation here to decentre the characters. By refusing to cut when the characters move out of shot, holding the camera instead to create *temps morts* by framing empty images of rocks, sky and sea, Antonioni shifts attention from characters to the landscape, which is not simply a location for the action, but has an identity and beauty of its own. When he does remain focused on his characters till the end of a sequence, Antonioni at times holds the camera just a little longer than the drama needs, catching the actors emerging from their roles, so that, as Michel Butor recalls, he can allow them 'to be seen in a different way than usual and to rejoin a more anonymous and spontaneous humanity in relation to what they had just done' (quoted in Rohdie, 1990: 52).

Towards the end of the first act of *L'avventura* the overt drama is progressively drained away, as attention shifts from the absent Anna to those left behind. In particular attention is paid to the growing connection between the two people most concerned with her dis-

appearance, Claudia and Sandro. Forced to spend a night together
sheltering in a fisherman's hut, they are edgy, tensely aware of each
other, even vaguely hostile. But the morning brings a closer connection, though there is no sense of a growing relationship being plotted
dramatically. Sandro's action in kissing her before he leaves and her
response in not resisting him come therefore as a shock to the
audience. Like the characters we are uncertain: there is something in
the air, a shift in emotion has occurred, but how important this is or
what its consequences will be remain uncertain. The effect is
paradoxical, partly an de-dramatisation, partly an intensification of
the drama's demand on the spectator, since, as Italo Calvino has
noted, 'nothing is demonstrated, nothing is clearly stated; the viewer
receives no help or satisfaction; narrative style is barren, with no
ornament or digression; the spectators are forced to make the same
efforts and judgements they normally do, or ought to do, when
confronted by reality' (Antonioni, 1989: 196).

   The almost equally long second act is much more fragmentary and
diffuse than the first, but has a structure that allows some progression, in that the first half shows Sandro and Claudia apart, while
the second half brings them together to realise their love for each
other. What is deliberately missing, however, is the carefully contrived and plotted development of situations and character to create
the suspense, tension and increased dramatic force which typifies
conventional film making. The first four scenes follow Sandro's vain
efforts both to find Anna and to ensnare Claudia. It is soon apparent
that the hapless fishermen caught smuggling in Milazzo have nothing
to do with Anna's disappearance, but Sandro has a second lead, a
reporter called Francesco Zuria, who has written about the disappearance. On his way to meet him in Messina, Sandro manages to catch
up with Claudia and to board her train. She tells him he must go and
resists his advances ('Is it possible so little can make one change,
forget?'). Watching a young Sicilian couple strike up an acquaintance
softens her anger, but she still insists that Sandro must get off the
train: for her there is to be nothing more between them. The scene
ends with a characteristic long-held shot of the empty station and the
railway line, and then suddenly, without transition, Sandro is in the
midst of a crowd of men engaged in a near riot on the streets of
Messina, provoked by a pretty girl who flaunts herself, pretending to
be in trouble with a slit in her tight skirt. Zuria, who is in the crowd,
tells Sandro her name is Gloria Perkins and that if he wants her, it

will cost him 50,000 lire. But he is unable to help Sandro with news of Anna, saying that she is yesterday's story.

The abrupt transitions in this section of the film are characteristic of the whole second act, which offers a variety of moods and locations, some fascinating secondary detail, but virtually nothing about the ostensible central concern, Anna's fate. We leave Sandro taking Zuria off for a drink, with no fresh leads and clearly (from his scenes with Claudia) with a less than total commitment to finding Anna. There is therefore no tension or suspense about what he may be doing, while the film now offers us four consecutive scenes of Claudia staying with the Montaltos. Though there are a few conversational references to Anna – Giulia betting she will turn up, and the Princess Montalto wondering aloud whether Sandro may perhaps have done away with her – Anna's fate has now shifted from being the centre of concern.

The real focus of these four scenes is a new budding romance, between Giulia and the Princess's seventeen-year-old grandson, Goffredo. In her room, first alone and then with Patrizia, Giulia toys with her appearance, trying on wigs in a scene which, in its play on movement and mirror images, recalls the earlier scene on the yacht with Anna. After Giulia has allowed herself to be seduced by Goffredo (partly as a way of punishing Corrado), Claudia learns that Ettore, Patrizia's husband, will be sending a car to fetch Sandro, who is needed for business meetings, next day. At this point, roughly midway through the second act, the two main strands of the action – the search for Anna and the potential romance between Sandro and Claudia – seem to have both come to a halt. In place of the usual sequential pattern of developing scenes tightly bound by causal links, Antonioni has created a pattern of what Umberto Eco aptly calls 'willed chance', designed 'to provoke a feeling of suspension, of indeterminateness, in his audience' (1989: 116). Perhaps Anna will be found, perhaps the couple will come together again, either way there will be dilemmas to be faced and decisions to be made: there is no narrative engine driving the action towards a predictable ending and no compulsion on the characters to act.

In fact the couple do meet up again, since Claudia takes a ride out to Troina with the chauffeur sent to fetch Sandro, and the last eight scenes of the act trace the immediate consequences of her action. She finds Sandro talking with a chemist and his wife about a newspaper report of a foreign girl who passed through the town and later took a bus to Noto. Claudia and Sandro now set out to follow up this final clue and stumble on a totally uninhabited town, which Claudia finds totally depressing, like a cemetery. As they leave, the camera stays on the deserted square. Then, in an astonishing cut – as striking as the earlier transition from the silent railway station to the turmoil of Messina – we are shown Claudia's ecstatic face as she and Sandro make love in the open air and, as it turns out, next to a railway line.

Later, in Noto and now feeling ashamed of herself, Claudia is too frightened to go into the hotel in case Anna is there. As she admits to Sandro, she needs desperately to hear his words of love, though she knows he must have said them many times before to Anna. On the church roof in Noto, surrounded by the extravagant façades of the baroque buildings around the square, Sandro recalls the days when he was an architect, not someone who makes a fortune drawing up estimates. Almost on impulse, it seems, he asks Claudia to marry him, but she is too confused to give a coherent reply. Back in their hotel room, Claudia is happier than we have ever seen her before, play-acting and demanding compliments from Sandro. He cannot capture her mood, however, and goes to wait for her on the square, where his true feelings at this moment are revealed when he tips ink over a student's exquisite architectural drawing. Returning to the hotel and now needing Claudia, he finds her thoughtful, worried about their friends. Quickly they pack and leave.

In this central act of the film Antonioni has made no attempt to create tension by intercutting the actions of Sandro and Claudia when they are separate. Nor has he created the conventional pattern of gradually rising involvement that is used to express the chains of cause and effect – and hence the seeming inevitability of actions and outcomes – in conventional film structure. This act is full of harsh and abrupt transitions on the one hand, and of dead-ends on the other. There is no inevitability about Claudia's action in seeking out Sandro, so their affair seems more a matter of chance than of logical inevitability, and far from their love possessing the sense of a unique experience, they both know that Sandro is using words which he has used many times already with Anna. The love is real, but the lovers are subtly out of synchronisation with each other. At the end of act one Sandro was ahead of Anna, who found his advances troubling. Here in act two they can achieve their moment of ecstatic connection, but already, as the act comes to an end, Sandro is already moving on, forced by the self-awareness created in him by his love, to confront the barrenness of his own professional life. As they leave for Taormina everything is in balance.

The last act (just six scenes and twenty-three minutes) is both shorter and, like the opening of the film, more conventionally dramatic. When they arrive at the hotel Claudia is worn out and decides to go to bed rather than join their friends for the evening. Her parting with Sandro is tender and loving, but as he goes downstairs to join Ettore and resume his business life, he passes Gloria Perkins, the girl from Messina, who eyes him seductively. When Claudia wakes, she finds herself unable to get to sleep again, and, at daybreak, goes to find Patrizia, worried by Sandro's absence from his room and fearful of Anna's return. Patrizia dismisses her fears as melodramatic, but when Claudia goes down into the hotel lounge, she finds Sandro wrapped around Gloria on one of the sofas. She runs off, Sandro follows her outside, then sits on a bench and weeps. Slowly Claudia returns to put a hand on the back of his head, and the film ends with a long shot of the two of them, wordless and almost motionless in the dawn.

By refusing conventional plotting and psychological explanation, Antonioni creates a paradoxical sense of separation from, and involvement with, his characters. On the one hand, we have to watch their actions, listen to their words, and come to our own conclusions about them; on the other, because no explanations are offered, we share the lovers' own sense of incomprehension about the emotions which bring them together and then separate them again. Here we are far from the all-too simplistic pattern of unhampered individual decision-making (allowing the comfortable structure of transgression, recognition and redemption) which characterises Hollywood. If we look for explanations of the lovers' behaviour in their own words and actions, or in the responses of those around them, we shall be dissatisfied. The answers lie less in some system of self-contained human will and determination than in the very landscape of Southern Italy: in the precipitous rocks of Lisca Bianca, which seem to demand a fall, an accident; in the sea apparently ready to swallow evidence of a death or a flight; in the barren town which prompts Claudia's surrender to passion; or in the glamorous amorality of a luxury hotel, which (with the memory of Messina) prompts Sandro's act of betrayal. The lengthy landscape shots, the *temps morts* which would be deemed errors in a Hollywood narrative, are here the key to *L'avventura*'s meaning.

Shot breakdown

L'AVVENTURA

(Overall: credits + 474 shots: 133 minutes)

ONE [credits + 224 shots: 55 minutes]
   Credits
1 *Outside the Villa* (1–6)   6 shots
   Anna argues with her father about Sandro
2 *Sandro's Apartment* (7–35)   29 shots
   Anna and Sandro make love, while Claudia waits
3 *The Yacht* (36–72)   37 shots
   Swimming: Anna claims to see a shark
4 *Inside the Cabin* (73–80)   8 shots
   Anna and Claudia: the shark was a joke
5 *On the Island* (81–90)   10 shots
   Anna talks of her need to spend time alone
6 *The Cliffs* (91–118)   28 shots
   The weather changes: Anna is missing
7 *The Island* (119–41)   23 shots
   The search for Anna begins
8 *The Hut: Night* (142–59)   18 shots
   Hostility between Sandro and Claudia
9 *The Hut: Next Morning* (160–78)   19 shots
   A boat is heard: first real contact of Sandro
   and Claudia
10 *The Rocks* (179–217)   39 shots
   The arrival of the police and Anna's father
11 *Departure from the Island* (218–24) 7 shots
   Sandro kisses Claudia before the group separates

TWO [188 shots: 55 minutes]
12 *Police Station* (225–33)   9 shots
   While Sandro listens, a group of smugglers is
   interrogated, but they deny knowledge of Anna
13 *Railway Station* (234–9)   6 shots
   Sandro meets up again with Claudia who is
   also seeking Anna
14 *On the Train* (240–58)   19 shots
   Sandro and Claudia are brought together watching

a young couple on the train, but separate again

15 *Messina* (259-83)   25 shots
    In Messina Sandro meets up with a journalist
    he hopes can help and witnesses a near riot
    provoked by the sexy Gloria Perkins

16 *The Princess's Villa* (284-95)   12 shots
    Claudia rejoins the yacht party at
    Princess Montalto's villa

17 *Claudia's Room* (296-302)   7 shots
    Claudia and Patrizia try on wigs

18 *Goffredo's Studio* (303-18)   16 shots
    Claudia watches as Giulia allows herself to be
    seduced by the Princess's seventeen-year-old
    grandson, Goffredo.

19 *The Villa* (319-26)   8 shots
    Claudia with the yachting party –
    a car will be sent for Sandro

20 *Chemist's Shop* (327-37)   11 shots
    Sandro gets no help from the squabbling
    chemist and his wife – Claudia joins him

21 *The Empty Village* (338-46)   9 shots
    Lost, they explore an uninhabited village

22 *The Countryside* (346-55)   9 shots
    The couple make love for the first time,
    passionately, by a railway line

23 *Street in Noto* (356-364)   9 shots
    Claudia full of self-doubt, fearing she may
    meet Anna

24 *Church Roof* (365-75)   11 shots
    Sandro questions his life style and
    proposes marriage

25 *Bedroom* (376-88)   13 shots
    Claudia, in love, dances, poses and pleads
    for words of love

26 *The Piazza* (389-400)   12 shots
    Sandro deliberately spills ink to spoil
    a young man's drawing

27 *The Hotel* (401-12)   12 shots
    The couple, uncertain, decide to go back

THREE [62 shots: 23 minutes]

28 *The Hotel at Taormina* (413–35)		23 shots
	Claudia and Sandro very much in love	
29 *The Hotel Lounge* (436–40)		5 shots
	Sandro meets Ettore; Gloria Perkins reappears	
30 *Claudia's Bedroom* (441–3)		3 shots
	Claudia, alone, is unable to sleep	
31 *Patrizia's Room* (444–7)		4 shots
	Claudia talks of her fears of Anna's return	
32 *The Hotel Lounge* (448–59)		12 shots
	Claudia finds Sandro and Gloria Perkins making love	
33 *Daybreak Outside the Hotel* (460–74)		15 shots
	A muted reconciliation	

7 Plot and narration: *Rashomon*

> It is reality itself (that is, our apprehension of it) that is being questioned
> and rendered relative. At stake is the validity of subjective experience.
>
> DONALD RICHIE (1972)

The representation of action

It has been argued here that the conventional feature film shares the
general characteristics of the dramatic mode of story making. A good
example of this mode of narrative is the first scene of the embedded
story concerning rape and killing in Akira Kurosawa's *Rashomon*.
This is quite unproblematic, a typical film opening. If we ignore the
framing shots at the beginning and end, where the woodcutter is
shown telling his story, there are twenty-nine shots (numbered as 26–
54 in the published script, and numbers 40–68 in my own breakdown
of the film as a whole, set out at the end of this chapter). We follow
the woodcutter as he walks through the forest, and the sequence
conveys, at first, a sense of movement through a landscape without
terrors, of sunshine and well-being – until the woodcutter is brought
to a halt by the successive pieces of evidence of a crime, culminating
in the discovery of the body itself. He then rushes off to tell the
authorities. The scene is an apparently simple one, lasting just three-
and-three-quarter minutes, yet it requires twenty-nine shots. Breaking
the scene down in this way allows Kurosawa to show the action from
a variety of perspectives and angles. As spectators, we have a sense of
empathy with the woodcutter – we share his horror – but at the same
time we are not limited by his literal perceptions. Indeed, as
spectators, we have no difficulty in occupying a dazzling array of
viewing positions: in front of or behind the woodcutter, from a static
position or moving with him, close or distant, above or below, seeing
the character from the outside or sharing his viewpoint. Though we
have an increasing sense of involvement with the character, the
climactic shot of the sequence is not his point-of-view, but a shot of

him from behind the body, showing his horrified face framed by the corpse's outstretched arms. Here we have the secret of film's power to generate emotion: its ability to offer the spectator a magical kind of seeing, the ability to move seemingly freely and invisibly within the action. Provided certain editing rules (which allow us to orientate ourselves in space) are adhered to, we experience no difficulty in adopting such a variety of viewing positions, indeed we hardly notice the abundance of shots.

With the multiplicity of shots comes the possibility of creating patterns and rhythms of a kind equivalent to those in music. Looking at the sequence as a self-contained unit of twenty-nine shots, we find that virtually every shot in the sequence has a repetition, an echo or a variant. The part of the sequence preceding the uncovering of the evidence (shots number 1–16) is made up of the weaving together of three strands of imagery: overhead shots of sun and trees (shots number 1 and 12, 7 and 10), a series comprising close-ups – of the axe (shot number 2), the woodcutter's face (shots number 3, 15 and 16) and his back (shots number 8 and 14) – and tilting, tracking and panning shots from the side (shots number 4, 5, 6, 9, 11 and 13). The discovery of the evidence brings in new types of imagery (shots number 17 and 20), but some shots from the beginning continue to find their echoes: the close-ups (shots number 19 and 24) and the side shots (shots number 27, 28 and 29), so that the sequence as a whole has a unity of pattern.

Moreover the patterning is not static and does not have a simple one-to-one relationship to the enacted drama. At the beginning of the scene, the cutting pattern reflects the woodcutter's carefree movement. But as he unwittingly approaches the body, a separation between his experience and that of the spectator takes place. Both the music and the visual organisation take on a new intensity, hinting at the horror to come: the tracking movements from the side become more involved, crossing his path (shot number 11) and coming in close (shot number 15), while the normal close-ups of the opening become extreme close-ups (shots number 14–16). Then, with the discovery of a first piece of evidence (shot number 17) and then a second (shot number 20), the rhythm slows. The pace comes to a virtual halt in the long-held shot of the woodcutter picking up the rope and looking earnestly off-screen (shot number 21). Then, as we share his point-of-view of the amulet (shots number 22 and 23), see him stumble (shot number 24) and view the body (shot number 25).

Then the sequence picks up pace again and keeps it, as we follow his panic-stricken flight through the forest (shots number 26–9). In all, the last eight shots (shots number 22–9) take in total just thirty seconds, that is, an average of just three-and-three-quarter seconds apiece, as against the overall average for the sequence of around eight seconds per shot.

Kurosawa's elaborate cutting and editing clearly shapes the spectator's emotional response to the sequence. By giving us prior warning of the disaster through the use of music and increasingly agitated and intense camerawork, he turns what is a surprise for the woodcutter (who does not anticipate discovering a body) into a piece of suspense for us (since we are cued to wonder what disaster is awaiting him). But the complexity of the directorial style does not alter the fact, that in this sequence, *Rashomon* – like most Holly-wood movies – uses the very simplest dramatic storytelling approach, more akin to a fairy-tale than a novel. What a character does is everything, what he or she thinks or feels is never directly accessible to us, though it may be revealed through dialogue or more frequently, as here, through gestures and actions.

But our response, as spectators, is not purely emotional. Robert Scholes argues that in attempting to decipher a film and hence to 'realise' the narrative, we bring to bear our 'narrativity', our active participation, by which we construct the story from the fictional data provided by the film (1982: 60). In Scholes's view, 'the images presented to us, their arrangements and juxtapositions, are narratio-nal blueprints for a fiction that must be constructed by the viewer's narrativity' (1982: 69). Not only do we register the images, we 'categorise them and assign them value according to whatever cultural codes we have available' (1962). This is a view of the spectator's activity which is very much in line with that of much contemporary film theory, attributing enormous power to the images and their organisation. My own view is that, at a first viewing at least, the precise organisation of the images passes us by to a large extent. We are not conscious of the multiplicity of shots: what we consider and attribute value to is the action.

David Bordwell (1985: 33–40) bears out this view with his notion that we bring our judgements to bear not on the images as such, but on the events, questioning not camera position, but causality. We test what we discover against a number of grids or sets of criteria (what Bordwell calls 'schemata'). Though it is exaggerated to claim that

Hollywood movies are suspect because they attempt to pass off their cosy, constructed world as reality, it is certainly true that one of the ways in which we test a film – as a story about human beings – is by reference to our everyday experience. In this sense the opening sequence of the embedded story of *Rashomon* causes us no problems: the woodcutter's reaction is what we expect from a person who has found the body of a murder victim in a forest. While watching *Rashomon*, however, we know that we are watching a film, so the discovery of the body has also to relate to our experience of film viewing and of storytelling in general. Here too we are again likely to be satisfied: the discovery of a body may be a rare event in our real world, but it is something with which we are familiar from the opening minutes of a great number of films, particularly in view of the popularity of detective fiction in cinema and television. We may not anticipate discovering a body when we ourselves venture into a forest, but we know this can be the source of interest and involvement at the beginning of a work of fiction. *Rashomon* is, however, also a Japanese period film, a genre virtually unknown in the West when Kurosawa's work was first shown at the Venice Film Festival in 1951. For anyone with a knowledge of Japanese cinema, the film presents itself as a variant on the *samurai* film, and hence some killing is to be anticipated. The ordinary viewer, lacking this knowledge, may still find this opening sequence – and the following ones – acceptable, since there are clear analogies with Hollywood's own favourite period genre, the western. Indeed the film was subsequently remade in Hollywood, as a western, by Martin Ritt in 1964. The fascination of *Rashomon* is that, despite the fact that this sequence – and those that follow – individually meet all these criteria, the film still emerges as highly enigmatic, giving rise to what Donald Richie calls 'The Great Rashomon Murder Mystery' (1965: 74).

Rashomon

Set in twelfth century Kyoto, *Rashomon* has a complex system of on-screen narrators and off-screen narrating voices, of a kind which, according to Avrom Fleishman (1992: 191), figures in one in six fiction films. It also has a complex double structure, deriving from the two separate stories, 'Rashomon' and 'In a Grove', by Ryunosuke Akutagawa on which it is based. In the framing story, set at the great gate, Rashomon, two characters, a woodcutter and a priest, discuss with a third, a commoner, events which they have seen and testimony they have heard at a magistrate's court summoned to investigate a murder. The embedded story, heralded by the woodcutter's walk into the forest, largely comprises a series of four enactments of the events in the forest three days earlier. Though the precise nature and interpretation of these events is disputed by those involved, the central action is clear. Following a chance meeting in the forest, the bandit Tajomaru (Toshiro Mifune) succeeded in tricking and tying up a samurai (Masayuki Mori). Then, in front of his eyes, the bandit assaulted the samurai's wife (Machiko Kyo), who may or may not have eventually submitted willingly. Subsequently the samurai died, though whether he was killed in a duel with the bandit, was stabbed by his wife, or committed suicide is in dispute. It would be artificial to impose a conventional three-act structure on the film, but there is a clear dramatic pattern, as the evidence given by the bandit is first refuted by testimonies of the wife and the dead samurai (the latter speaking through a medium), and then these conflicting accounts are in turn questioned by the woodcutter, who finally admits to having witnessed the aftermath of the events. Though the testimony given at court subsequently complicates the issues involved, the embedded story itself begins in classic film drama style, with a small, chance event – the breeze blowing aside the wife's veil as she rides past the bandit – setting the whole tumult of death and assault underway.

After the woodcutter has described finding the body, we hear the testimony of other witnesses at the magistrates court. The priest tells of passing the samurai and his wife in the forest, and a police agent describes the arrest of Tajomaru, discovered writhing in agony on a river bank, still in possession of the samurai's bow and arrows and the horse on which the wife had been riding. The police agent's assertion that Tajomaru had been thrown from the horse provokes a violent response from the bandit, who claims to have been poisoned by water from a stream where he stopped to drink. Then we see the enactment of his story, with four returns to the court where he is shown giving his testimony (shots number 84, 104, 146, 189).

In the bandit's own account, he is aroused by the brief glimpse of the woman's beauty as she rides past him, accompanied by her husband on foot, on a path through the forest. Determined to take her, even if he has to kill the husband, he tricks the samurai with a story about an old tomb filled with swords and daggers and lures him into the depths of the forest. There he overpowers him and returns to the woman, still waiting by the pathway. Telling her that her husband has been bitten by a snake, he leads her to the clearing where she sees her husband tied to a tree stump. When she attacks Tajomaru with her dagger, he overpowers her and pushes her to the ground. Resisting at first, she eventually submits and gives herself to him. When he is about to leave, the woman pleads that one of the men must die to lessen her dishonour. She will go with whoever wins. The fight between the bandit and the samurai is hard-fought and, back at the magistrate's court, Tajomaru declares his admiration for the samurai, who crossed swords with him twenty-three times. He says he has no further use for the woman who 'turned out to be just like any other woman', and claims to have forgotten to pick up her dagger, which looked valuable ('the biggest mistake I ever made').

Tajomaru's story is contested, first by the wife and then by the dead samurai, speaking through a medium. The wife takes up the story with the bandit sneering at her husband in the aftermath of the rape. When she turns to her husband for sympathy, he looks at her with cold hatred and even when she cuts him free he remains motionless. His attitude unnerves her to such an extent that, hardly knowing what she is doing, she stabs him. Then – she tells the magistrate – she fainted. Coming to her senses, she says, she ran away and threw herself into a pond in a vain attempt to kill herself. The husband, by contrast, in an enacted account marked – like that of the bandit – by constant returns to the magistrate's court where the medium is presenting his version (shots number 290, 293, 297 and 303), claims that his wife falls in love with her assailant. Looking more beautiful that he has ever seen her, she begs the bandit to kill her husband and to take her off. Tajomaru, disgusted, offers to kill her for the husband (words for which, the medium states, he 'almost forgave the bandit'). But the wife escapes and later the bandit returns to cut him loose. Hours later he hears someone crying, and finds that it is himself. Slowly he gets up and kills himself with his wife's dagger. Later, he tells the magistrate through the medium, someone crept up and removed the dagger from his chest.

Forced to admit that, rather than just finding the body, he also witnessed the aftermath of the assault, the woodcutter now gives a quite different account. Far from being indifferent to the woman after the rape, Tajomaru begs her on his knees to go off with him, even offering to give up stealing if she will marry him. It is the wife who cuts her husband free and provokes the two very reluctant men into fighting over her. The samurai is totally scornful of his wife, calling her a shameless whore and saying he will regret the loss of his horse more than the loss of her. Only by taunting them, saying they are neither of them real men, does the wife get the two of them to confront each other. But far from being the glorious duel of Tajomaru's account, the fight is a clumsy, unskilled affair between two frightened men who constantly fall over as they try to evade each other's blows. It ends with the samurai begging vainly for his life and with Tajomaru half-crazed after the killing and too exhausted to go after the woman when she runs off. While we might be inclined to believe the woodcutter's story as the truth of the events in the forest, particularly as Kurosawa and his co-scriptwriter, Shinobu Hashimoto, have added it to Akutagawa's original array of testimony, it proves – if accepted – that the woodcutter's evidence to the magistrate's court was a lie. It is also notable that this account, produced only in response to the commoner's accusations, breaks off before the point when the woodcutter may have become involved, by stealing the dagger. If this second account – like the first – is a lie, the woodcutter may even – conceivably – have murdered the samurai himself.

How we respond to the events in the forest is partly shaped by the words of those gathered at the gate, who comment on them and discuss their meaning. Though Robin Wood surely goes too far when he asserts that the woodcutter (Takashi Shimura) is 'the real hero of the film' (1984: 384), the scenes involving him, the priest and the commoner at the Rashomon gate do have more importance than that of a mere narrative framing device. The five scenes at the gate, occupying about a quarter of the film's length in all, open and close the film, and separate the four versions of events. Throughout the film the comments made by the trio reflect their differing states of mind – the woodcutter's troubled involvement, the priest's despair at men's actions and the commoner's cynical desire merely to be amused ('I only wanted to know about this strange story of yours because I thought it might amuse me' and, later, 'I don't mind a lie. Not if it's interesting').

The opening scene at the gate in the pouring rain sets the pattern, introducing us to the contrasting attitudes of the trio and promising us a story which will capture our attention, with the priest claiming that 'There was never anything as terrible as this. Never'. After we have seen Tajomaru's version of events, we return to the gate, where the woodcutter, who has presumably told the story (though this is not wholly clear) rejects it, together with the next version – that of the wife – as a lie. When faced with this clash of evidence, the commoner gives a response which may perhaps point to the film's meaning: 'Well, men are only men. That's why they lie. They can't tell the truth, not even to themselves'. The priest, who tells the wife's story, presumably believes this to be the truth, since he comments that he 'found her very pitiful' and 'felt great compassion for her'. When, after the wife's story, we return for the third scene at the gate, the commoner is unimpressed: 'Women lead you on with their tears, they even fool themselves'. The woodcutter is more concerned with the dead man's story, which is to follow and which he rejects as another lie, though the priest asserts his belief that 'dead men tell no lies'. In the fourth scene at the gate, after the dead man's story, the drama there is heightened, as the commoner forces the woodcutter to admit that he lied to the magistrate's court and was, in fact, a witness to the aftermath of the rape. But in the final scene of the film, the commoner rejects this version too as merely a further lie, and the woodcutter has no answer when accused of stealing the woman's ornate dagger. Clearly whatever truth one is to find in the film must come from a balancing of the events in the forest and those at the gate. *Rashomon* ends, after all, not with the woodcutter's story of female scorn and male cowardice, but with the commoner's act of stealing the clothes from a baby left abandoned at the gate and the woodcutter's response: to take the baby home to his own family.

Crucial to the meaning of *Rashomon* is the question of how we understand its complex structure of internal narrators. The story of the finding of the body is retold by the woodcutter to his companions sheltering at the gate and ends, after three tracking shots showing him running away accompanied by voice-over comments, with a 'wipe' which translates him to the prison courtyard, where he is seen giving his original evidence to the unseen magistrate. The evidence of the priest and the police agent is similarly given to the magistrate and the much longer testimony of the bandit not only begins and ends in the courtyard, but also has its stages marked by returns there. After comments by the group at the gate, the priest retells the wife's story, which he introduces sympathetically. This story too begins and ends in the prison courtyard, where the wife is shown telling it to the magistrate, with the woodcutter, the priest and the police agent visible in the background. Further discussion at the gate precedes the retelling of the dead samurai's story – itself told through a medium – though it is not clear who narrates this time. Again the medium's narration begins and ends in the courtyard, and its stages are marked by returns there. The final story, that of the woodcutter who turns out to have witnessed the aftermath of the affair, is told uninterrupted and without transition to the courtyard (since the woodcutter admits to having lied there), and the film returns to the gate for the final stage of the framing story.

The distinctiveness of *Rashomon* does not lie simply in this pattern of multiple storytelling, but in the unresolvable discrepancies between the four versions of events. Avrom Fleishman has drawn attention to the variety of storytelling situations which exist in cinema, especially in films of the 1940s and 1950s: external and internal narrations, single and multiple narrators, the use of letters and diaries, and inner (ostensibly unspoken) musings. His examples include such films as Jean Cocteau's *Orphée* and Robert Bresson's *Journal d'un curé de campagne*, as well as such Hollywood movies as Billy Wilder's *Sunset Boulevard*, Orson Welles's *Citizen Kane* and Max Ophuls's *Letter from an Unknown Woman*, along with the David Lean-Noel Coward collaboration, *Brief Encounter*. In Fleishman's view, when we view this cinema within the context of contemporary modernism, 'the role of narration [in cinema] will come to higher prominence, for just as modern writers were delving into newly opened psychological strata by innovations in narrational technique, film makers were experimenting with narration in pursuit of similar ends' (1992: 196).

For Fleishman, such films as those listed above – and especially the Hollywood ones – constitute a hitherto unrecognised stage in filmic modernism, bridging the gap between, on the one hand, the 1920s experiments of the French 'First Avant-Garde' and Soviet generation using montage techniques and, on the other, the 1960s break with traditional Hollywood norms achieved by such directors as Antonioni, Bergman and the members of the loosely grouped French New Wave: 'In the years immediately before and after World War II, as we have seen, extensive literary-inspired narrational innovation took place, at least as remarkable as the breakthroughs in *mise en scène*, acting and cinematography associated with neo-realism' (1992: 203). One of the problems with such a formulation is touched upon briefly by Fleishman earlier in his study when he notes, with regard to the subjective transitions in Edward Dmytryk's *Murder My Sweet*, that 'movie audiences seem to have had little difficulty in following even the more complicated of these transitions' (1992: 45). In more general terms, he has to concede that 'audiences seem to have little difficulty – although innovative film makers give them reason to have some difficulty – either in relating certain scenes to others as the telling and the told, or in placing voice-overs as later renditions of earlier events' (1992: 16).

Such ease of reception should make us wary of conferring the status of modernist works on the films with which Fleishman deals and must prompt us to query the actual weight attached to the narrational stances which he probes so acutely. Clearly, in a narrative form in which everything is told in words – in a novel or a short story, for example – the key to enigmas of the kind which *Rashomon* presents would lie in probing the nature of the telling or retelling, and the 'voice' of each narrator would be crucial. It would be important to ascertain whether any particular version of the events in the forest is told or retold, whether it is presented directly (by the participant) or indirectly (through a medium), and whether the teller or reteller is a detached witness or someone implicated in the events. Each account would have its own particular verbal form, reflecting the gender and social status of the speaker, and this too could be probed for clues in order to establish its credibility. In *Rashomon* as a written text, the social distinctions between samurai, bandit and woodcutter, and the gender identity of the wife (vividly reflected in Japanese language usage) would be crucial. And indeed, even in translation, the different speaking styles of those who make statements in Akutagawa's original story, 'In the Grove' are very apparent. But in the film *Rashomon* none of this differentiation is to be found. All four versions of the events in the forest are enacted with apparent conviction and none is depicted subjectively in terms of the handling of camera placement or viewpoint. Fleishman argues early in his study that 'while films in general are not narrated but mimetically performed, some films employ coded signals to give the impression that their images and sounds proceed from a narrator' (1992: 21–2). What he fails to analyse in any detail is the precise organisation of the images and sounds which follow the (often elaborate) signals indicating that a sequence is a narration of events by one of the characters.

The sequence of the woodcutter's entry into the forest, which we examined earlier, is clearly marked as the woodcutter's personal story. It is introduced by him in close-up at the Rashomon gate (shot number 39 in my numbering) as he begins the story: 'It was three days ago. I'd gone into the mountains for wood. . .'. The story then unfolds in a dramatic enactment which allows us to see the events he is presumably describing. But we see these events from the outside, sharing his viewpoint in only two shots out of twenty-nine (those showing the amulet). The voice re-enters after the climactic discovery of the body, as he begins to run off in panic – 'I ran as fast as I could to tell the police. That was three days ago. Then the police called me to testify' – and immediately a wipe translates us to the court (shot number 69), where we see him concluding his testimony to the (unseen) magistrate – 'Yes sir. It was I who found the body first. . .'.

At first sight the subjectivity of the woodcutter's account might seem strengthened by this double anchoring (as both told and retold). But in fact, though the film implies that what we see and hear is both his evidence and his subsequent retelling, we know from all analysis of oral storytelling that narratives vary as they are told and retold. Logically therefore the woodcutter's account to his companions at the gate must differ in detail (if not in substance) from the version he gave to a magistrate of whom he is clearly in awe. The fact that the same images and sounds can serve as both telling and retelling – even more strikingly in the subsequent accounts by bandit, wife and dead husband all of which begin and end at the court though they are ostensibly those told at the gate – points to the fact that the events are not in fact told, narrated, at all.

Obviously an on-screen narrator or an off-screen voice can tell us stories, but as soon as we switch to the enactment of what is told, the narrator loses all control. The actions of the character, and indeed the shaping of the images and sounds themselves, bear no trace of the past tense of the spoken voice-over. They show us events as they happen, unmediated by a narrator. Though at the end of the sequence we hear the woodcutter's voice, as he speaks three days after the events in the forest, what we see and hear on screen is him running off in panic at the very moment of finding the body. Avrom Fleishman's query about how it is that audiences seem to have no trouble with even immensely complex storytelling situations can be answered simply. Though the narrating voice may focus our attention or arouse our interest – much as the camera does – we have no more need to ask ourselves where this is told from, than we have to question camera position and angle.

Just as we can empathise with the woodcutter on his entry into the forest without sharing his literal point-of-view, or even occupying a logically consistent spatial position with respect to his movements, so too we can appreciate enacted events without troubling ourselves about where they are ostensibly told from. Our role is to probe the actions of the characters and the workings of the plot – drawing what hints we can from voice, image and sound – so as to realise the dramatic action.

The mystery of *Rashomon* stems partly from the deliberate concealment of evidence – since even the priest has seen the body, it should surely be possible to tell us whether the weapon used was a small dagger or a *samurai* sword, but the film's authors refuse to do so. The main cause of puzzlement, however, is that we have no way of resolving the contradictions posed by the four versions of the events in the forest. Since these are all presented objectively and in exactly the same style, it is no help to probe the alleged narrators, to ask whether the wife should be believed (as the priest clearly believes her) or to question whether dead men do indeed tell lies. We are left with four enactments, each of which is as plausible as the others. Alfred Hitchcock, in his conversation with François Truffaut, finds it strange with regard to *Stage Fright*, that though, in movies, 'people never object if a man is shown telling a lie', they refuse to accept a flashback that lies (1968: 231–2). The answer, with respect to *Stage Fright*, is surely that we feel cheated if the lie is enacted and used as the premise for the whole plot, and we do not have the subtlety of analysis and historical awareness which allow Kristin Thompson to justify such 'duplicitous narration' in her account of the film (1988: 135–61).

The response to the systematic use, in *Rashomon*, of flashback enactments, some of which must be at least partial lies, is very different. In a sense, the visualisation of the woodcutter's entry into the forest (later revealed as a lie) could potentially be as off-putting as Hitchcock's inclusion of Johnny's lies in a seemingly objective flashback at the beginning of *Stage Fright*. But at least it does tally with the key event in the forest (the *samurai* did indeed die), and the revelation of the deceit leads to a fourth account (which initially seems to promise us the truth) at a moment in the narrative when the audience is desperately in need of some means to reconcile the conflicting accounts of bandit, wife and *samurai*. The four enactments themselves remain unreconcilable and this can have a powerful impact upon us, since this questions the assumptions on which all conventional (Hollywood-style) film narrative is based, namely that the world is wholly decipherable, that people's motivations can be understood, that all events have clear causes and that the end of a fiction will offer us the chance to fuse all elements of the plot into a single coherent dramatic action. *Rashomon*, by depicting events four times while not giving us the information we would need to evaluate each enactment, calls into question the very dubious claims to 'truth' of conventional film narrative.

Shot breakdown

RASHOMON
(Overall: Front title + 421 shots: 84.5 minutes)

Credits (front title + 1–11)	11 shots: 1.5 minutes
1 *The Gate* (12–39)	28 shots: 5 minutes

Priest, woodcutter and commoner discuss a murder

2 *The Woodcutter's Story* (40–69)	30 shots: 5 minutes

The discovery of the crime

3 *The Priest's Story* (70–72)   3 shots: 1 minute
    The samurai and his wife enter the forest
4 *The Policeman's Story* (73–78)   6 shots: 1 minute
    The bandit's capture
5 *The Bandit's Story* (79–224)   146 shots: 21 minutes
    The bandit's own account of his arrest (79–83)
    The first encounter in the forest (84–103)
    The bandit tricks the samurai and returns
    to the woman (104–145)
    The wife is seduced in front of her husband (146–88)
    The bandit and the samurai fight (189–223)
    The bandit claims he forgot the woman's dagger (224)
6 *The Gate* (225–232)   8 shots: 2 minutes
    The woodcutter rejects the bandit's story,
    and the wife's too
7 *The Wife's Story* (233–268)   36 shots: 10 minutes
    A different story: her rape provokes her husband's
    contempt: she kills him with her dagger (233–67)
    She tells of her own suicide attempts (268)

8 *The Gate* (269–276)   8 shots: 2 minutes
    The woodcutter disputes the dead man's story
    (told through a medium)
9 *The Samurai's Story* (277–319)   43 shots: 10 minutes
    The medium summons up the dead man (277–287)
    His wife begs the bandit to take her away (287–93)
    She even urges him to kill her husband, but is scorned
    Freed by the bandit, the samurai kills himself (294–318)
    While he lies dead, the dagger is withdrawn (319)
10 *The Gate* (320–4)   5 shots: 3 minutes
    The woodcutter protests that the samurai was killed
    with a sword: he saw it all
11 *The Woodcutter's Story* (325–89)   65 shots: 14 minutes
    After the rape, the bandit pleads with the woman (325–31)
    Untied, her husband scorns her (332–48)
    She mocks them both as cowards: reluctantly
    they fight and the samurai is killed (249–289)
12 *The Gate* (390–421)   32 shots: 9 minutes
    The commoner rejects the woodcutter's story,
    accusing him of stealing the dagger (390–406)
    The woodcutter takes home the abandoned baby (407–21)

N.B. The shot numbering adopted here differs from that of the published script (Kurosawa, 1969), which – presumably because of differences between release prints in the UK and the USA – does not number the credits nor the first three shots of the action. My own numbering here differs therefore by fourteen shots.

8 The refusal of plot: *L'année dernière à Marienbad*

> This present which is continually inventing itself, as if it were at the mercy of the writing, which repeats itself, bisects itself, modifies itself, contradicts itself, without even accumulating enough bulk to constitute a past – and thus a 'story', in the traditional sense of the word – all this can only invite the reader (or spectator) to a different sort of participation from the one he is accustomed to.
>
> ALAIN ROBBE-GRILLET (1965)

Time, causality and the generation of narrative

One of the key dates in the history of modern drama is the first production in Paris, on 5 January 1953, of Samuel Beckett's play, *En attendant Godot (Waiting for Godot)*. It had an immediate and enormous impact on audiences and critics alike throughout the world, and its influence continues to be felt forty years later. Indeed, in a recent study of modern drama and the modern imagination, John Peter goes so far as to speculate that 'this play may turn out to be the single most important event in the theatre since Aeschylus'. Here we have a totally paradoxical success, since *Waiting for Godot* is:

> a play which defies most of the rules of what we understand by drama. It has structure, but virtually no plot. Its characters have little in the way of personality, and practically no social background. There they are in no particular place and no particular time; much of what they do seems to be purposeless; how long they have been here is obscure and irrelevant (1987: 17).

If the play seems static, it is not because nothing happens, but because the events 'are not clearly caused or explained', occur not once but twice, and have a very dubious status in reality: 'the same things may already have happened, we do not know how often, and may all happen again' (1987: 15). This temporal ambiguity is possible because the play is written in such a way as 'to function in an endless present. It conveys an experience of time as to which actual length of time is irrelevant' (1987: 8). *Waiting for Godot* is a play which 'has a story, though it does not have a plot'. The grip of causality is 'relaxed, almost non-existent', so that it is held together 'not so much by the causal pressure of events as by its rhythms' (1987: 262).

An immediate impact akin to that of *Waiting for Godot* in the theatre was achieved in cinema some eight years later with the screening of *L'année dernière à Marienbad* (*Last Year at Marienbad*), a work which has striking similarities to *Waiting for Godot* in its handling of time and causality, character and plot. The film, directed as his second feature film by Alain Resnais from a script by the novelist Alain Robbe-Grillet, is fascinating from many points of view. For example, it offers remarkable insight into the relationship between a dramatic text and its realisation in cinema, since in many ways the direction works against the text in precisely those areas in which it is most innovative, an issue I have explored elsewhere (Armes, 1981: 24–44). But since Resnais's modifications to the text presented to him by Robbe-Grillet essentially involve changes to the proposed musical score and an attempt to separate out the level of reality to be accorded to each of the various events, rather than the dramatic structure itself, it is with the work of the writer that we are most concerned here. Significantly Samuel Beckett is one of the authors who make up 'The Elements of a Modern Anthology' in Robbe-Grillet's collection of critical and theoretical writings, *Pour un nouveau roman* (*Towards a New Novel*), published in 1962 and translated into English in 1965.

As we have seen, the poetics of Hollywood cinema is fundamentally Aristotelian. We are given dramatic actions in which everything is precisely plotted to exploit to the full the interweaving of consecutiveness and causality in the construction of the story. We can say we understand the story, when we understand the causal connections between events. Action and character are locked indissolubly together in the unfolding of the story, so that the one reveals and confirms the truth of the other. The plot may be highly patterned in terms of its repetitions, parallels and variations of events and characters, but the meaning is assumed to lie elsewhere, in the subject of the story rather than the structure itself. As a form, the Hollywood movie functions in a manner akin to nineteenth century popular drama or novels, and Robbe-Grillet's critique of the latter can be applied word for word to the movie, if we simply substitute 'spectator' for 'reader'. Judgement of a film, as of a novel, 'consists above all of an appraisal of its coherence, its development, its balance, the way the breathless reader [or spectator] is surprised or kept guessing. A gap in the narrative, a badly introduced episode, a break in the interest, a passage that merely marks time, will be major defects' (1965: 61–2). In both conventional forms, to tell a story well, 'is to make what you write resemble the prefabricated synopses that people are used to; in other words, to make it resemble their ready-made idea of reality' (1965: 62).

Though Robbe-Grillet came to the cinema with an international reputation as a leading figure of the New Novel, the *nouveau roman*, and as a writer with four major novels published in the 1950s, he was in no way interested in creating a novelistic form of film making. As he later put it, 'the two languages, film and book, have in fact so little in common that the eternal discussions on "novel and film" cannot claim more precision than if one were to speak of "music and painting" or "architecture and poetry"' (1967: 131). What attracted him to cinema were those creative possibilities not open to the novelist. The first of these was not simply the possibility of working with images, but also with the sound track – 'voices, noises, different effects, different kinds of music' – and above all, 'the possibility of playing on two senses at the same time, the eye and the ear' (1965: 146). In conventional cinema the sound track is always subordinated to the images and even if there is a notional narrator – Walter Neff, say, in Billy Wilder's *Double Indemnity* – the narrating voice has no power to command the images. What interested Robbe-Grillet in *L'année dernière à Marienbad* was to create a structure in which the voice confronts and eventually commands the images. One of the simplest ways to see the film as a dramatic structure is to follow the suggestion made by Robbe-Grillet in his introduction to the published screenplay and to understand it as the story of a persuasion: 'it deals with a reality which the hero creates out of his own vision, out of his own words' (1962: 9). The film is thus, in one sense, a confrontation of word and image: when the voice is in complete control, and the male narrator has imposed his will on the woman, the film can end.

The second major attraction of cinema for Robbe-Grillet was the possibility of exploiting the fact that the action of a film unfolds in the present: 'what we see on the screen is *in the act of happening*, we are given the gesture itself, not an account of it' (1962: 11). In conventional cinema the unfolding moment is held in a web of cause and effect which calls into being a remembered past and an anticipated future. In conventional cinema, as Robbe-Grillet notes, the duration of the work is 'a résumé or a condensed version of something of longer and more "real" duration' (1965: 149). But for him, in his own work, 'the breaks in the montage, the repeated scenes, the contradictions, the characters suddenly immobilised as they are in an amateur's photos, give this perpetual present all its force and all its violence' (1965: 147). When the film was first shown, Alain Resnais as director was concerned to explore the varying levels of reality and dimensions of time implied in the film. Robbe-Grillet, by contrast, presented *L'année dernière à Marienbad* as an exploration of the power of immediacy:

> The universe in which the whole film takes place is, characteristically, that of a perpetual present which makes any recourse to memory impossible. It is a world without a past, which at every instant is self-sufficient, and which obliterates itself as it goes along. The man and the woman don't start to exist until they appear on the screen for the first time; before then they were nothing, and the moment the film is over they are again nothing. Their existence only lasts as long as the film lasts (1965: 149).

A third aspect of Alain Robbe-Grillet's approach to the film, which he did not talk about at all at the time of its release, was the application to film of some of the methods used to generate narrative in many of the written texts of the New Novelists (*nouveaux romanciers*). There is no coherent geography in *L'année dernière à Marienbad*, with, for example, the statue which plays a key role in the story of X (Giorgio Albertazzi) and A (Delphine Seyrig) being constantly located at different spots in the grounds of the *hôtel*, sometimes overlooking the fountains, sometimes placed away from them. Equally there is no extractable chronology, no possibility of separating this year from last year. As Robbe-Grillet puts it, 'This love story that we are being told, as if it were a thing of the past, was in fact taking place under our very eyes, here and now' (1965: 149–150). In exactly the same way, there is no external subject matter. Instead the narrative events linking X and A are drawn from elements already present in the narrative before the two of them meet.

The procedure of auto-generation of narrative is perhaps taken to its extreme in the work of the novelist and theorist of the *nouveau roman*, Jean Ricardou. He has explained that he saw his task in his novel *La prise de Constantinople* (1965) as being to generate all the principal elements of the narrative (settings, characters, events) from the future title page of the book when it was published by the Editions de Minuit. Bruce Morrissette has spelt out what this involved:

> From JEAN RICARDOU, the numerical division into four and eight, as well as the principle of the half, the smaller, minor component (giving adults and children); the syllable ARDOU, suggesting VILLEHARDOUIN, the chronicler of the siege of Constantinople (generating VILLE and IN, 'dans la ville'); the CONST of Constantinople leading to the word and idea of CONSTELLATION (reinforced by the star of the Editions de Minuit's printer's sign) or referential 'constellations'; the little *m* (for Minuit) by the star, from which emerges the section of the novel dealing with the 'mystère dans les étoiles', the space travellers, and the like; and in Editions de Minuit itself the Ed of Ed Word, the Edith of the dedicatee, the *tion* of Sion (Jerusalem, the Crusades), the *mi* of demi or half, and the *nuit* of the novel's initial nocturnal scene (1985: 5).

Robbe-Grillet's procedures in *L'année dernière à Marienbad* are by no means as esoteric as this, though we do find a twenty-two shot 'generative segment' of the Ricardou kind at the beginning of his next feature film (the first he directed himself), *L'immortelle* (1963) (*see* Armes, 1981: 45–65). Robbe-Grillet's later 'serially' based films, such as *Glissements progressifs du plaisir* (1974) and *Le jeu avec le feu* (1975), also possess a self-referential dimension as complex as anything in Ricardou's work. Here in *L'année dernière à Marienbad* Robbe-Grillet includes all the major elements of the story of A and X in the initial play sequence and in the overheard fragments of conversation among the guests at the *hôtel*. In the play, a woman waits for a clock to chime and then yields to the man beside her, just as A will do at the end of the film. There is one anonymous couple whose situation seems to parallel what will be that of X and A, with the man pleading, 'Then listen to my complaints. . .'. and again, looking forward to the end of the film, describing the two of them living, 'side by side, you and I, like coffins laid side by side underground in a frozen garden'. Another couple appears, with the woman saying 'I've already been here before' and giving her father as the reason for being there. Snatches of conversation are heard, such as a reference to 'a shoe with a broken heel', and repeated statements that 'there's no way of escaping', which obviously tie in with the future relationship of A and X. Above all, there is the story of Frank: 'Don't you know the story? It was all anyone talked about last year. Frank had convinced her he was a friend of her father's and had come to keep an eye on her. It was a funny kind of an eye, of course. She realised it a little later: the night he tried to get into her room'.

When initially confronted with the film, most critics tried to understand it in conventional terms, to construct the missing 'last year' and to come up with plausible psychological explanations for why the woman does not remember (he is a mythomaniac, she is an amnesiac, etc). But a truer understanding of the film can be reached if we accept that the story of X and A is generated by these fragments, with X attempting, in particular, to relive with X last year's story of Frank. In support of this thesis, it is worth noting that the fragment about Frank peters out when he enters her bedroom and in the unfolding story of A and X it is precisely at this point that the hitherto assured narrating voice of *L'année dernière à Marienbad* falters, unable to state what happens next.

A key element in this postmodern world of highly self-conscious fictional creation is the notion of the game, a rigorously rule-bound activity, capable of giving immense pleasure and satisfaction to those who submit to its conventions. There is a ludic aspect to virtually all Robbe-Grillet's work, whether in fiction or film, and in *L'année dernière à Marienbad* the game of Nim, at which X opposes M (Sacha Pitoëff, who 'may be' A's husband, 'le mari' in French), plays a key role. The game involves objects (cards, matchsticks) laid out in rows of seven, five, three and one. Each player takes in turn as many objects as he or she wishes from a single row, the loser being the person who takes the last object. At the time of the film's presentation this was described as an ancient Chinese game (adding to the film's air of mystery), but more recently it has been plausibly identified as a German children's game, *Nimm* (in English: 'take'). In *L'année dernière à Marienbad* the game allows the confrontation of X and M to be played out in a totally stylised, ritual manner: M wins every game in which he confronts X, but loses the woman, A. As Bruce Morrissette has pointed out, the notion of the game – whether literally, as in Nim, or more widely as the play of elements in a narrative – has a crucial role in Robbe-Grillet's work:

Game for Robbe-Grillet has come to mean structural freedom, absence of traditional rules of transition, viewpoint, chronology, and other parameters of previous fiction, and, on the constructive side, an invitation to create new models, to develop new combinations, to push ahead even further the aptly termed *nouveau roman* (1985: 164).

L'année dernière à Marienbad

On one level, *L'année dernière à Marienbad* is a highly complex work which presents formidable barriers to any attempt at analysis. The three central characters, played by Delphine Seyrig, Giorgio Albertazzi and Sacha Pitoëff, for example, are nameless in the film, though the script designates them as A, X and M. While these designations are used here for convenience, it is notable that in his conversations and interviews about the film, Alain Resnais never employs such terminology, invariably referring to the character by the name of the performer. It is equally impossible to break down the flow of images into entities which in any way resemble the scenes of a classic Hollywood movie, and it has none of the fades to black which can guide us in the dissection of a film like Robert Bresson's *Un condamné à mort s'est échappé*. We cannot divide the film in terms of units of spatial continuity, since successive shots in any sequence may range over a whole series of spaces, which may be 'real' or 'imaginary', and which may, or may not, be logically consistent. It is even more hazardous to attempt divisions in terms of a presumed time scheme, since Robbe-Grillet's structuring deliberately makes the imposition of an external chronology impossible.

The flow of images is unbroken through the film, and any breakdown of the action into sequences must stem as much from the intuitive search for a pattern, as from the observation and tabulation of the 350 or more shots that go to make up the whole. In accordance with the stance adopted here, namely, that *L'année dernière à Marienbad* is to be seen as the story of a persuasion, I have segmented the film in terms of the various stages of voice-over narration spoken by Giorgio Albertazzi (X, the stranger, in the script). Other analyses, taking different starting points, would undoubtedly arrange the shots somewhat differently. But it is interesting to note that the only other detailed analysis of the film of which I am aware, that by Manfred

Engelbert (Faulstich and Korte, 1990, 386–406), which uses a slightly different print and breaks the film down into five 'acts', using the successive games of Nim as break points, comes up with thirty-one segments which in general terms correspond broadly with my own twenty-five part division. The differences between us are less those of substance than of detail (he includes the credit sequence in his numbering, for example, and breaks it into two parts, making a separation before and after the entry of X's voice).

L'année dernière à Marienbad's complexity lies partly in the incredible visual sophistication which Alain Resnais as director brings to the film. But at the same time, with its story of a stranger arriving to remind a woman that they met a year ago and agreed go off together, the film has an archetypal simplicity, akin to that of fairy tales about the prince and the sleeping beauty, or death coming to claim his victim after a year and a day. Accordingly this analysis is based on the proposition that the underlying structure is equally simple, comprising, in fact, a set of symmetrical relations. Accepting Robbe-Grillet's assertion that the characters come from nowhere – and therefore have nowhere to go – this analysis traces how X's story is built up from (or generated by) words he overhears in the early part of the film, and then looks at the successive stages by which it is imposed on the reluctant woman, A. Since, by definition, there is no reality outside the film and causality is abolished within its boundaries, the only pattern which the subsequent stages of the relationship of X and A can take is one which mirrors or echoes the ways in which they have come together. The pattern by which the story of X and A is generated must be echoed in the pattern of its ending, and, as X entered unseen at the beginning, so too the pair must depart unseen at the end (see Figure 8.1).

If we need confirmation that symmetry is at least one key to the dramatic structure of *L'année dernière à Marienbad*, we need look no further than the two scenes depicting the performance of the play for the guests at the *hôtel*. These are located at the beginning and the end of the film (sequences two and twenty-four in my analysis). As X enters from the garden at the beginning of the film, his voice is caught up in the dialogues of the play which is just coming to an end. On stage, in a garden setting, a woman finally yields to a man: 'And now – I am yours', and the curtain comes down. As X and A, without exchanging a word, prepare to leave the *hôtel* at the end of the film and enter the garden, we see the beginning of the same play, the scene

A: *Credits*
Music ends, X is heard

B: *The Play*
1. Unseen entry
2. End of play
3. Frozen figures

C: *Conversations*
4. Appearance of X
5. Story of Frank's intrusion
6. X meets A

D: *Separation*
7. Verbal fragmentation

E: *The Statue*
8. First evocation
9. Second evocation

F: *The Room*
10. A's terror
11. A's acceptance

M: *End Title*
Music surges

L: *Resolution*
25. Unseen exit
24. Beginning of play
23. A's farewell to M

K: *False Ending*
22. Disappearance of X
21. X's intrusion
20. M shoots A

J: *Doubt*
19. Visual fragmentation

I: *Departure Planned*
18. Second plan
17. First plan

H: *Terror*
16. A's reassurance
15. A's terror

G: *The Concert*

12. First kiss   14. Second kiss

13. The walk in the garden

Figure 8.1 The symmetry of *L'année dernière à Marienbad*

set this time in a salon of some kind. Though we do not hear the dialogue, it is clear that the woman is resisting the man's entreaties. On one level, the two characters can be seen to represent A and X, and so constitute a perfect example of the interior duplication (*mise en abyme*) so beloved of the practitioners of the *nouveau roman* (*see* Morrissette, 1985: 141–156). The two scenes thus parallel the main action, but they also contest it: threatening to 'short-circuit' the film at its opening – 'This whole story is already over now. It came to an end – a few seconds more – it has come to close. . .' – and promising a new beginning at the end, when the main action is already virtually over. As Figure 8.2 shows, there is a complex interaction between all four elements: principally between the opening of the film and the ending of the play and between the end of the film and the opening of the play, but also between the opening of the film and its end set against the end of the play and its opening.

Looking at the film as a whole, the credits (section *A*) are marked by the rhythmical interplay of music (present from the start) and voice (entering on the sixth title, the name of the film). There is a clear anticipation of the overall rhythmical structure of the film, as X's words, beginning 'Once again – I walk on, once again, down these corridors. . .', emerge from the music, impose themselves and are then dissolved again. In section *B*, the film presents a series of fused tracking shots (sequence 1), accompanied by the rhythmical alternation of voice and music established in the credit sequence: X himself remains unseen, but the words carry the implication of an entry from the garden. The camera moves on into a doorway and total darkness. It passes over the frozen figures of the audience to an actress on stage (sequence 2). The narrating voice we have heard is 'captured' by the play, fusing with that of the actor who responds to the woman. As the play comes to an end, the camera pulls back to show the audience applauding. The camera now begins to move amid the audience (sequence 3), with an alternation of frozen poses and snatches of conversation. The voice of X is silent.

Section *C* shows more extensive passages of conversation among the guests and contains most of the remaining generative material. X is seen for the first time (sequence 4), in the foreground by a mirror in which is framed a couple, deep in conversation about the difficulties of their relationship. The narrating voice of X, lost during the play sequence, now reasserts its authority, taking over from the man's words. The camera continues to move among the guests (sequence 5).

OPENING OF FILM

- **hotel**: interior visible
  described as animated

- **garden**: invisble
  described as frozen

- **situation**: entry to hotel
  man and woman invisible
  narration heard:
  'advancing, as if to meet'
  man seeks

END OF FILM

- **hotel**: exterior visible
  not described
- **garden**: visible
  described as frozen
- **situation**: exit to garden
  man and woman invisible
  narration heard:
  'lost, alone with me'
  man has triumphed

END OF PLAY

- **hotel**: invisible
  described as frozen

- **garden**: visible
  seen as decor

- situation: static exterior
  man and woman visible
  dialogue heard:
  'this story is over'
  woman yields

OPENING OF PLAY

- **hotel**: interior visible
  seen as decor
- **garden**: invisible
  not described
- **situation**: static interior
  man and woman visible
  no dialogue heard:
  silence
  woman resists

Figure 8.2 *The opening and end of play and film*

showing the game of Nim for the first time. We hear the story of
Frank, X loses to M at Nim, and we see yet another couple, discussing
freedom. The passage is interwoven with X's words establishing the
theme of last year, 'You are still as beautiful. But you scarcely seem to
remember'. X and A are brought together for the first time as he
explains a detail of the ceiling to her (sequence 6). Then they are seen
dancing together. Shots of the guests culminate in a scene in the
shooting gallery. Over a long-held shot of A, X's voice describes their
first meeting by a statue in the gardens of Fredericksbad. A denies that
she is the woman concerned, but adopts, on an interior balustrade,
precisely the pose he has described: the imposition onto A of the story
generated by the various snatches of conversation has begun. But in
section D the momentum is lost: ' And once again we were separated'
(sequence 7). X loses to M once more at the game of Nim. The voice
of X stresses the emptiness of the *hôtel*, enumerating objects without
links between them.

Section E relates the couple to the statue which, according to X,
formed the setting for their first meetings. The statue is evoked and
A's movements in relation to it 'directed' by X (sequence 8). The
statue itself is animated and described in terms that relate it directly
to A and X. Then M intervenes with the 'true' explanation: 'This
statue represents Charles III and his wife. . . . The classical costumes
are purely conventional'. But a subsequent shot shows A by the
statue, exactly as described by X. Now A is seen walking alone
through a group of figures (sequence 9). She is alone and lost in the
garden when X accosts her and she asks for the continuation of their
story. The scene he describes is recreated and the couple is translated
to the salon, where they dance together once more. Section F also has
a double pattern, relating this time to A's room. X's first reference to
entering A's room triggers off an elaborate sequence which intercuts
steadily lengthening flash images of A in her room with much darker
shots of A and X at the bar (sequence 10). Her nervous laugh in her
room carries over to the bar and another passage of intercutting which
culminates in A dropping her glass. In the sudden silence X is seen
entering A's room, then a servant picks up the fragments of glass in
the bar. In the interpretation of the film proposed here, sequence F
concludes the first stage of the action and significantly it ends with a
kind of résumé of the film to date (sequence 11). Frozen groups of
guests and X's voice, intoning 'There were always walls. . .'. We see
X as we first saw him in sequence 4 by the mirror, which this

time contains the image of A. The couple walk together in the garden, which is now firmly established, and a repeat reference to X's entry into her room does not this time provoke terror. As X takes A to the concert, his voice-over commentary echoes the dialogue of the opening play sequence.

Section G is the pivot on which the symmetrically patterning of the whole film hinges and is itself symmetrical shaped, with A and X kissing in the first and third of its sequences. The concert takes place in the same room as the play, and the guests in the room and in the garden have the same immobility. Against this background A and X embrace tenderly by flowing water. Then they walk together in the empty garden (sequence 12). A meeting by the statue (sequence 13) precedes another embrace by water (sequence 14). Then X grows more distant, 'Always walls, always corridors. . .'. A is seen alone at the concert, with X's voice-over, 'It is already too late'.

Section H follows the same pattern as the corresponding section F, but this time it is X's fears that have to be resolved. X is now haunted by fears of A's death, allusions to which are strengthened in the dialogue (sequence 15). Four times he tries to banish the thoughts, 'It's not true'. His talk of A's fear leads back to the scene where she screams. But their discussion of A's room (sequence 16), shows that she can 'see' it too. X offers a photograph as evidence, and again talks of entering her room, denying that he took her by force. Running away, A finds the garden – here and now. There is a resolution in the scene in which they walk back together after she has broken the heel of her shoe.

In section I, which corresponds symmetrically to the evocation of the statue (section E), X proposes that they leave together, but at this point begins to grow uncertain. He talks of departure (sequence 17), but not of where they might go to. A's fears and denials continue, but now, sitting side by side in the garden, they 'see' the room together. X attempts to direct A's movements in the room (sequence 18), but she constantly disobeys his voice. There is an increasing air of uncertainty, even when X again produces the photograph as evidence and it is animated. Like section D, to which it corresponds, section J constitutes a pause in the action, with A alone in her room (sequence 19). In a brilliantly edited sequence, mutually inconsistent shots of A's movements are brought together to create a paradoxical continuity. X is now totally uncertain and three times his voice repeats, 'I don't remember any more'.

In section K, which corresponds to section C, where the various beginnings used to generate the story of X and A were successively given to us, a set of possible endings is tried out. First there is a scene between A and M (sequence 20). A in a gown of white feathers tries to warn X of something before she is shot by M. The fourth shot of her lying apparently dead stretched out at the foot of the bed shows her with her eyes open and a finger on her lips. X rejects this, 'No, this isn't the right ending'. He again confronts M at the game of Nim, and again loses. A, looking in a drawer, finds hundreds of identical photographs of herself. Then X enters the room (sequence 21) and she recoils in terror. X rejects the idea of rape (detailed in the script but not shown in the film); 'No, no no. . . . That's wrong', as the images show overexposed shots of A welcoming him with open arms. There is an abrupt transition to a dark garden (sequence 22). Now A is in black feathers and utters the words fixing the meeting for a year's time. Then as M approaches, X jumps astride the balustrade, which crumbles to ruins. A's scream at finding him vanished takes her back to the bar.

Now the film can find its appropriate ending in section L, with the couple leaving to enter the garden from which X had entered in section B. X in the corridor (sequence 23), begins once more, 'And once again I was walking down these same corridors. . .'. A tenderly says goodbye to M and does not obey the voice that intrudes. Shots of the *hôtel* and the beginning of the play (sequence 24) give way to images of A waiting to leave. X arrives and the pair set out together in silence. But the departure merely leads them into a new labyrinth (sequence 25), a garden resembling a cemetery, where, X tells A, she was 'now already getting lost, forever, in the calm night, alone with me'. Over the end title, section M, the music swells up with a new beginning, emphasising the circularity of the action.

Shot breakdown

L'ANNÉE DERNIÈRE À MARIENBAD
(Overall – including credits: 355 shots: 90 minutes)

A CREDITS (1–19)   19 shots
   The music comes to an end and the voice emerges

B THE PLAY (20–64)   45 shots
  1 *Down these corridors* (20–29)
    Voice-over as the camera tracks down corridors
  2 *I am yours* (30–46)
    Audience and players on stage: X's voice 'captured'
  3 *Really, that seems incredible* (47–64)
    Audience conversation and frozen poses

C CONVERSATIONS (65–94)   30 shots
  4 *Then listen to my complaints* (65–72)
    X is seen for the first time and his voice takes over
  5 *Don't you know the story?* (73–86)
    Fragments of conversation: the first game of Nim
  6 *The first time I saw you* (87–94)
    X and A are brought together for the first time

D SEPARATION (95–104)   10 shots
  7 *And once again we were separated*
    X loses again to M; enumeration of isolated objects

E THE STATUE (105–144)   40 shots
  8 *It was in the gardens of Fredericksbad* (105–17)
    The statue is evoked; A's movements 'directed' by X
  9 *You were in the middle of a group* (118–44)
    A asks for the rest of their story

F THE ROOM (145–199)   55 shots
10 *At night, most of all* (145–85)
    A in her room; X enters
11 *One evening I went up to your bedroom* (186–99)
    A résumé of the film to date

G THE CONCERT (200–220)   21 shots
12 *Let me alone* (200–7)
    The discordant concert and the first embrace
13 *We were talking about anything at all* (208–13)
    The couple walk in the garden
14 *Come here* (214–20)
    Meeting by the statue and second embrace

H **TERROR** (221–236)   16 shots
15 *You are afraid* (221–7)
        X tries to banish his fear of A's death
16 *I loved your fear that evening* (227–36)
        The room again: flight and reconciliation

I **THE DEPARTURE PLANNED** (237–258)   22 shots
17 *I've come now, to take you away* (237–48)
        X talks of departure, A hesitates; they 'see' the room
18 *We are going to leave* (249–58)
        X tries to direct A's movement in her room

J **DOUBT** (259–282)   24 shots
19 *I don't remember any more*
        Fragmented shots of A in her room

K **FALSE ENDINGS** (283–332)   50 shots
20 *You should get some rest* (283–94)
        A is shot by M, but comes alive
21 *It wasn't by force* (295–319)
        The idea of rape is rejected: blinding shots of A
22 *In the middle of the night* (320–332)
        X vanishes as the balustrade crumbles

L **RESOLUTION** (333–354)   22 shots
23 *Where are you. . my lost love* (333–41)
        X again in the corridors; A bids farewell to M
24 *I came at the time we set* (342–51)
        The play begins, and they leave together
25 *The park of this hotel* (352–354)
        Departure into a new labyrinth

M **END TITLE** (355)
        The music swells up to begin afresh

Part three PROTAGONISTS

Whether the hero be ridiculous or sublime, Greek or barbarian, gentile or Jew, his journey varies little in essential plan. Popular tales represent heroic action as physical; the higher religions show the deed to be moral; nevertheless, there will be found astonishingly little variation in the morphology of the adventure, the character roles involved, the victories gained.

JOSEPH CAMPBELL (1975)

9 The individual as protagonist: *The Big Sleep*

The extraordinary popularity of detective fiction since Poe is based upon the way in which this fictional form incorporates the principles of narrativity within the narration itself.

ROBERT SCHOLES (1982)

The Hollywood Protagonist

The conventional Hollywood movie is an example of enacted storytelling in one of its purest forms. Extraneous influences, such as the lessons of history or the pressures of society, are not permitted to intrude into what is essentially a personal conflict fought out between notionally free individuals. This conflict is expressed through a single action, which unfolds with inexorable narrative logic and with a rigorously worked out trajectory. Within this dramatic world, as the scriptwriting manuals constantly tell us, the hero or protagonist plays a key role. In David Mamet's words, 'screenwriting is a craft based on logic. It consists of the assiduous application of several basic questions: What does the hero want? What hinders him from getting it? What happens if he does not get it?' (1992: xv). There can be only one protagonist, whose outer motivation – what he or she visibly wants to achieve or accomplish before the end of the movie – drives the film forward. This outer motivation, as Michael Hauge points out, is 'the spine on which the entire plot, each of the other characters, and each individual scene will be built' (1989: 50). The incident which triggers the plot gives the protagonist a clearly defined goal. To reach this, the protagonist is compelled to make a series of decisions, each of which is translated into action. In this way, the protagonist's character under pressure is revealed as the film's plot progresses. The action of a Hollywood movie has a simplicity akin to that of a fairy-tale, but, as Bruno Bettelheim admirably demonstrates in *The Uses of Enchantment*, a simple narrative form presenting an action without interiority or overt explanation can possess a rich variety of meaning.

In the Hollywood system of narrative, action and character are locked indissolubly together. As Syd Field constantly reiterates, action is character. Field makes a useful distinction, in his advice to potential screenwriters, between interior and exterior aspects of character: 'The interior life of your character takes place from birth until the moment your film begins. It is a process that *forms* character. The exterior life of your character takes place from the moment your film begins to the conclusion of the story. It is a process that *reveals* character' (1982: 23). Action in a movie is significant only in so far as it is an expression of character. In turn, character shapes the action, by defining possible outcomes and events, and thereby justifying the story logic. In so far as the plot is built up into a three act structure with clearly defined climaxes and turning points, these are, at the same time, the stages in the progress and development of the central character, the protagonist. As Ken Dancyger and Jeff Rush observe, the three act structure gives the character 'maximum opportunity for redemption and restoration' (1991: 25).

Beyond possessing constant energy and a willingness to act whatever the threatening danger – the protagonist will always go resolutely and alone down that dank stairway to the cellar in the old dark house – the most striking aspect of this character is the space afforded to him or her to make decisions. Within the structure of the conventional Hollywood movie, the protagonist has a complete freedom to decide, during a whole series of clearly defined moments of either-or choice, which in turn lead up to the major decision: how to cope with the Act Two crisis. This decision-making, and the actions into which the choices are promptly translated, allow us to appreciate the protagonist's outer motivation (what he or she wants), but it gives us very little indication of the character's inner motivation (why he or she wants it), that is to say, how what is sought and achieved relates to the particular values held by the character (one role of the music is to convey this). To quote Michael Hauge's advice to screenwriters again: '*Exploration of inner motivation is optional.* All of your characters, including your hero, will do whatever they do for a reason, but you may choose not to examine their particular desires for self-worth' (1989: 53).

The fact that inner motivation may be concealed from us, does not mean, however, that the protagonist is incapable of change. In general, the Hollywood protagonist succeeds in his or her endeavour, or redeems an earlier error, so that Ben Brady and Lance Lee are compelled to observe in their screenwriting manual, 'if you can't conceive your story in terms of survival for your protagonist, then you will be left to write in the shallows' (1988: 189). Usually there will be an accompanying growth in maturity, a deepening of values, a strengthening of commitment. But we will judge this solely by the specific actions of the character. A Hollywood character does not pronounce, 'I must become a better person', he or she undertakes some premeditated action which we, the spectators, may judge as demonstrating a new resolve. Nor do the words of other characters within the drama carry any weight. As Irwin R. Blacker rightly notes, 'Nothing said about a character has any significance in the viewer's understanding of him if it is different from what the viewer has seen. The character is understood in the context of his actions' (1988: 36).

Just as the protagonist's values have to be deduced from his or her actions, so too any character development in the Hollywood system must be understood from a changed relationship with the other characters. These latter have no individual autonomy but, in this form of narrative organisation, exist only in fixed roles in relation to the protagonist. In a useful if somewhat schematic analysis, Michael Hauge allows only three other primary character roles in addition to that of the protagonist (or hero). The first is the character who stands in the way of the hero in his pursuit of his goal. This character – the 'nemesis' in Hauge's terms – may be a villain, an opponent, or a rival, but, whatever the case, the film must show a scene of final climactic confrontation between the two. The second character role, which Hauge calls the 'reflection', is the adjunct or helper in other classificatory systems, basically someone who supports the hero in his or her struggle, and who, to some extent, plays a role akin to that of the confidant(e) in classical tragedy. More interesting is Hauge's third category, the 'romance', which he defines not simply as someone with whom the protagonist is linked in a romantic or sexual relationship, but as a character who, in addition, alternately helps and is at cross-purposes with the protagonist.

In Hauge's view, while it is possible to have more than one character in any category, it is impossible for a secondary character to undergo a major development and so to change categories, though the revelation to the audience of a character's true role may be held back for dramatic purposes. Hauge also denies that anyone but a human being can occupy these supporting categories – animals and natural forces are explicitly excluded – which leads to the distinctly odd view that the 'nemesis' in *Jaws* is not the shark but the mayor (1989: 102). Character development – and hence a clarification and illustration of the film's theme – can occur in this system only through a realignment of the protagonist's relation with one of the other characters (1989: 81). Hauge deals only with the protagonist who comes to realise similarity to the nemesis and difference from the reflection, but a new relation with the romance figure is surely the most common form of character development and growth in this type of film structure.

Our understanding of the relationship between spectator and protagonist is bedevilled by film theory's use of the term 'identification'. Identification with the characters is one of the supposed pillars of theatrical illusionism, attacked by Bertolt Brecht because it prevents us from regarding a character in a truly critical way. Yet the dictionary definition of the intransitive verb to identify – 'to be made, become or prove to be the same' – indicates that this is not a precise way of describing our link with characters on either stage or screen. The viewing problems caused by Robert Montgomery's adaptation of the Raymond Chandler novel, *The Lady in the Lake*, are one proof of this. This film, Hollywood's most radical attempt at first person narration, uses the camera as the protagonist's eye, so that we see what he sees and are only shown his appearance when he looks at himself in a mirror. The attempt to impose a literal, physical identification with Marlowe on us in this way merely underlines our sense of separation from the protagonist (*we* do not smoke a cigarette, get punched etc.) and lays stress on the striking differences between human perception and the way a camera records reality. Certainly characters on stage and screen may arouse strong emotions in us, but as Noël Carroll notes, 'the relation is asymmetrical; the characters, in part through their emotions, *cause different* emotions in the spectator' (1988: 246). We may at times weep, laugh or be frightened with them, but we do not fall in love as they do, nor do we feel their pain.

Moreover, even in a conventional three-act structure, there is a systematic separation of levels of knowledge, so that at some times we know more than the protagonist, at others (particularly towards the end of a film) he or she leads us on. A much better term for our involvement is surely empathy, defined by the dictionary as 'the

power of projecting one's personality into, and so fully understanding, the object of contemplation'. Certainly Hollywood narratives
make it easy for us to empathise, with the scriptwriter's aim defined
by Michael Hauge as to 'enable a sympathetic character to overcome
a series of increasingly difficult, seemingly insurmountable obstacles
and achieve a compelling desire' (1989: 4). Yet the emotional
involvement is only part of our response . Since there is no narrator to
explain the action, and the inner motivation of the character may be
only lightly sketched in, we have to work out our own understanding,
make our own judgments about meaning and value.

The Big Sleep

Because the the conventional tight linking of plot and protagonist in
the Hollywood movie, one needs a film where the plot is generally
agreed to be nonsensical but in which the hero role is nevertheless
particularly strong, if one is to be able to isolate the power of the
protagonist from the customary onward drive of the plot. For this
reason I have chosen to discuss *The Big Sleep*. Any analysis of this
film must account for two things: the film's legendary impene-
trability and its cult status. If we follow Tzvetan Todorov's
observation that all detective fiction 'contains not one but two
stories: the story of the crime and the story of the investigation'
(1977: 44), it seems at first sight that the problems with the plot in
The Big Sleep lie basically in the 'first' story and so concern the crimes
which Marlowe is investigating. Most critical investigation of this
has focused on the unexplained murder of the chauffeur, Owen
Taylor, a figure who does not actually appear in the film, though we
do see the car in which he met his death being pulled out of the ocean.
There is the doubtless apocryphal story of the telegram which Hawks
claims to have sent to Chandler to ask who the killer was, to which
Chandler is supposed to have replied that he didn't know either.
Gerald Mast quotes an even more unlikely tale by the film's editor,
Christian Nyby, that 'the entire company stopped production for two
days to sit around on the set and try to deduce some killer who might
answer to this question' (1982: 277).
    But this is to treat the film as an Agatha Christie-style whodunit,
in which the detective proceeds from clue to clue, working purely
cerebrally, insulated from the aura of crime, and immune to the

outside world (who can imagine Hercule Poirot mugged by hoodlums?). In fact, of course, *The Big Sleep* is a thriller, a form in which the balance of the two stories is quite different. To quote Todorov again, 'this kind of detective fiction fuses the two stories or, in other words, suppresses the first and vitalises the second. We are no longer told about a crime anterior to the moment of narrative; the narrative coincides with the action' (1977: 47). Actually there is an anterior crime in *The Big Sleep* – the murder of Sean Regan – and the film comes to an end when this is resolved. But the real focus is on the succession of crimes, the murders committed during the action, and if there is a real problem with the plot – sufficient to trouble virtually everyone who has ever written about the film – then it must surely lie in the investigation undertaken by Marlowe (Humphrey Bogart).

There is considerable disagreement about why the plot of *The Big Sleep* is as it is. Gerald Mast sees the suppression of information and answers as a deliberate strategy which 'generates the entire film of *The Big Sleep*; Hawks deliberately leaves mysteries mysterious rather than supplies explanations' (1982: 277). Robin Wood sees it as simple 'indifference to plot' – 'the treatment of plot in Hawks's film is casual. Hardly anyone can follow it, including apparently Hawks' – and argues this is 'evidence of Hawks's strength rather than weakness' (1968: 170). Annette Kuhn, who offers a Proppian analysis to show that 'there is a high degree of closure in the film's narrative, in that only one of its moves remains finally unresolved', sees the confusion as the result of censorship (1985: 78–9). I shall here be arguing, more prosaically, that the confusion stems simply from the rewriting of the script and the shooting of new scenes during the production, in order to shift the focus from Carmen to Vivian (Lauren Bacall) and to transform the latter's role from co-villainess to romantic interest. The source of the confusion is that *The Big Sleep* begins as one film, shifts into quite a different story midway through, and is then given an admittedly exciting conclusion that really has little to do with the film's beginning.

This is not to argue that *The Big Sleep* is in any way an aberrant Hollywood movie, in the manner of Robert Montgomery's Chandler adaptation, *The Lady in the Lake*. It contains all the elements of patterning – the repetitions, variations and parallels – which we would expect from a tightly plotted 'closed' drama. Gerald Mast points out that, though there is very little such patterning in Chandler's original novel, everything in the film of *The Big Sleep* comes in pairs: two car scenes between Marlowe and Vivian, two scenes in which a woman waits for Marlowe to arrive, two lying phone calls from Vivian to Marlowe, two witty women outsiders who aid Marlowe's search, two male goons who work for Mars and two waitresses at the casino, two beatings that Marlowe receives from Mars's men, two bluff phone calls and two real telephone calls to the police, two calls by Marlowe to arrange a meeting with Mars, two scenes in which one character watches another take a beating, and two scenes in which a character threatens to count to three 'like they do in the movies' (1982: 292–3). There are also consciously worked out parallels in the shaping of the various acts. The question is, how are these elements put together?

Gerald Mast argues convincingly that 'in over forty years of film making, Howard Hawks builds every story in an identical four-part structure (1982: 30). This would seem at first sight in contradiction to the three-part structure explored in the chapter on *North by Northwest*, but in fact a closer examination shows that the difference is merely one of emphasis, with a greater than customary stress put on the act two midpoint, which conventionally redefines the direction of the action and hence divides act two into two distinct halves. In Mast's definition of Hawks's practice, the first part is a 'prologue', and the fourth a resolution, while 'the second and third parts develop the central conflict established in the first, either by letting one of the conflicting characters or life styles dominate in the second part, then the other in the third, or by letting one of the characters work alone in the second part, then both of them together in the third' (1982: 30-1). Usually, in Hawks's work, the result is 'the firmness of shape, the elegance, economy, and symmetry that allow surprising events to transpire within the firm logic and structure of a controlled pattern' (1982: 31) – a perfect definition of the best Hollywood narrative practice. But here in *The Big Sleep* the four parts fall apart, so that the film is held together only by the will and action of the protagonist.

The first words of the film set the pattern: 'My name is Marlowe'. Marlowe has come to see General Sternwood, but first he encounters the younger daughter, Carmen, who flirts with him and (literally) throws herself into his arms. Carmen's appearance here at the outset is, in terms of conventional 1940s Hollywood structure, a clear indication that she is a key figure in the crime to be investigated and that when her role is resolved, the action will be complete. The commission which the General has for Marlowe strengthens the importance of Carmen to the narrative. A number of her signed IOUs – allegedly gambling debts – have been sent for payment. There is some talk of the General's former assistant, Sean Regan, whom he describes as 'my friend, my son almost', but the task for Marlowe is clear. Months before, Regan had handled a similar request, for $5,000, from a gambler called Joe Brody. Now Marlowe is to get the new blackmailer, a rare book dealer named Arthur Gwynne Geiger, off the General's back. A subsequent meeting with the second daughter, Vivian Rutledge (Lauren Bacall), who assumes his visit concerns the disappearance, a month earlier, of Regan, in no way clouds the issue: the film is to deal with Marlowe's handling of the blackmailing bid by Geiger.

Accordingly Marlowe pays a research visit to the library, checks out Geiger's book shop (meeting his assistant, Agnes), and whiles away the time awaiting Geiger's appearance drinking rye with the bookseller in the shop on the opposite side of the street. When Geiger does emerge, accompanied by his sidekick, Carol Lundgren, Marlowe follows them to Geiger's house. There he watches Carmen arrive, but does nothing until shots ring out from the house. But by the time he enters the house, the killer has made his escape, and Marlowe finds only Geiger's dead body and a drugged Carmen, who has evidently been posing for photographs of some kind. When he returns Carmen to the Sternwood residence, he again meets Vivian, whom he provokes by bringing up the name of Sean Regan. Returning to the Geiger house, Marlowe finds to his amazement that the body has disappeared.

Running some twenty-six minutes (seven scenes), this first act is a perfectly coherent, if somewhat bland, opening for a 1940s Hollywood film, with the pervading air of corruption – Geiger's pornographic book shop, his homosexuality, Carmen's drug addiction – only lightly touched upon, in accordance with contemporary censorship requirements. Hawks has devised the film so that we follow the action as Marlowe experiences it, though he spurns such devices as a voice-over commentary (used in so many *film noir* adaptations) and the subjective camera favoured by Robert Montgomery. Bogart brings a pleasing style of self-deprecating authority to the role of Marlowe, which is weakened only by the tendency of women (here Carmen and the bookseller, later a female taxi driver) to find him instantly irresistible. A further weakness is the absence of a tangible adversary. Marlowe sets the pattern for the film as a whole by arriving just too late (unable to stop the killing or, later, to stop the removal of the body). Lauren Bacall, as Vivian, provides a potentially worthy foil for Bogart's Marlowe, but at this point her role is peripheral in plot terms and her father's description of her – 'spoilt, exacting, smart, ruthless. . . and with all the usual vices' – makes her in some ways an unlikely 1940s heroine. The addition of the second scene between her and Marlowe, which was shot and inserted only after the film had been released for army viewing, in no way alters the balance of the film decisively in her favour.

In act two Bernie Ohls, the cop who recommended him to General Sternwood, summons Marlowe to the Lido, where the Sternwood limousine is being pulled from the ocean. Later Vivian visits Marlowe with news of a second blackmail attempt (this time one using the photographs of Carmen) and the two enjoy sparring together. Retracing his steps to Geiger's book shop, Marlowe finds that the stock is being removed and follows the van to the flat of Joe Brody, author of the earlier blackmail of General Sternwood. Going back to Geiger's house, Marlowe finds Carmen and meets the gangster Eddie Mars for the first time. When Vivian later phones to say that the blackmailers have not called, Marlowe rightly guesses she is lying and goes to Brody's place. A series of confrontations there, with Brody, Agnes (the assistant from Geiger's book shop) and Carmen, culminate in the totally unexpected shooting of Brody. Marlowe chases and captures the killer, Carol Lundgren, and takes him to Geiger's place to hand him over to the police. Geiger's body is back, laid out on the bed.

The structure of this second act (thirty-one minutes, ten scenes) echoes that of the first. This time we begin with the nameplate, 'Philip Marlowe. Private Investigator', and again the action involves Marlowe going to Geiger's book shop, making, potentially at least, an easy sexual conquest (the female taxi driver), and twice visiting Geiger's house. The notorious scene where the Sternwood limousine is pulled from the sea turns out to be dramatically interesting for quite other reasons than 'Who killed Owen Taylor?' It allows the police to question Marlowe's involvement and brings the first hint that Sean Regan might be dead (when Marlowe queries whether he is the driver). If we need a killer for Taylor, the obvious candidate is Brody, who admits to having followed him, knocked him out and taken the photographs of Carmen.

The end of the act is the midpoint of the film (317 shots out of

607, seventeen scenes out of thirty-four). The body is back and the narrative has run out of steam. Those involved in the blackmail attempts Marlowe is supposed to be investigating are either dead (Geiger, Brody) or in custody (Lundgren). Eddie Mars has made his first appearance, but with his two comic henchmen he is hardly a figure of menace. Apart from the fact that he owns the Geiger house, there is nothing at this point to link him to the blackmail or to the Sternwoods (he does not recognise Carmen), though it seems his wife has run off with Sean Regan. Carmen herself is marginalised, making just two peripheral appearances. Vivian and Marlowe have discovered they enjoy playing games with each other, and Vivian has had the chance both to lie to him and to see him at work, but there are no plot questions linking them. Marlowe has shown himself adept at finding his way around in this dark and mysterious world, but at the end of the act there is no obvious step for him to take nor any particular mystery for him to solve.

Vivian gets the action under way again, ironically by trying to pay Marlowe off. His sense is that Eddie Mars is behind it all and that somehow Sean Regan is involved. His question to Vivian is, 'What's Eddie Mars got on you?'. Going out to confront Eddie, he sees Vivian singing in the club and then watches her act out a scene of winning at the tables. Outside, in the car park, Marlowe foils a hold-up and in the car he and Vivian establish two things: their love and the fact that she is still lying to him. Back home he questions Carmen about Sean Regan and then throws her out of his flat (and out of the narrative). Bernie Ohls summons him to tell him that Vivian has persuaded the D.A. to instruct Marlowe to lay off. When Marlowe phones Vivian, she lies again, telling him Sean Regan is safe and well in Mexico. In the street Marlowe is beaten up as a warning to keep off the case, but Harry Jones, who has been following him, offers a vital clue: Agnes knows the whereabouts of Eddie's wife. Marlowe has to watch as Eddie's chief henchman, Canino, makes Jones drink poison, but the information bought from Agnes gives him the clue he needs.

In this third act (thirty-three minutes, eleven scenes), *The Big Sleep* finds its focus as Marlowe's personal quest. From now on the film generates real dramatic power and interest, as the romantic story of a man intent on discovering the truth that will break the hold which he believes an evil man has over the woman he loves. Marlowe has to find the reason why Vivian tries to buy him off and even gets the D.A. to order him off the case, why she refuses to tell him about Sean

Regan and even lies blatantly to him. His instinct is that Eddie Mars is somehow behind it all, and though Eddie denies it, the beating up Marlowe himself receives and the murder of Harry Jones confirm his suspicions. At the end of the act he has a clear focus: his purpose is to avenge Harry Jones and to settle matters with Eddie Mars. But he is still uncertain about Vivian, about the hold Eddie has over her.

Act four (six scenes, eighteen minutes) is a swift move towards resolution. Knowing that Eddie Mars's wife is hiding away in a garage near Realito, Marlowe drives there, fakes an accident and seeks assistance. But Canino is not deceived, knocks him unconscious and ties him up in the house behind the garage. There Marlowe indeed finds Mrs Mars, but also Vivian who unties him. In the confrontation with Canino, she plays a key role in helping Marlowe kill his adversary, and in the car afterwards they finally admit their love for each other. Phoning from Geiger's house, Marlowe allows Mars to choose this as the site of their meeting. For the first time in the film, Marlowe is ahead of his opponents, armed, in the right place, and with time in hand. He is thus able to create his own *mise en scène*. Vivian had been lying to him to protect Carmen, because she had been convinced that her sister had killed Sean Regan. Marlowe proves that the killer is Mars, and then drives him out of the house to be gunned down by his thugs waiting outside. Vivian and Marlowe are united.

Hawks and his writers (William Faulkner, Leigh Brackett and Jules Furthman) had great difficulty in devising this fourth act. Initially, it seems (Mast, 1982: 273–4), they kept to the ending of Chandler's novel and the logic of the film's opening: a confrontation with Carmen, exposed as the killer of Sean Regan, and a return to the Sternwood mansion and the General. But this left no space to resolve the Vivian-Marlowe romance, which as the shooting had progressed had become one of the strongest aspects of the film and a major potential selling point. Various unsatisfactory attempts were made before the final pattern was reached, one which takes the action back not to the origin of Marlowe's quest (the Sternwood mansion) but to the location of his first set-back (Geiger's house). By making Mars responsible for Sean's death, the authors can show Vivian's concerns for her sister to be misplaced, and hence able to be resolved by Marlowe. And by keeping the two together for the last fifteen minutes, they can allow Vivian to redeem herself during the shoot-out with Canino and the couple to affirm their mutual love. All that is then necessary for the climax is for Marlowe to prove Mars's guilt and to contrive his death without actually shooting him in cold blood.

The plot of *The Big Sleep* is full of gaps and obscurities, inhabited by episodic characters and given a comparatively weak villain as the source of evil. But Marlowe's role as protagonist is perfectly coherent and provides a consistent thread through the film. We experience the world as Marlowe does, not literally, by seeing it through his eyes, but in true Hollywood fashion by following his actions. We have no insight into his mind, except when he reveals his hunches or convictions in the course of the dialogue, but he is constantly taking us forward. As is so often the case, the protagonist is under pressure or on the defensive for much of the action: in this case from the trivial instance in the opening scene, when Carmen accuses him of not being very tall, to the culminating moment of weakness when he is unable to prevent Harry Jones being killed in cold blood by Canino. But with a final burst of energy and total commitment, Marlowe as protagonist can resolve all doubts about the woman he loves and set up a totally satisfying final confrontation. The Hollywood movie is a reassuring form: Harry Jones may die, but his actions will be respected and his death both mourned and avenged. In the overall pattern of reassurance the role of the protagonist is crucial. As a lone individual he may be perplexed and led astray, but ultimately he will have the chance to redeem himself, and with redemption comes the opportunity to win true love.

Why does such a simplistic formula offer such satisfaction? Partly because it gives pattern and meaning to events which, in our own lives, are often random and haphazard. Partly because the focus on external action, uncluttered by interiority and subjectivity, gives the action the purity of a fairy-tale. Chandler has to make explicit in his novel the symbolic dimension of the action. But in the film we do not need to see the glass panels over the doorway of the Sternwood place depicting 'a knight in dark armour rescuing a lady who was tied to a tree and didn't have any clothes on but some very long and convenient hair': any film protagonist is automatically the gallant knight rescuing his fair lady.

To give life to the contrivances of the plot, we have the performances of the players. If the main plot line is flawed in *The Big Sleep*, the romance sub-plot is strong and cohesive. From the moment they first meet, in Vivian's bedroom, they are a well-matched pair, though their potential interaction gets little scope for expression in the complex plotting of the first two acts. But from the moment at the beginning of act three, when Vivian enters the nightclub to flirt with Marlowe and also to buy him off, it is the scenes between the two of them that provide the central focus for the action. It is while they are separated, after the first car scene, that Marlowe is beaten and finds himself impotent in the face of the vicious Canino. Reunited at Realito, the pair can work together to rout evil and show themselves worthy of the love they share. The fact that many of the scenes between Bogart and Bacall have been devised with scant regard for the demands of a thriller plot and are presented in an almost improvised manner gives the film its air of freshness and spontaneity. The playful vitality of the interaction of the two performers encourages us to share the enjoyment and to play our own games with our memories of other films and our awareness of the off–screen romance: a key requirement for a film destined for cult status.

Shot breakdown

THE BIG SLEEP
(Overall: credits + 609 shots: 108 minutes)

ONE [168 shots, 26 minutes]
  Credits
1 *Sternwood House* (1–73)   73 shots
    Marlowe is hired and meets the General's two daughters
2 *Library* (74–7)   4 shots
    Marlowe begins his research
3 *Geiger's Shop* (78–88)   11 shots
    Marlowe investigates Geiger's operation
4 *Book shop* (89–106)   18 shots
    Marlowe keeps watch (and shares rye
    with the bookseller)
5 *Geiger's House* (107–47)   41 shots
    Marlowe fails to prevent a murder, but finds Carmen
6 *Sternwood House* (148–62)   15 shots
    Marlowe returns Carmen to her sister, Vivian
7 *Geiger's House* (163–8)   6 shots
    Marlowe returns: the body of Geiger has vanished

TWO [149 shots, 31 minutes]

  8 *Marlowe's Office* (169–74)   6 shots
     Bernie Ohls summons Marlowe

  9 *Lido Quay* (175–82)   8 shots
     Owen Taylor's car is pulled from the ocean

10 *Marlowe's Office* (183–202)   20 shots
     Vivian brings news of the second blackmail
     attempt

11 *Geiger's Shop* (203–09)   7 shots
     Marlowe finds Geiger's stock being removed

12 *Taxi* (210–19)   10 shots
     He follows the van to Joe Brody's place

13 *Geiger's House* (220–42)   23 shots
     Marlowe finds Carmen and meet Mars
     for the first time

14 *Marlowe's Office* (243)   1 shot
     Vivian phones to lie about the blackmailers

15 *Randall Place* (244–83)   40 shots
     A series of confrontations culminates in Brody's
     death

16 *Corridor, Street* (284–303)   20 shots
     Marlowe captures the killer, Carol Lundgren

17 *Geiger's House* (304–17)   14 shots
     The body of Geiger is back

THREE [167 shots, 33 minutes]

18 *Bar* (318–34)   17 shots
     Vivian tries to put Marlowe off the case

19 *Mars's Gambling Joint* (335–74)   40 shots
     Marlowe questions Mars and has two
     encounters with Vivian

20 *The Car park* (375–99)   25 shots
     Marlowe foils the hold–up

21 *Car Interior* (400–10)   11 shots
     Marlowe and Vivian establish their love,
     but not their trust

22 *Marlowe's Flat* (411–27)   16 shots
     Marlowe gets rid of Carmen

23 *Bernie Ohls's Office* (428–34)   7 shots
     Vivian has arranged for the D.A. to warn off Marlowe

24 *Bar and Restaurant* (435–6)   2 shots
    Vivian again lies to Marlowe, this time about Regan
25 *Street Exterior* (437–48)   12 shots
    Marlowe is beaten up by Eddie Mars's men
26 *Marlowe's Office* (449–59)   11 shots
    Harry Jones offers to sell the whereabouts
    of Eddie's wife
27 *Fulwider Building* (460–80)   21 shots
    Jones is killed by Mars's henchman, Canino
28 *Agnes's Car* (481–4)   5 shots
    Agnes sells the information Marlowe needs

FOUR [125 shots, 18 minutes]
29 *The Road to Realito* (485–96)   12 shots
    Marlowe fakes an accident
30 *The Garage* (497–508)   12 shots
    Marlowe is knock unconscious by Canino
31 *The House* (509–33)   25 shots
    Vivian frees Marlowe
32 *Outside the House* (534–60)   27 shots
    With Vivian's help, Marlowe kills Canino
33 *Car Interior* (561–72)   12 shots
    Marlowe and Vivian confess their love for each other
34 *Geiger's House* (573–609)   38 shots
    Marlowe outsmarts Eddie Mars, the real killer
    of Sean Regan
    End Title.

10 The hand of God: *Un condamné à mort s'est éschappé ou Le vent souffle où il veut*

The real is not dramatic. Drama will be born of a certain march of non-dramatic events

ROBERT BRESSON (1977)

A figural realism

Erich Auerbach begins *Mimesis*, his study of the representation of reality in Western literature, with a comparison of two styles, which he terms the Homeric and the Old Testament. The first style, defined as comprising 'fully externalised description, uniform illumination, uninterrupted connection, free expression, all events in the foreground, displaying unmistakable meanings, few elements of historical development and of psychological perspective' (1957: 19), finds one echo – among many others – in examples of the Aristotelian tradition of 'closed' dramatic art, of which the dramatic structures of the Hollywood movie are a contemporary example (cf. Eco, 1989: 105–22). The evolution of the second and more enigmatic approach, the Old Testament style, is characterised by Auerbach as possessing 'certain parts brought into high relief, others left obscure, abruptness, suggestive influence of the unexpressed, 'background' quality, multiplicity of meanings and the need for interpretation, universal-historical claims, development of the historically becoming, and the preoccupation with the problematic' (1957: 19). He explores this latter style through the use of the concept of the mediaeval *figura*, deriving from the tradition of interpretation according to which episodes in the Old Testament are interpreted as 'figures or phenomenal prophesies' of events in the New Testament (1957: 64). One example of this connection which Auerbach gives is the linking of Eve ('mankind's primordial mother after the flesh'), born from Adam's rib, that is, from a wound in his side, with the Church ('the mother of all men after the spirit'), born from the wound inflicted in the side of the crucified Christ (1957: 42–3).

A key feature of figural representation was the refusal to separate the earthly and the divine, the grotesque and the sublime, or to treat them as two separate entities. Instead stress was placed on the interconnection of the two. Figural representation in no way under-played the claims of the physical and tangible, giving 'a presentation which carefully interrelated the elements of history, which respected temporal and causal sequence, remained within the domain of the earthly foreground'. But, sumultaneously, there was also 'a vertical connection, ascending from all that happens, converging in God', so that the presentation of the earthly was 'constantly seeking an interpretation from above' (1957: 65). As a result, in figural representation, 'an occurrence on earth signifies not only itself but at the same time another, which it predicts or confirms, without prejudice to the power of its concrete reality here and now. The connection between occurrences is not regarded as primarily a chronological or causal development, but as a oneness within the divine plan, of which all occurrences are parts and reflections' (1957: 490).

Robert Bresson is no mediaeval artist, but his work has an analogous double focus, which may appear paradoxical if we do not see it as part of a lengthy Christian tradition of representation (a view also put in Hanlon (1986), which I had not read when this chapter was written). The two elements are explicitly brought together in the double title of Bresson's fourth feature film, made in 1956: the earthly level in the main title, *A Man Condemned to Death Has Escaped*, and the divine in the secondary title, *The Wind Bloweth Where It Listeth*. A constant emphasis is placed on the authenticity of the film's action. Bresson has based his film on the published account of an actual escape in 1943 and prefaces his film with the signed statement: 'This story is true. I give it as it is, without ornament'. In his presentation of the film at the Cannes Film Festival in 1957, Bresson laid stress on the documentary aspects: 'I wanted it to be almost a documentary. I've kept to a tone close to the documentary in order to preserve this aspect of the truth, all the time' (1957: 4). His own practice bears this out. The film was shot partly in location at the actual prison, Fort Montluc, using non-professional actors, including German students to play the guards. When the cell was rebuilt in the studio, Bresson insisted on the use of real materials, not simply plasterboard. But despite Bresson's concern with authenticity, his central purpose is not to give a simple realistic portrayal of a human achievement, but rather to explore what might lie behind this surface reality. As he stated at Cannes:

> What I feel in a prison, that is to say, as the second title, *The Wind Bloweth Where It Listeth* indicates, are these extraordinary currents, the presence of something or someone, call it what you wish, which means that there is a hand guiding everything (1957: 7).

Overt Christian elements are discreetly employed in *Un condamné*, though Bresson does use fragments of Mozart's Mass in C Minor to give a new dimension to routine activities within the prison, and to celebrate the final escape by the protagonist (here called Fontaine), as well as to underline the failed escape attempt of another prisoner, Orsini. A comparison between the film and the authentic account by André Devigny, on which it is based, shows that Bresson has in fact made less explicit, and perhaps more mysterious, the Christian references. Devigny admits in his account to having prayed in prison, but we never see Fontaine either praying for help or giving thanks for his success, though he does ask for the prayers of the pastor before beginning his final escape attempt. There is an interesting nuance in the shift from Devigny's statement. 'There were two parts, mine and God's', to Fontaine's comment in the film, 'It would be too easy if God took charge of everything' (Prédal, 1992: 65). And Jean Sémolué underlines the importance of the change in the biblical text passed by the pastor, from the simple encouragement, 'Ask, and it shall be given you; seek, and ye shall find; knock, and it shall be opened unto you' (Acts, 3.8), in Devigny's account, to the passage used in the film: 'The wind bloweth where it listeth, and thou hearest the sound thereof, but canst not tell whence it cometh, and whither it goeth: so is everyone that is born of the spirit' (Matthew, 7.7), (*see* Sémolué, 1959: 151). To understand the interrelationship between human action and the divine will in *Un condamné* we need to look at both the overall dramatic structure and the shaping of sequences, as well as the detailed use of such elements as editing and camera placement.

Un condamné à mort s'est échappé

Robert Bresson's film preserves the simplicity and clarity which he has said he admired in André Devigny's published account. Hence *Un condamné* is one of the director's most accessible works. Indeed the shaping of the action and the focus on the protagonist with his single-minded quest is so close to the precedures of conventional Hollywood cinema, that the film is best understod as both a utilisation and a subversion of these conventions. Bresson himself, in his interviews and his collection of aphorisms – *Notes on Cinematography* – is always at pains to distance himself from this kind of conventional acted cinema, which he equates with filmed theatre: 'bastard theatre lacking what makes theatre: material presence of living actors, direct action of the audience on the actors' (1977: 3). Yet though he rejects the use of actors on screen (writing off, at a stroke, ninety-nine per cent of world cinema: Renoir, Cukor, Mizoguchi, Welles, Resnais, Kurosawa, Ray, Spielberg . . .), Bresson's approach to the conventional (and extremely powerful) model of classical, highly plotted drama, typified in cinema by the Holywood movie, is much more nuanced. Indeed it is easy to find in the overall structure of *Un condamné* a three-act pattern linking action and character in the manner advocated by the Hollywood scripting manuals, such as Field (1982) or Seger (1987).

The first act (six sequences; seventeen minutes) opens with the protagonist, Fontaine, and his first failed escape attempt from the car bringing him to prison. It follows him through his initial beating to the cell into which he is thrown, bruised and bloody. His first deception of his guards here (feigning unconsciousness) perhaps saves his life, and certainly it sets the pattern of his actions for the whole of the film. In the cell, initial despair gives way to hope and fresh determination, largely thanks to the help and support he receives. He gets encouragement through the bars of cell window, when Terry, a prisoner allowed to exercise in the yard, enables him to communicate with the world outside. Another prisoner, himself waiting to be shot, teaches him how to open his handcuffs. Freeing his hands is Fontaine's first triumph and leads to the decision to escape which will drive the whole action of the film (in precisely the same way that, say, a bereaved cowboy's search for revenge may propel the action in a Western). Then unexpectedly Fontaine is transferred to another cell, in the upper floor of the prison.

The second act (sequences number 7–29; forty-nine minutes) begins with the routine life of the prison, given fresh significance by Bresson's use of passages from Mozart's Mass in C Minor, which recur several times during the act. In the second sequence of the act, Fontaine begins the meticulous preparation of his escape by starting to dismantle his cell door. Terry makes an unexplained (and inexplicable) appearance in the corridor outside Fontaine's cell, but in act two the focus of Fontaine's relationships shifts to his new neighbour, M. Blanchet, to whom he gives new hope, and his friend, the pastor, with whom he discusses his plans to escape and debates the role of God. The third key person is Orsini, who keeps watch for Fontaine from his cell opposite, initially hopes to join him in his escape, and then decides to go it alone.

Orsini's failed escape (sequence 23) is the crucial mid-point of the act, giving Fontaine the key knowledge which will permit his own escape attempt to succeed and also strengthening his resolve. But most of act two is concerned with Fontaine's meticulous preparations as he ransacks everything in his cell to provide the necessary ropes and hooks for the escape. The fortuitous arrival of a parcel saves him by distracting the guards who are supposed to search his cell and also aids his escape by providing new materials. Everything is now ready, his friends warn him not to delay, but Fontaine hesitates. Then, at the act's climax, two blows rain down on Fontaine: he is told by the Germans that he is to be executed and, on returning to his cell, finds he has a new companion, Jost, a scruffy individual dressed half in French and half in German uniform. Fontaine is in the classic position of a Hollywood protagonist at a similar state in the narrative: forced to make a life-or-death decision in circumstances where a clear way out is difficult to see.

Act three (sequences number 30–3; 29 minutes) opens with a visit to the washroom, where Fontaine's friends again urge him to leave, but from then on the focus is almost exclusively on Fontaine and Jost. Fontaine interrogates the young man, then broods on whether to kill him or take him along. Again he is paralysed by self-doubt. Fontaine makes a last visit to the washroom, where he leaves his 'testament' (details of his plan of escape) with the pastor and asks for prayers from the pastor and the latter's cell mate, the abbé. This is followed by a tense scene in which Fontaine reveals the plan to Jost and makes the final preparations. In the long concluding sequence of the film (an unbroken sixteen and a quarter minutes), the pair make their escape, though their progress to the outside takes several hours to accomplish, as Fontaine is wracked with doubt, particularly about the killing of one of the German guards. But the escape is finally completed, and the film follows the conventional Hollywood pattern by concluding with the very briefest of resolutions, a single shot of Fontaine and Jost walking off over a railway bridge and becoming hidden by smoke from a passing train, as we hear the renewed strains of Mozart's C Minor Mass.

At one level, therefore, *Un condamné* gives us a pattern of the conventional type: a first act which offers immediate introduction to a protagonist whose predicament is severe (Fontaine must make his escape if he is to survive) and subsequently following him through his first response (freeing his hands). At the beginning of act two a shift of location (to a new cell, where handcuffs are no longer required) leads to a new strategy being needed, and we follow Fontaine as he makes his elaborate plans. The failure of Orsini's solo effort in the middle of act two redefines the problem and adds a greater impetus. As members of the audience we share the opinion of Fontine's friends that he must act immediately, only to find ourselves caught in the double crisis with which act two ends: death is imminent, but Fontaine is no longer alone in his cell. We do not see a clear way out: Jost is clearly untrustworthy, but to kill an unsuspecting boy would be immoral. Fontaine interrogates Jost, but finds it hard to reach a decision. Then finally he makes up his mind, leaving Jost no choice but to accompany him. On the rooftop there are many further hesitations, but Fontaine's determination and the sureness of his preparations finally carry him through to the moment of triumph, whereupon the film promptly ends.

The locking of the protagonist into this action is as tight as in any Hollywood film: Fontaine's personal trajectory and the unfolding of the plot are one. Fontaine enters the story from nowhere (we never learn the circumstances of his arrest, for example) and we come to know him only through his actions (his words in voice-over generally offer a commentary on these actions rather than an insight into Fontaine's inner self). Bresson is quite clear about his intentions, both in this film and his others: 'Not to shoot a film in order to illustrate a thesis or to display men and women confined to their external aspects, but to discover the matter they are made of' (1977: 20). But we are given very little insight into Fontaine's thoughts: we never learn, for example, how he makes the decision to take Jost along with him, though this is a crucial moment in the film. Instead we see his actions: in the very first shot we see Fontaine's hands, his determined face and appreciate that he will try to escape. Alert, intelligent and infinitely resourceful, he is initially the archetypal film hero. Even his wavering towards the end of act two – when his friends urge him to leave – can be seen as part of the conventional pattern of increasing pressure on the protagonist throughout act two. Faced with a life-or-death crisis he makes his decision, reasserts his authority, first over Jost and then over himself, and acts.

Only during the actual escape, on the roofs, walls and parapets of the prison, do Fontaine's doubts and hesitations distinguish him sharply from a conventional film protagonist, who at this point would be totally self-confident and wholly involved in the action. In *Un condamné* something else – beyond the courage and the meticulous preparations – is needed for Fontaine's success. It is here that the conventions of the Hollywood action film are particularly useful to Bresson. In this system of narrative, which Bresson has largely followed up to this point in the film, outer motivation (what the protagonist wants) must always be clear, but inner motivation (why the protagonist wants it, how he makes his decisions) is optional. Now we are given no explicit explanation of Fontaine's hesitations and how he overcomes them. There is a gap, as it were, in the narrative that members of the audience in their interpretation of the film can either ignore (by concentrating on the eventual success of the escape) or fill with a religious explanation (the hand of God). Bresson leaves the decision open to us.

Though Bresson subverts conventional movie structure at key moments, the overall system of tight classical dramatic plotting is itself extremely apposite for his project. As Noël Carroll notes, the Brechtian assault on classical theatre focused in part on its compelling momentum 'which suggests not only that what was enacted was a "real event" but that the way it was presented was the way *it had to happen*, which implies, purportedly, that society, the social world, cannot be changed' (1988: 92). This is precisely the tone which Bresson wishes to capture in *Un condamné*. The echoes and parallels, anticipations and repetitions, which characterise conventionally plotted drama (and which were inherited by Hollywood) emphasise this sense of inevitability. This narrative system requires a failure to be set against a success, a small victory to herald a major triumph, help received to be repaid through help given, and so on. In *Un condamné*, there is the pattern of Fontaine's own initial failure set against his ultimate success, with Orsini's attempt forming a crucial parallel. Fontaine initially receives hope from the help of Terry, and in return gives hope to his new neighbour, M. Blanchet. The rather odd first shot from outside the cell door (as Fontaine tidies the wood shavings inside) prefigures the uenxpected visit of Terry, which in turn prefigures Fontaine's own sortie into the corridor, which is equally inexplicable to the neighbour to whom he gives words of encouragement. Both these moments of freedom find their culmination, of course, in the final escape by Fontaine and Jost. Above all classical drama makes potent use of dramatic irony: Oedipus himself being the murderer he is seeking, or, here in *Un condamné*, the arrival of Jost in Fontaine's cell, which seems initially a disaster for his plan, eventually turning out to be crucial to its success (encountering an unexpectedly high wall during the escape sequence, Fontaine admits, 'Alone, I might perhaps have been stuck there').

While such patterning is often used (certainly in Hollywood) to build up the protagonist's ultimate invincibility, Bresson here intersperses a more than usual number of coincidences and chance events, which perhaps hint at some unseen hand guiding Fontaine's efforts. Thus, the pastor's acquisition of a bible (which he describes as a miracle) is instantly followed by Fontaine's finding of the second spoon which is vital to his efforts in dismantling his cell door. Similarly, the providential arrival of the parcel saves Fontaine from having his cell searched after he has recklessly defied the guards. Just occasionally Bresson is more explicit: immediately before the escape, the failure of the guard to search the pastor's jacket (which contains a note detailing Fontaine's plan) is perhaps also mere chance, but the tiny cross clearly visible on the lapel perhaps points to another reason.

Though Bresson has claimed that there are no sequences in the film, since the whole work forms a single sequence (Sémoulué, 1959: 130), there is in fact a precise structure of thirty-three sequences of very varied length (ranging from two shots to sixty-two), all separated by fades to black and comprising, as we have seen, an overall three act pattern. It is in the construction of these sequences that Bresson distances himself most from Hollywood practice. In conventional cinema the basic building block is the scene: a self-contained entity which comprises a confrontation of some kind, which will turn the direction of the plot (in however minimal a way), and which occurs in a more or less continuous time and space. The construction of a dramatic action out of discrete units of this kind is one reason why Hollywood cinema shares with the nineteenth century novel the ideological stance attributed to it by Alain Robbe-Grillet, namely, that of 'imposing the image of a stable universe, coherent, continuous, univocal and wholly decipherable' (1965: 63).

The communication of a world-view of this kind is not Bresson's intention, and the units out of which he builds his dramatic action – which I have termed sequences, to distinguish them from Hollywood scenes – are very differently constructed. Of the thirty-three sequences, only five of the shorter ones (numbers 3, 9, 10, 13, 18) are scenes of the classical type implying (if not literally constituting) a clear continuity of time and space. All the rest are made up of smaller units linked by dissolves, which have the effect of linking discrete spaces or compressing much longer timescales. The effect, in a film ostensibly about physical barriers and inexorable daily routines, is a breaking down of all the external barriers of space and time. The impact of this form of structure can be seen in the very first sequence which comprises three distinct actions: Fontaine makes a failed attempt at escape, he is beaten almost unconscious, and he is thrown into a cell where he admits he may have wept. Shot as three separate scenes these events could easily constitute three successive failures. But by using dissolves, firstly, to underplay the blow from a revolver which concludes the escape attempt and, then again, to elide the actual beating, Bresson is able to reverse this meaning. By giving greater prominence to the positive elements in the resolution of the sequence – the emergence of the narrating voice of Fontaine and the sight of his alert face – he turns a series of disasters into an ultimate triumph of the human spirit.

Later in the film, a single sequence may propel Fontaine seemingly effortlessly throughout the prison. Sequence 19, for example, in which Fontaine recruits Orsini as his co-escapee, shows him in his cell, on the stairs, in the yard, in the washroom, in his cell, looking out across the corridor, and back at his window. In spatial terms, the effect of dissolves from one part of the prison to another within a sequence is to translate Fontaine around the prison as if the barriers of walls and locks, corridors and stairways, are as nothing. Fontaine is literally a prisoner, confronted with real obstacles in the shape of the door that needs to be broken down, the ropes and hooks that need to be made from the few materials at hand. But there is a narrating instance in the film – a force which shapes the sequences, and hence the narrative – that clearly tells us that such barriers are not unsuperable. In Hollywood cinema the enactment of the story can be 'innocent', in that the characters themselves seem to be the sole authors of the events which constitute the story. But here, in *Un condamné*, we have a highly self-conscious style of film making, in which the shaping of the narrative calls attention to itself and posits itself – rather than simply the characters themselves – as a source of meaning controlling the action.

The same is true of the handling of time. The two sequences in which Fontaine finalises his preparations for his solo escape, towards the end of the second act (numbers 24 and 25), contain little movement through space but an enormous fluidity of time. In the first sequence, Fontaine acts on the information given him by Orsini and, in a series of seven shots linked by dissolves, fashions an appropriate hook, before the passage of a guard in the corridor makes him stop. In the later sequence, which begins with the arrival of the parcel which is searched by the guards, Fontaine turns the entire contents of the parcel into additional ropes in just seven shots, again all linked by dissolves. The effect of this compression of time is, in each case, to give an enormous dynamism to Fontaine's efforts.

Even more interesting is the handling of time in the final sequence of the escape. Fontaine's voice-over narration aknowledges his continual doubts during the escape – in some instances hours pass before he feels able to make the next move. This hesitancy, as Fontaine submits to a rhythm which is not that of his own will, is, of course, the narrative gap which we are invited by Bresson to fill with a sense of the divine power shaping the outcomes of human action. But at the same time the flow of images, through which the progress of the escape is depicted, erases the hours of doubt and waiting through a series of dissolves and depicts a smooth, flowing (and hence seemingly inevitable), sweep towards the escape. Human frailty – in even as strong a character as Fontaine – is acknowledged, but the film sweeps on with its own almost lyrical rhythm to its seemingly preordained ending.

Bresson's placing of the camera in *Un condamné* is as consciously thought-through as his shaping of sequences. French film theory, beginning with Albert Laffay and followed by Christian Metz and, more recently, André Gaudreault and François Jost, is fond of the notion of 'the Great Image-maker' as the organising power behind narrative images which otherwise seem to have no narrator. In

Laffay's definition, the Great Image-maker:

> . . . is not strictly speaking the director, nor any of the film makers, but a
> fictional, invisible figure to whom their communal work has given birth
> and who, behind our backs, turns the pages of the album for us, directs
> our attention with a finger pointing discreetly at some detail or other,
> slips us the necessary information at the right moment and, above all,
> gives rhythm to the flow of images (1964: 81–2).

Believing, like David Bordwell, in the principle that 'we ought not to
proliferate theoretical entities without need' (1985: 62), I feel that
such a concept is basically unnecessary. The absence of a definable
narrator in conventional cinema is in no way odd, but is simply a
characteristic shared with virtually all Western stage drama, in which
the voice of the author can be defined only from the polyphony of
conflicting voices and actions of the characters.

But for Bresson's *Un condamné* we do need some such entity since,
far from the camera being effaced, the placing of it displays what one
can only describe as an overtly expressed *knowledge* of the outcome of
the action. The opening section of the first sequence, depicting
Fontaine's failed escape from the car (shots 1–24), gives a clear
insight into Bresson's stylistic approach. The first shot shows us
Fontaine's situation: his hands free, his face alert, in the backseat of a
car alongside two men handcuffed together (we see only the hand and
arm of the second of these). The depiction of the escape attempt is
deliberately fragmented, with alternating shots of Fontaine's face and
hands interspersed with oddly angled shots of the gear lever being
changed and shots purporting to be Fontaine's point-of-view forward
through the windscreen which are slightly disturbing, because the
point-of-view is literally that of the unseen third prisoner. This kind
of editing, built up by capturing and intercutting gestures in close-up,
is conventional in the action film, when the outcome of the hero's
efforts is uncertain.

But in the final shot (number 24), when Fontaine leaps from the
car, the camera does not follow him. Instead Bresson holds the
camera focused on the space which Fontaine has just vacated and on
the emotionless face of his neighbour, who does not even turn his
head. In a tiny corner of the rear window we see Fontaine pursued and
captured by guards from a following car. Still the camera remains
motionless, until Fontaine is brought back to the car, pushed inside
and brutally clubbed, whereupon Bresson dissolves to the next scene,

in the prison yard. Though the decision to shoot the scene in this way is self-evidently that of the director, the effect of such an obtrusively immobile shot, calling attention to itself by the refusal to show us clearly what we want to see (the escape), is to anthropomorphise the camera, seemingly to give it a kind of intelligence. Why is there no shot of Fontaine from outside the car? We are tempted to answer, because the camera 'knows' that he will be caught and returned. Certainly there is an order, a knowledge, in the film which is quite outside the powers of the human protagonists.

If this seems an exaggerated interpretation of a single shot, we can see the same process of construction used in the sequence depicting Orsini's failed escape. The sequence in question (number 23) comprised thirty-one shots variously linked by six dissolves. It opens with Fontaine, alone in his cell, hearing shots and fearing for Orsini. A dissolve takes us to a point a week later when, in a series comprising nine individual images, Fontaine tries to make contact with Orsini, who hurries ahead into the prison yard. As we again hear the music of Mozart, we see that Orsini is equipped with hooks, but as he moves off, the camera stays behind to wait for Fontaine. Orsini breaks into a run and turns around a corner, but again the camera stays to frame Fontaine's face. A dissolve takes us to the pastor in the washroom, who expresses the hope that Orsini may succeed. We dissolve again, this time to an eleven-shot series in Fontaine's cell. Through the peephole Fontaine sees Orsini brought back and learns the crucial fact that hooks are needed to conquer the outer wall. Mozart's C Minor Mass is heard again as a dissolve takes us to the corridor, where Orsini is taken away by the guards. A fresh dissolve takes us to a four-shot series in the washroom, where the pastor gives Fontaine a piece of paper. One final dissolve, for the last three-shot series, as Fontaine reads the biblical text to M. Blanchet – 'The wind bloweth where it listeth' – and hears the execution of Orsini.

Here both camera immobility and sequence structure are used to convey the futility of Orsini's attempt (though, as M. Blanchet later observes, it was necessary for Orsini to fail, in order that Fontaine might succeed). Like Fontaine in the opening sequence, Orsini makes his dash for freedom, but the camera does not follow him, twice remaining immobile to focus on Fontaine. In terms of the sequence as a whole, Orsini is condemned from the start, with Mozart's mass acting as his requiem. By beginning the sequence with the shot of Fontaine hearing what he wrongly thinks is Orsini's execution –

though it is a week before the actual death – Bresson is already condemning Orsini, since, in the kind of classical plot structuring employed here, the real execution is the only satisfactory conclusion to follow such an opening. Despite the wishes of Fontaine and the hopes expressed by the pastor, Orsini cannot succeed, but his death can be given meaning both by the music and the biblical quotation.

This treatment of the two failed escape attempts contrasts strongly with the depiction of the successful escape of Fontaine and Jost. Here the camera is constantly in advance of the characters, focused on the space into which they will emerge. The pattern is set in the brief sequence number 17, when the camera is outside in the corridor waiting for Fontaine to emerge from his cell. At a moment like this – and throughout the final sequence – suspense of a conventional kind is removed, since we, as spectators, do not move forward with the characters into an unknown danger, but are placed in advance of them, waiting for them to enter a space which is shown to be empty before they venture forward into it. When this kind of camera placement is combined with the way in which Fontaine's hours of waiting are obliterated by a pattern of dissolves which keeps the action moving smoothly ever forward, the effect is precisely that which Bresson has intended: an unseen hand leads the hesitant characters smoothly forward without any real doubt or set-back towards a preordained ending. The will to succeed and total preparedness are necessary, but not sufficient, requirements for the escape. There is an additional need for the characters to submit themselves to a rhythm outside their control, which welcomes them and carries them forward as they make their tentative advance. Only in the single shot of the resolution is the camera behind the characters as they set their own rhythm and stride off into the unknown future they must construct for themselves outside the prison.

Shot breakdown

UN CONDAMNÉ Á MORT S'EST ÉCHAPPÉ
(Overall: credits + 507 shots: 95 minutes)

ONE [credits + 97 shots: 17 minutes]
Credits

1 *Car, Prison, Cell* (1–29)   29 shots
  Fontaine tries to escape, is captured, beaten
  and imprisoned
2 *Cell, Window, Prison Yard* (30–49)   20 shots
  Fontaine fakes injury and finds allies in the
  prison yard
3 *Cell* (50–1)   2 shots
  Fontaine makes contact with his neighbour
4 *Cell, Window, Prison Yard* (52–71)   20 shots
  Fontaine gets help from Terry and frees his hands
5 *Window, Prison Yard, Cell* (72–91)   20 shots
  Fontaine makes his decision to escape
6 *Cell, Corridor, New Cell* (92–7)   6 shots
  Fontaine is moved to a new cell, his handcuffs
  are removed

TWO [250 shots: 49 minutes]
7 Cell, Washroom, Yard, Cell (98–108)   11 shots
  The routine of prison life
8 *Cell* (109–16)   8 shots
  Fontaine begins work on dismantling his door
9 *Cell* (117–22)   6 shots
  Fontaine receives a visit from Terry
10 *Washroom* (123–67)   shots
  Fontaine makes contact with the pastor
11 *Cell, Peephole, Window* (127–31)   5 shots
  Fontaine gets help from the cell opposite
12 *Cell, Corridor, Yard, Window* (132–41)   10 shots
  Fontaine makes contact with his neighbour Blanchet
13 *Cell* (142–7)   6 shots
  Fontaine works at dismantling the door:
  the spoon breaks
14 *Washroom, Cell* (148–67)   20 shots
  Two 'miracles': a bible from the curé
  and a new spoon
15 *Window, Cell, Washroom* (168–79)   12 shots
  Conversation with Blanchet, first meeting with Orsini
16 *Cell, Peephole* (180–3)   4 shots
  More people work on the door

17 *Corridor, Cell* (184–6)   3 shots
    Fontaine's first exit from his cell, visiting a neighbour
18 *Window* (187–90)   4 shots
    Fontaine communicates with Blanchet
19 *Corridor, Yard, Washroom, Cell,*
   Peephole, Window (191–212)   22 shots
    Fontaine recruits and vows to leave his cell
20 *Corridor, Washroom, Cell* (213–26)   14 shots
    Free again, contact with Orsini, preparations
21 *Washroom, Cell, Window, Yard* (227–39)   13 shots
    Orsini rejects his plan, Fontaine talks with Blanchet
22 *Washroom* (240–1)   2 shots
    Curé to be interrogated; Orsini to be freed?
23 *Cell, Corridor, Yard, Cell, Peephole,*
   Washroom, Window (242–72)   31 shots
    Orsini fails his escape, but aids Fontaine
24 *Cell* (273–82)   10 shots
    Fontaine makes further preparations
25 *Window, Cell, Courtyard, Stairs, Corridor* (283–96)   14 shots
    Orsini crucial to his success; warned about a search
26 *Cell* (297–304)   8 shots
    The arrival of a parcel saves Fontaine
27 *Corridor, Stairs, Yard, Washroom* (305–11)   7 shots
    Blanchet assists; Fontaine passes a message
28 *Window, Cell, Corridor* (312–16)   5 shots
    Orsini's replacement rejects the plan,
    Fontaine warned
29 *Window, Hotel Terminus, Stairs, Cell* (317–47)   31 shots
    Fontaine is condemned to death; Jost moved
     into his cell

THREE [160 shots: 29 minutes]
30 *Cell, Washroom, Cell* (348–95)   48 shots
    The interrogation of Jost
31 *Cell* (396–9)   4 shots
    To kill or not to kill?
32 *Washroom, Cell* (400–45)   46 shots
    Fontaine passes a note and decides to escape with Jost
33 *Roof, Parapet, External Yard, Wall, Bridge* (446–507) 62 shots
    The German guard is killed and the escape completed

11 The group as protagonist: *Ceddo*

> The key concept in understanding African social organisation is that of the corporate group. Every individual belongs to several overlapping groups which provide the frame of reference for his daily life.
>
> JOLAYEMI SOLANKE (1982)

The individual and the group

It is a commonplace of African studies that the crucial distinction between African and Western societies lies in the different relationship between the individual and the communal group. As Jolayemi Solanke observes:

> Social control within African society rests on the seminal concept of the individual as part of a corporate group. The perception of belonging to a group – whether family, age-grade, village, clan or nation – is almost always paramount of a sense of individuality. One acts as a member of a group and is responsible to that group (1982: 35).

In passing it is perhaps worth noting that the notion of the 'tribe' (with its pejorative adjective 'tribal'), which is not mentioned by Solanke, is, of course, a colonial 'invention of tradition'. To quote Terence Ranger, the societies of pre-colonial Africa 'had certainly valued custom and continuity, but custom was loosely defined and infinitely flexible. Custom helped to maintain a sense of identity, but it also allowed for an adaptation so spontaneous and natural that it was often unperceived' (1983: 247–8). Ranger further notes that almost all recent studies of nineteenth-century pre-colonial Africa have emphasised that:

> far from there being a single 'tribal' identity, most Africans moved in and out of multiple identities, defining themselves at one moment as subject to this chief, at another as a member of that cult, at another moment as a part of that clan, and at yet another moment as an initiate of that professional guild (1983: 247–8).

What is crucial is that they did not define themselves as notionally free individuals.

This individual/community duality can be explored at a number of levels in African literature. The work of the Nobel prize-winner, Wole Soyinka, is controversial in the respect. Pointing to a tendency in contemporary African playwrights to show the individual as 'almost wholly self-determined, even when they pay lip service to the force of African communalist custom and tradition', the Nigerian critic Biodun Jeyifo argues that, despite his enormous talent, Soyinka is 'the greatest exemplar of this tendency'. For him, Soyinka's works show 'the pumping heart of the individual, the lines of experience and destiny on his face and in his person, the consciousness of personal moral choice and responsibility', so that Western liberal critics can 'see, with eminent justification, Western bourgeois individualism incarnate' (1985: 48). This is a view which the playwright himself would no doubt strongly dispute. In his own exploration of 'drama and the African world view', he rejects the definition of the divergences between a traditional African approach and the European one in terms of an opposition between creative individualism and communal creativity, yet stresses that, for the audience faced with the tragic hero of ritual theatre:

> the real unvoiced fear is: will the protagonist survive confrontation with forces that exist within the dangerous area of transformation? Entering that *microcosmos* involves a loss of individuation, a self-submergence in universal essence. It is an act undertaken on behalf of the community, and the welfare of that protagonist is inseparable from that of the total community (Soyinka, 1976: 42).

For Soyinka, the divergence between the European and the African cast of mind is the divergence between a view which 'sees the cause of human anguish as visible only within strictly temporal capsules' and one 'whose tragic understanding transcends the causes of individual disjunction and recognises them as a reflection of a far greater disharmony in the communal psyche' (1976: 46). Taking as his example *Song of the Goat* by the contemporary Nigerian dramatist, J. P. Clark, Soyinka stresses that 'the death of an individual is not seen as an isolated incident in the life of a man (. . .). The sickness of one individual is a sign of, or may portend the sickness of, the world around him' (1976: 51).

At a different level, the Ugandan Shatto Arthur Gakwandi, seeking reasons why 'in essence and technique the African novel has borrowed so heavily from the European novel', thereby proving comparatively shy of experiment (1977: 127), he finds at least a partial answer in the fact that the social realist tradition of the European novel has allowed African writers to 'analyse the basic social structure of a given society and show how the total life of the individual is affected by the conditions in which he lives' (1977: 129). No such possibility was offered by the traditions of Western cinema, and especially the Hollywood film, which reflects a view of the relationship of the individual and society widely held in Europe and the United States, and perhaps most graphically summed up in Mrs Thatcher's memorable phrase, 'There is no such thing as society'. Mrs Thatcher's is the approach that underlies the basic Hollywood view of narrative, as the screenwriting manuals make clear. As we have seen, movies are *only* about individual characters, whose progress and relationships are not shaped by social forces, but structured into clearly defined, stereotypic roles, in order to meet the needs of accessible and emotive dramatic patterns and to foreground individual motivation and action.

As Milan Kundera has noted, the origins of the European novel lie in Boccaccio's tales of actions and adventures which are based on the assumption that, 'it is through action that man steps forth from the repetitive universe of the everyday where each person resembles every other person; it is through action that he distinguishes himself from others and becomes an individual' (1988: 23). Similarly the key assumption about characters in the Hollywood movie is that they are essentially individuals, able to make choices as the basis for action. Whatever the pressures or dangers, these choices are ultimately freely made by the individual, and cannot be blamed on background, family upbringing, heredity, or even social or economic pressures. There is always a space for individual decision-making and an opportunity to turn decisions into the individual actions by which we – the spectators – can recognise the worth of the character in question. These decisions and actions have consequences that flow logically from them, and, in essence, a human being is the sum of his or her free decisions and actions.

Clearly this model of dramatic narrative is very closely linked to the ideas and aspirations of individualism in American society, in the context of which its cinematic expression was devised and refined. African film makers tend to have been trained in the West – in the USA or, more usually, at one of the European film schools – and some have used the standard Hollywood model as the basis for their own portrayals of African society. For others, such as Souleymane Cisse in *Yeelen*, seeking to translate to the screen their own versions of African myths and traditional tales, the fairy-tale simplicity of the Hollywood structure has allowed them to use many elements of the traditional Hollywood pattern in their work, much as such European directors as Antonioni and Bresson have done. As we have seen, with comparatively small changes in structure, the whole ideological stance of the Hollywood system of narrative – except its stress on the individual protagonist – can be transformed.

But there remain those who feel that a wholly different model of narrative is needed to convey the realities of an African society emerging from colonisation into neo-colonial dominance, facing enormous problems of economic development, held in an unresolvable tension between modernity and tradition, but where individuals are brought together into supportive groups by the traditional social organisation in terms of the web of familial, kinship and social relationships. The result has been the creation of quite a different dramaturgy, one which its authors feel reflects more adequately than the imported model the realities of African social organisation.

A useful starting point is offered by an early film by Ousmane Sembene, *Emitai*. This is a film which depicts two assaults by French colonial troops on a Diola village community, the first to persuade one of the young men of the village, who has fled into the forest, to return and to do his military service, the second to find and confiscate the year's harvest of rice, needed by the French to feed their troops. Among the soldiers used in the operation is a young African recruit, regarded by his European superiors as the finest black NCO in the district and, by chance, a native of this particular village. There is no doubt as to how a Western film maker would shape the story. The focus would be on this individual, whose situation – one might say, fate – embodies both the clash of cultures and the conflict of values between regiment and family. One can easily imagine the plot line: the inner torment of the protagonist, the characters he loves and admires pulling him in different directions, the false step taken unthinkingly and then repented, the ultimate life-or-death decision he has to make and act upon, the final gestures which may not preserve his own life, but will show his concern for the aged and the helpless. The film would conclude, of course, with a death which would stand as a symbol of the wickedness of colonial oppression.

But such a film is a depiction of social forces – the conflict between traditional culture and colonialism, the role of group solidarity in shaping political events – *only* in so far as these are reflected in and through the fate of a single individual. If one does not share the West's particular focus and emphasis on the role and fate of the individual, a new film dramaturgy is required and this is what Ousmane Sembene pioneers in *Emitai*. The pattern is set in the seventeen minute opening pre-credit sequence showing the methods used by the French to recruit Africans into the *tirailleurs*: a mixture of brutality (press-ganging lone passers-by) and psychological pressure. In the latter case, a village elder is left tied up in the village square until his son, who has fled into the forest, surrenders himself for military service. The French can rely on the young man's traditionally-minded sisters to do their work for them and summon the young man back. But when the young man gives up his individual revolt and rejoins his age-grade as a recruit, he is never singled out again. There is no focus on him, as an individual, as the young recruits are marched off to a chant of 'Maréchal nous voilà', and his reactions go unrecorded when the men are addressed by a French officer, whose theme is 'France is doing you a great honour'.

From a European or American perspective this vanishing of the individual into the anonymity of the group is likely to seem like a defeat, but this is not the way that the episode is intended. African films continually make it clear that the individual protagonist alone is powerless. African cinema is full of characters who reject, or are expelled from, a group, and who are doomed unless they can find an alternative group into which they can be absorbed. All value is incorporated in the group, and an individualistic response can lead only to disaster. In narrative terms the result is often not just marginalisation, but literal exclusion from the drama.

Returning to *Emitai*, the main body of the film constitutes an extended restatement, a year later, of the themes of the pre-credit sequence. The tactics of the French as they attempt to obtain the rice needed to feed their troops are similar, but more subtle. The primary opposition is, of course, between colonisers and villagers. The traditional division of labour (the women growing the rice, the men acting as warriors) is translated into spatial terms through the separation of the two groups. The women who have hidden the rice in the forest are being held captive in the village square. The men, denied access to them, become locked in debate at the shrine of the gods who seem to have deserted them. The debate among the men gives rise to a further division within their ranks (between warriors and appeasers). It is between such groups – and not between individual figures that represent them or embody their values – that the drama is acted out. The characteristic lack of interest by Sembene in a division into plot and subplot, means that some potentially interesting secondary conflicts (such as the clash of interests between white officers and black soldiers) are ignored. The focus is unflinchingly on the central conflict of colonisers and villagers, presented without the personalisation of issues which invariably colours Western treatments of the themes of repression and colonial brutality.

The substitution of the group for the individual as protagonist has important implications for dramatic structure, since it inevitably results in a slow and measured pace and rhythm. While an individual's life can be subject to rapid change, groups shift much more slowly over time, in response to long-term social, economic and political forces. We are used, in Hollywood movies, to an action which constantly throws the individual protagonist into new situations and confronts him with unexpected pressures and complications, thereby allowing him to discover and affirm values in the course of the unfolding narrative. But when groups are the focus, this form of development through revelation is denied, since groups openly embody from the start the values which hold them together. Whereas an individual Hollywood protagonist develops over time through a cycle of transgression, recognition and redemption, a group will co-exist in time with groups embodying other values. African culture is not characterised by a simple movement from tradition to modernity, but a co-existence of these two conflicting sets of values in the same moment of time within groups and, indeed, within the individuals who comprise them. Whereas in Hollywood the successive stages of the action reveal a clear temporal line or trajectory for the protagonist, a system concentrating on groups will show a contemporaneous spatial intermingling. An individual will, at one and the same time, inhabit several different groups and value systems (family, age-group, workplace, caste, class, religion, etc.), so that the principle of organisation is one characterised by a simultaneity of conflicting values, not a succession of events revealing values.

If all narrative is a balance of some kind between showing and telling, the particular approach of Hollywood is not the only one possible. As André Gardies puts it, reversing the normal process of

Hollywood narrative cinema, African cinema 'tells in order to show, in order to allow the spectators to see what other cinemas do not show them: images of themselves' (1989: 171). Often a plot is little more than the journey of an individual from one group to another (which may receive or reject the newcomer), that is from one space to another. Given the comparative simplicity of the interaction of groups (compared with the complex interplay of psychologically defined individuals), more attention can be focused on the organisation of the space which groups inhabit. From the very beginning of African cinema one finds what I have called elsewhere 'an organising eye', a system of organisation of dramatic narrative in which sets of spatial binary opposites are identified and become the bearers of meaning (Malkmus and Armes, 1991: 186). Thus, in Sembene's first film, *Borom Sarret*, the physical contrast between the Plateau (the former white quarter now inhabited by the black bourgeoisie) and the Sangara market (where the poor cart-driver lives), becomes the underpinning for the sets of conflicting values which structure the narrative: Europe/Africa, modernity/tradition, corruption/virtue. The shift from the individual as protagonist to the group as protagonist implies, in short, what one can only call a spatialisation of narrative.

Ceddo

Ousmane Sembene's *Ceddo*, though essentially driven, I shall argue, by other dramatic imperatives, bears enough resemblance to a conventional Western film narrative for us to be able to measure the extent of its radical innovation. The action is set in motion within the first five minutes by an event which could qualify as the 'triggering incident' in any Hollywood movie: Princess Dior, the king's only daughter, is kidnapped. Similarly the film ends when the repercussions of this act have been worked through and the Princess is returned to the village. The first thirty-one minutes of the film, in which we are introduced to the full range of characters, can be seen as building up to a fairly conventional first act climax: the council which ends with the king deciding that his son Biram is to be sent to recover Princess Dior.

The longer second act (forty-seven minutes) begins with the failure of Biram's mission, followed by a second attempt by Saxewar, one of the claimants to Princess Dior's hand in marriage. Saxewar, who represents the traditional warrior values of the people, has already shown himself able to tame the ambitions of the Christian missionary, but he too is defeated in combat by the kidnapper. This double failure plunges the village society into turmoil, creating a situation analogous to the 'progressive complications' of conventional second act dramaturgy. In the aftermath of these failures, the second council shows how far the balance of power has shifted away from the king, and towards the imam, who represents militant Islam. The common people, the *ceddo* who refuse to be converted to Islam, find their community split apart by these events: some favour accepting the inevitability of conversion, some opt for exile, and others even contemplate the more fateful step of selling some members of their families into slavery as a way of obtaining the guns which will allow them to resist the imam and his growing band of armed followers.

The final act of thirty-three minutes begins at night in the imam's compound, when a holy war on the *ceddo* is declared, and ends in the bright light of day with the imam's death at the hands of Princess Dior. Here, as in conventional film dramaturgy, the pace quickens. The third council – at which the imam, after the as yet unexplained disappearance of the king, shows himself to be the supreme power in the village – is the shortest of the three public discussion scenes. In place of the ritual interplay between the kidnapper and the king's champions, we now have a very brief scene in which the kidnapper is coldly shot down from beyond the range of his arrows. The latter part of the act, building up to the climax, is marked, for the first time in the film, by the intercutting of parallel actions, moving between the burial of the dead kidnapper and the forcible conversion of the *ceddo* people. The film ends, as it had begun, with a personal act which, though perhaps viewable as an expression of the will of the *ceddo*, is highly ambiguous in its meaning.

But if it has similarities to the classic Hollywood model in terms of its basic dramatic structure, in most other ways *Ceddo* shows a highly distinctive approach. Certainly the overall structural pattern is not linked in Hollywood style to the transgression, recognition and redemption of a single protagonist. *Ceddo* is a fable which turns its back on the conventional realist approach, with its setting, for example, only loosely located in either time or place. Sembene's publicity material points to a seventeenth-century setting, but in fact the events which form the background to the action – the penetration of Islam, the European slave trade and the missionary activities of the Catholic church – tended to be separate in time and place. What Sembene offers is less a historical study than an exemplary present-ation of power politics, marked by ritualised gesture and formalised speech, with many of the major verbal interactions (such as those between the Princess and her captor or between the king and his people) enacted through *griot* intermediaries. To underline the stylisation, Sembene includes numerous anachronisms, both in terms of the images (such as the use of a thoroughly modern sunshade as a mark of the king's authority, subsequently usurped by the imam) and sound (exemplified by Manu Dibango's aggressively modern sound-track and the use of American Negro spirituals). In addition, the priest is allowed a startling anticipatory vision of Catholicism's eventual triumph in twentieth century Africa. Those who seek in the film a literal truth in its rendering of historical events can only be disappointed, with Jean Copans, for example, accusing the film of schematisation, idealisation and caricature (1985: 58). As so often in African cinema, what is important spatially is not the historical or geographical specificity, but the symbolic value accorded to the fundamental oppositions of space, such as Inside/Outside the Village, which contribute so much to the shaping of the drama.

The very opening scene of *Ceddo* locates three potential threats to the traditional life of the *ceddo* or ordinary people, embodied in the figures of the European slave trader, the Catholic priest and the imam. The (probably unhistorical) location of these three and an active indigenous culture in the same time and space is indicative of the way in which Sembene presents African reality: as a location for the interaction of the forces of tradition and modernity, the indige-nous and the external, which co-exist in conflict. Since neither can overcome the other totally, there can be little or no sense of progress. In this perspective, the treatment of the slave trader, the first of the three figures we see in the film, is fascinating. He is not a personalised character and though we see him branding his slaves, we never learn of his fate when the village is burned by the imam's followers. Presumably he survives, since no-one opposes his activities, and he is never shown in a scene which puts the blame for the evil of slavery on him, the outsider, the white man. It is an African who brings in slaves to trade for a gun in the opening scene. Madior Fatim Fall, the king's nephew, casually sells a girl into slavery in order to buy the wine with which he wishes to make a public display of his break with Islam, and

Saxewar, the warrior and defender of tradition, offers slaves for the honour of taking Biram's place as the king's champion. On the eve of the destruction of the village, the imam's supporters are instructed to sell into slavery – in exchange for guns – those who oppose them, while offering the chance of conversion to those who acquiesce. More crucially of all, the *ceddo* themselves, who do not own slaves, consider selling members of their own families into slavery, as a way of getting the guns they need to oppose the imam, as if this were an option on a par with giving in to the pressure to convert or responding by going into exile. Clearly Sembene's message is that slavery is an African responsibility, which, unlike Islam, cannot be blamed on outsiders.

The two religious figures in *Ceddo* are treated in very different ways. The Catholic priest is a pathetic figure, who clearly represents no threat to the *ceddo* and who can indeed be publicly patronised and humiliated by Saxewar, the traditional warrior hero, at the king's council. Though he lacks followers and is killed when the imam's supporters burn the village, he is allowed a vision of a glorious future (the twentieth century) which is striking in that it breaks with the film's temporal framework, though it figures Madior as an African bishop. The repeated use of Negro spirituals, with their words of hope, over scenes depicting the slaves, also seems to point to a positive long-term impact of Christianity on black life and culture. By contrast, the imam is given no redeeming traits and no long term vision. The cultural benefits which Islam brought to the lands it colonised are never shown. The imam is depicted as a ruthless impersonal force for the destruction of traditional beliefs, indifferent to any values the *ceddo* culture might have, and a figure all the more frightening for the cold efficiency with which he pursues his aims. Nothing could be more telling than the contrast between the ritual combats undertaken against the kidnapper by the king's two champions, his son Biram and the warrior Saxewar, and the calculated shooting down from a distance which makes them safe from his arrows, which characterises the response of the imam's soldiers. The imam is not a personalised character, but he represents a dynamic force lacked by the other two outsiders.

The African figures in *Ceddo* are given equally little personal development and their relationship with the dramatic narrative line shows that it is not they, but the groups to which they belong, which form the focus of the film's attention. The action is triggered by what is an individual action: there is no clear indication that the kidnapper's act is in any way a reflection, or outcome, of the *ceddo* community's own views of what needs to be done, though later the imam will call for a collective punishment of the *ceddo* for the threat made to authority. The king's response to the kidnapping is to summon a council at which the various conflicting voices can all be heard – those of the *ceddo*, expressed by the village elder, Diogomay; the nobles and members of the king's family; and the group of white-clad converts led by the imam. The symbolic pole, the *samp*, planted by Diogomay at the outset of the council, calls for the settlement of grievances in conformity with traditional practices. The proceedings of the council, where participants address each other through an intermediary, the *griot* Jaraaf, the traditional praise-singer of the community, are formal and ritualised, as is the departure, preceded by the *samp*, of each of the king's champions. We are shown a society with its own accepted rites and hierarchies, roles and customs, which has now been fractured by the growing coercive power of Islam.

The role of the kidnapper is complex. In political terms, his individual act of revolt, combined with the skill and ingenuity with which he defeats the king's champions, leads only to the very opposite conclusion to the one he desires: the destruction of the king's authority, the disintegration of the *ceddo* community and the full imposition of Islamic rule. But in a non-political fable he would of course be the hero, the handsome young man who, through acts of courtesy and courage, wins the Princess's love. Holding her against her will, he nevertheless treats her with elaborate politeness, and together they agree to respect the symbolic prison he marks out in the sand. His acts of valour win her affections and he is drawn to her, as we see when he watches as she bathes naked. But when she offers herself to him, he spurns her, mindful of his wider mission. Yet when he dies, the Princess has a vision of their being man and wife, and it is his death which motivates her act of violence which ends the film.

Meanwhile, in the central portion of the film, the key figure seems to be Madior Fatim Fall, the king's nephew who has converted to Islam without realising the implications for his personal position. Certainly Madior is the character who would be the centre of attention in a conventional Western narrative. When we first meet him he has already transgressed, by unthinkingly deserting the traditional ways and converting to Islam. At the council, dressed in the white garb of a convert, he has his moment of realisation, withthe discovery that, under Islamic law, he, the king's nephew and hence traditional heir, can no longer claim the succession to the throne, which will go instead to Biram, the king's son. At a stroke he loses his royal position, his claim to Princess Dior and his chance to act as the king's champion. His response is a flamboyantly individualistic one: he sells a slave girl to buy wine which he drinks before the imam and his followers as a symbol of his renunciation of his adopted faith. Subsequently he reverts to traditional garb and we anticipate some action on his part which will redeem him, even if at the cost of his life. He can share the priest's vision of Christianity's triumph, seeing himself as a bishop, but turns his back on the idea of yet another conversion. In a system of narrative in which the lone individual is powerless (cf. Malkmus and Armes, 1991: 210-6), he quickly becomes a marginalised figure, an observer of events and occasional messenger, but not a participant in the action of political struggle between Islam and the traditional way of life. When the village is burned, we do not learn his individual fate, any more than we do that of the other purely symbolic figure, the slave-trader: the personal destinies of such figures are of no consequence and none has a role in the last thirty minutes of the film, which deal with the imposition of Islam on the *ceddo*.

In the light of the thesis advanced here about the powerlessness of lone individuals in a system of narrative concerned primarily with the interaction of social groups, the ending of the film might seem to cause some problem. What occurs in the four-minute final sequence (followed by a minute and a half of credits unfolding over a freeze frame) is simple, but the meaning is clearly ambiguous. The Princess is brought back before the imam, walks proudly past the converted *ceddo* and abruptly seizes a gun. The *ceddo*, led by Diogomay, defend her by putting their mouths over the muzzles of the guards' single shot rifles, and she is able to advance and shoot dead the imam. The film ends with a mid-shot of her, with tears streaming down her face, which is frozen for twenty seconds before the credits begin to role.

In terms of the overall narrative patterning of the film, this individualistic act makes a very satisfying conclusion, echoing the equally individualistic act of kidnapping with which the film began and resolving both the major plot line (the actions set in motion by the kidnapping) and the sub-plot concerning the relation between the Princess and her kidnapper. But it is certainly open to conflicting interpretations. If one interprets the film with a value system which allows for the significance of individual actions, particularly those carried out by a woman, then the ending can be seen as a very positive one: Princess Dior carries on the revolt against Islam after the death of the king. Françoise Pfaff, in her study of the director's work, is positively lyrical:

> Although her final act may be seen as an isolated and individual one, she succeeds, whatever her motives are, in changing a political and religious order alien to a traditional African political and religious system. Her individual initiative has a collective range and far-reaching consequences. As she walks among the villagers, any pre-existing class differentiation is erased. She is now the agent of their common liberation (1984: 177).

My own interpretation of the film is somewhat different, though Pfaff's is certainly closer to the director's own public statements about the film's purport. Far from 'celebrating the prowess of heroes to whom he confers present-day significance and an allegorical morality' (Pfaff, 1984: 177), Sembene has in fact shown with remorseless logic throughout his film that an individual act cannot have a positive political impact, and this applies as much to the final act of slaying the imam as it does to the initial kidnapping of the Princess. The individual death of a leader is lacking in importance: a narrative which has not found it necessary to clarify the circumstances of the death of the last holder of power, the king, cannot lead us to attribute significance to the personal fate of his successor. The imam is not a personalised figure, and the balance of power at the end of the film still lies with the imam's armed followers, who have already exercised their will over the *ceddo*. While it might be agreeable if the response of the *ceddo* to the Princess marked the beginning of a classless society, the whole essence of traditional African life as depicted in the film is shown to lie in deference to existing rites and hierarchies. The *ceddo* response is surely more properly seen as a defence by those now lacking in power of the last remnant of their traditional system of authority. The Princess's act of killing *is* an isolated and individual one. The most likely motivation for her tears is surely the memory of the man she dreamed of marrying and whose death she has now avenged, and if the final focus is on her motionless figure, it is surely because her act has no real consequences beyond its personal impact on her. Here, as in the depiction of the doomed revolt of the villagers at the end of *Emitai*, Sembene's work is harsher and less optimistic than some of his supporters might wish.

Shot breakdown

CEDDO (Overall: 698 shots + end titles: 111 minutes)

ONE [162 shots: 31 minutes]
1 *The Village* (1–25)   29 shots
   The scene is set: Princess Dior has been kidnapped
2 *Outside the Village* (26–42)   17 shots
   The ritual dialogue of Princess Dior and her captor
3 *The Village* (43–55)   13 shots
   The king summons a council, the imam orders the
   ceddo to bring wood
4 *The Council* (56–162)   107 shots
   Ceremonial entry of Demba War (56–70)
   Diogomay, a *ceddo* elder, complains of oppression (71–94)
   Entry of the warrior Saxewar, Dior's betrothed (95–108)
   Madior Fatim Fall, the king's nephew, intervenes (109–13)
   Biram, the king's son and the new heir responds (114–21)
   The imam gives his ruling and the king concedes (122–35)
   Saxewar confronts the imam's 'lies' (136–41)
   Madior drinks wine and renounces Islam (142–53)
   Biram is to confront the *ceddo*, the council ends (154–62)

TWO [311 shots: 47 minutes]
5 *The Village* (163–8)   6 shots
   The slaves are fed
6 *The Village* (169–82)   14 shots
   Biram departs with the imam's blessing
7 *Outside the Village* (183–207)   25 shots
   Biram's battle with the kidnapper
8 *Into the Village* (208–40)   33 shots
   Biram's body is returned, Saxewar takes up
   the challenge
9 *Outside the Village* (241–85)   45 shots
   Saxewar's battle with the kidnapper
10 *The Village* (286–310)   25 shots
   The prayers to Allah and the branding of the slaves
11 *The Graveyard* (311–30)   20 shots
   Saxewar's body, rejected by the faithful,
   is taken out of the village

12 *The Church* (331–66)   36 shots
   Madior shares the priest's vision of Christianity's
   triumph
13 *The Second Council* (367–442)   76 shots
   The imam joins the king's council (367–78)
   The *ceddo* demand justice, but are ejected by the
   imam, who preaches holy war against the *ceddo* (379–405)
   Madior warns the king against the imam (406–30)
   The imam leads the way to prayer, the nobles discuss
   their problems, Madior alone stays with the king (431–42)
14 *Discussion among the Ceddo* (443–63)   21 shots
   The *ceddo* are torn between conversion, exile and
   selling members of their own families to buy guns
   and to resist
15 *The Village* (464–73)   10 shots
   The conversions begins

THREE [225 shots: 33 minutes]
16 *The Imam's Compound at Night* (474–91)   18 shots
   The imam preaches holy war
17 *The Village at Night and Next Morning* (492–529)   38 shots
   The destruction of the village and its aftermath
18 *Outside the Village* (530–40)   11 shots
   Princess Dior bathes, watched by the kidnapper
19 *The Village* (541–7)   7 shots
   The imam supervises the burial of the dead
20 *Outside the Village* (548–56)   9 shots
   Dior offers herself to her kidnapper
21 *The Imam's Council* (557–620)   64 shots
   The men's heads are shaved (557–74)
   The imam enters, now the sole authority (575–80)
   Jaaraf and the nobles are put to one side (581–96)
   The imam addresses his subjects and sends for
   Dior (597–612)
   The conversions begin (613–10)
22 *Outside the Village* (621–33)   13 shots
   A family in exile visits the kidnapper
23 *Outside the Village* (634–51)   18 shots
   The imam's soldiers kill the kidnapper

24 *The Village* (652–4)   3 shots
    The conversions continue
25 *Outside the Village* (655)   1 shot
    The kidnapper is buried upright with his weapons
26 *The Village* (656–61)   6 shots
    More converts – women and children now
27 *Outside the Village* (662–5)   4 shots
    The burial is completed
28 *The Village* (666–98)   33 shots
    Princess Dior is brought back and kills the imam
    End titles

12 The disintegration of the protagonist: *Pierrot le fou*

> The Americans are good at storytelling, the French are not. Flaubert and
> Proust can't tell stories. They do something else. So does the cinema. . . .
>
> JEAN-LUC GODARD (1969)

Questioning the protagonist's role

As we have seen, character and story, protagonist and action, are
indissolubly linked in conventional Hollywood narrative. The action is
shaped so as to reveal the protagonist, and the protagonist is structured
so as to motivate the action. This pattern has important implications
for both action and protagonist. As far as the action is concerned, it
means that the plot, the succession of incidents and events leading
through a series of climaxes (or plot points) to an unambiguous
resolution, is foregrounded and takes precedence over both the texture
and the detail of the action (Dancyger and Rush, 1991: 28).
Hollywood narrative is thus precluded from depicting life as we most
often experience it, not as a simple trajectory aimed at a single
predetermined destination, but as a random set of events, without
obvious inner coherence or focus, and making sense – if at all – only in
retrospect. Similarly, the consistent chain of explicit causality, linking
each incident unambiguously, which is so characteristic of Hollywood
film structure, cannot reflect adequately our frequent sense that life has
no pattern of this kind, that it comprises instead a contingent series of
events lacking a definable inner necessity.

The Hollywood system requires not simply that the protagonist is
foregrounded: as the first character we meet, as an active presence
who sets the action in motion, as a focus of the other characters'
desires and emotions, as the possessor of a look which organises the
action, or as source of the voice-over commentary which shapes
response to the depicted events. The Hollywood protagonist must
also be a decision-maker who, at a number of key, strategically placed

moments, is faced with the need to make clear-cut decisions as the basis for future action. In the conventional Hollywood format, 'the overall structure of the script builds to and is dependent on the decision-making moment. Often, the moment is slowed down, exaggerated, or frozen. This clear-cut articulation can be thought of as a decision-making space, a moment that is emptied of any distractions aside from the decision' (Dancyger and Rush, 1991: 29).

But it is very possible to argue that life does not offer us a sequence of clear-cut, life-or-death decisions of this kind. The decisions which turn out to have been of major influence on our subsequent lives are often not thought-through, or even seen in isolation at the time, but buried in a mass of other steps which seemed important then, even if they prove trivial in retrospect. Often decision-making, as such, is hardly involved at all, since we – unlike Hollywood protagonists – are at the mercy of social, historical or political events which are totally beyond our control. It is arguable, for example that in Europe in the early 1990s far more lives have been blighted by redundancy and unemployment than by ill-made personal decisions. Chance and coincidence – over which we have no control – play important roles in redirecting our lives at many key moments. We act on whim and impulse, take actions without thought for the consequences, are consistent only in behaving inconsistently, so that our lives inevitably lack any perceivable rational shape or order. Those potentially dramatic situations which do occur are not in their 'right' order, are separated by huge time gaps, or find us out of synchronisation with those most deeply involved. Though the Hollywood notion of romance as an inextricable mixture of pleasure and problem may be realistic, people in our lives do not in general fit the neat character roles demanded by Hollywood dramaturgy.

Even for a film maker who loves Hollywood and admits to being influenced by it, there is therefore always an alternative starting point, the chance to offer us (as with *L'année dernière à Marienbad*) an action without a plot, or (as is often the case in Jean-Luc Godard's work) a protagonist who lacks an elaborate mechanism of decision-making. Ferdinand Griffon (Jean-Paul Belmondo) in *Pierrot le fou* is undoubtedly the central character of the film and has many of the attributes of the conventional protagonist. His voice-over narration leads us into the film, just as his death concludes it. But the essence of the conventional protagonist's role – the ability to control his (or her) life through decision-making and action – is denied him.

As Tom Milne has noted, the film *Pierrot le fou* follows with surprising fidelity the novel, *Obsession*, by Lionel White on which it is based (1972: 179). The action has been shaped into a general form akin to that of mainstream Hollywood. The reappearance of Marianne Renoir (Anna Karina) in Ferdinand's life occurs within the first five minutes of the film and triggers the whole action, which ends when the full consequences of this meeting have been followed through. The intervening pattern of events follows a conventional rise and fall, and there is no difficulty in discerning the vestiges of a three act pattern: a first act of escape (coloured by hope and apprehension), a failed idyll by the sea at the film's core, and a final act of betrayal. The action has all the romanticism of a Hollywood tale of doomed passion (though coloured by Godard's literary tastes), with Marianne as a classic *femme fatale*, though she operates not in the shadows of the traditional *film noir*, but in the sunlight of the Côte d'Azur. Yet in detail the film is made in conscious opposition to the classic model, a stance which Godard clarified by a comparison with Luchino Visconti's *Senso*:

> In *Senso*, which I quite like, it was the scenes which Visconti concealed that I wanted to see. Each time I wanted to know what Farley Granger said to Alida Valli, bang! – a fade out. *Pierrot le fou*, from this standpoint, is the antithesis of *Senso*: the moments you do not see in *Senso* are shown in *Pierrot* (Milne: 1972: 222).

Jean-Luc Godard has admitted that he is not much interested in telling a story: 'I like using a story as the basis on which I can embroider my ideas. What people in the profession call "telling a story" has always troubled me. Setting out from scratch, making a beginning, reaching an ending. . .' (quoted in Douin, 1989: 93). Godard's interest is in piecing together fragments, and *Pierrot le fou* is a patchwork of action and repose, quotations and allusions, contrived incidents and moments of improvisation. Godard, who claims that only the beginning of the film was planned, describes it as 'a kind of happening, but one that was controlled and dominated'. It was, he says, 'a completely spontaneous film. I have never been so worried as I was two days before shooting began. I had nothing, nothing at all. Oh well, I had the book' (Milne, 1972: 218).

Pierrot le fou

It is Ferdinand's voice-over, reading from Elie Faure's history of art, which initially leads us into the world of the film. The essence of Godard's project in *Pierrot le fou* is indicated in Faure's comments on Velasquez, who, after reaching the age of fifty, 'no longer painted anything concrete and precise. He drifted through the material world, penetrating it, as the air and the dusk' (this and subsequent quotations are taken from the English translation of the script, published by Lorrimer). Here in *Pierrot le fou* the director wishes to tell his tale of romantic passion tangentially, through allusions and asides, by what is unsaid as much as through explicit comment, rather than through direct depiction or enactment. The same sentiment finds an even more forceful expression later in the film, during the couple's idyll by the sea (scene 16 in my listing), when Ferdinand explains his idea for a novel: 'No longer to write about people's lives. . . but only about life, life itself. What goes on between people, in space. . . like sound and colours. That would be something worth while'. Thus it is Ferdinand, as protagonist, who articulates the film's theme, but each time his words are undercut by forms of presentation which deny his authority: in the first instance he is shown sitting in the bath, reading Faure's work to his five-year-old daughter, in the second he talks directly to camera, but imitates the voice and mannerisms of the actor Michel Simon (apparently an unanticipated improvised contribution by Belmondo, cf. Milne, 1972: 218).

The very first scene shows Ferdinand as he will be throughout the film: malleable and indecisive. First he refuses, like a spoilt child, to go to the party, then he agrees when his wife insists. His meeting with Marianne, his friend Frank's so-called 'niece', is lightly handled and it is only in retrospect that we are able to recognise the spark between them. While this first scene is basically realistic, the second, by contrast, is violently caricatured. Echoing an incident in the first scene, where Ferdinand reads an advertisement for women's under-wear, the guests at the party converse almost exclusively in advertising jargon about their cars, clothes and perfumes. The exception is the American film maker, Sam Fuller, in Paris, he says, to make a version of *Les fleurs du mal*, who gives Ferdinand a definition of the movies, 'The film is like a battleground. Love. Hate. Action. Violence. Death. In one word. . . Emotion'. Following on from the quotation from Elie Faure, Fuller's statement confirms the way in which the meaning of the film will be conveyed, through verbal (and visual) quotations and allusions, far more than through the actions of the protagonist, who never seems decisively in command of his feelings.

At the party, however, Ferdinand does show himself active, leaving early to pick up Marianne from his flat and to drive her home. Though this third scene is given a portentous introduction by Ferdinand in voice-over – 'Next Chapter. Despair. Memory and Freedom. Sorrow. Hope. The pursuit of time passed away. Marianne Renoir' – it does not contain a true moment of decision (when Ferdinand might actually decide to go off with Marianne), nor does it constitute an instance of passion, the expression of which will sweep the two of them into a new course of action. Unlike the main characters in a Hollywood romance, Ferdinand and Marianne seem incapable of actively assuming their doomed roles. Their dialogue is mostly a banal discussion of what they have done during five years of separation, and for much of the scene they are virtually motionless. The sense that they are pinned down is emphasised by the choice of camera angle (the scene is shot in full frontal angle, through the windscreen) and by the way in which they describe acts of love – 'I put my hand on your knee', or 'I kiss you all over' – while doing, literally, nothing (this effect is lost in the English translation of the script, which uses the future tense, as well as misdescribing one shot).

The scene is further deliberately weighed down by Godard's decision to shoot it, though it lasts some two and a half minutes, in just three shots: a close-up of Marianne, a matching close-up of Ferdinand and a tight two-shot of the couple. Moreover, instead of foregrounding the emotions of his characters, Godard turns the scene into a formal exercise in colour composition. The party sequence itself was stylised, filmed in an abruptly shifting mix – from shot to shot – of normal colour and single hues (red, yellow or blue). Here in the car sequence Godard uses circles of primary colours sweeping in an arc across the screen as a highly stylised representation of the lights of passing cars. The pattern is totally symmetrical – red and green lights, right to left, for Marianne; orange and blue, left to right, for Ferdinand – with the result that it is impossible not to become as aware of the shooting style as of the situation and emotions of the characters. The effect is further heightened by Marianne's comments on the limitations of a photographic image of a person (prompted by a radio report about anonymous Vietcong guerrillas): 'At that precise instant when the photograph was taken, no one can say what he actually is, and what he was thinking exactly'. It is impossible not to apply this insight to Marianne and Ferdinand as we see them in this scene – a link which Ferdinand will make explicit later in the film.

A sense of movement is recovered next morning in Marianne's flat, when she moves around singing, though not of a love rediscovered but of a love withheld ('I never told you I would love you all my life. . . . Let us keep the knowledge that our love is a love. . . . That our love is a love with no tomorrow'). Marianne's sense of vitality is undercut by her casual ignoring of a dead body stretched out on a bed in the kitchen. Then, in a sequence introduced by inset postcard images and voice-over comments by Ferdinand and Marianne (a tactic which Godard adopts regularly in the film), the film plunges into confusing action: the waylaying and knocking unconscious of Frank and subsequent escape of the couple. While the first step (which presumably results in Frank's death, since he does not reappear in the film) is shot in a single long take, with the handheld camera moving intricately among the three characters, the escape itself is given in a multi-shot collage which presents the action with a confusing mix of time overlaps, anticipations and repetitions. While these two scenes show Godard as the virtuoso director, playing with the long take and complex cutting to undercut the violence of the action he is shooting (at this period Godard was keen to assert that there is no blood in his films, only red), the following scene, when the couple steals petrol from a garage, is handled in a naive style of shooting with seemingly improvised performances, showing Karina, as Marianne, trying out an old Laurel and Hardy gag and Belmondo, as Ferdinand, showing his boxing prowess.

These first six scenes of *Pierrot le fou* set the pattern for the work as a whole with their striking mixture of styles, using song and movement, improvisation and contrivance, colour and camera, postcard inserts and narrated stories to advance the action. The whole system of Hollywood cutting, whereby the interaction of two characters is depicted through a balanced pattern of shot and reverse angle shot, and through a constant shifting between viewer and point-of-view, is abandoned in favour of an approach which skirts around the apparent demands of the depicted action and emotions by applying an ever increasing and almost always surprising diversity of means. The characters are constantly together, but everything about the way they are depicted stresses their separateness. Already, in their first scene alone together (scene three, in the car), Marianne begins the undermining of Ferdinand's identity by her refusal to call him anything but Pierrot, an attitude which will be a feature of all their meetings. The romantic passion uniting the characters is simultaneously evoked and undercut by Godard's handling of the couple's scenes together.

The next six scenes trace the couple's progression across France to the Côte d'Azur in a similar array of fragmentary perspectives, each with a different stylistic manner of contributing to the depiction of the film's theme. There are two further, contrasting, car scenes. In the first of these, another night scene in which Marianne again insists on calling him Pierrot, the couple stop and embrace, but characteristically their major contact comes when each in turn addresses his or her own image in the driving mirror. Ferdinand sees 'the face of a man who's about to throw himself over a precipice at a hundred miles an hour', while Marianne sees ' the face of a woman who is in love with a man who is about to throw himself over a precipice at a hundred miles an hour'. Neither sees the other. In the second car scene, which shows them driving in daylight through the countryside, Godard includes flashbacks to their first meeting (the only time in the film this device is used) and abrupt transitions of mood. In one shot Ferdinand can sense 'the smell of death in the countryside, in the trees, in the faces of women, in cars', a couple of shots later he finds everything beautiful ('the sea, the waves, the sky. . .'). Here too we find the first real direct address to camera, when Belmondo/Ferdinand turns to address the audience with the comment, 'You see! . . .that's all they think about, enjoying themselves'. When Marianne asks who he is talking to, he explains and she too turns to look at us, the audience. The scene ends when Ferdinand, taunted as a little fool 'who's following a straight line', drives the car abruptly into the sea, signalling the end of their journey.

In between these two car scenes, the couple try to make money by telling exciting stories in a cafe, burn their first car and steal another, in a series of incidents linked by shots of postcards and book jackets, and images from the children's comic book they have brought with them, La bande des pieds-nickelés, usually with accompanying voice-over comments from the two characters. All the three sequences are to some degree marked by the patterns of symmetry which characterise Pierrot le fou as a whole and which, as in L'année dernière à Marienbad, give a structure which helps compensate for the lack of an external causality. The storytelling sequence contains both a fake *cinéma-vérité* interview (with the actor Lazlo Kovacs, who appears in several Godard films) and two (presumably) real ones, with a shop assistant and a peasant. The stories considered include both the real suicide of the painter Nicholas de Staël and the fictional death of William Wilson, who met and killed his double, only to find that he had in fact killed himself and that the double remained alive. As Marianne talks – unheard – to a group at one table, Ferdinand's voice informs us what she is talking about, and when Ferdinand talks to another group, it is Marianne who gives us his words.

In the car burning scene, which has images which anticipate the motorway carnage of Godard's later film, *Weekend* (1967), the two begin the business of defining their differences, this time in terms of the destinations they would have chosen if Ferdinand had not allowed the $50,000 hidden in the car boot to burn: Chicago, Las Vegas and Monte Carlo for Marianne; Florence, Venice and Athens for Ferdinand. The stealing of a new car, a Ford Galaxie, follows a further moment when Marianne addresses Ferdinand as Pierrot, but the theft is lightheartedly and easily accomplished. In this sense the scene clashes strongly with the portentous verbal title that introduces it – 'Chapter Eight – A Season in Hell' – accompanied by the postcard image of the cafe where Van Gogh decided to cut off his ear. The final sequence of this first part of the film (scene 12), which depicts them on the beach at night after Ferdinand has ditched the car in the sea, offers a perfect example of the way in which Godard can move effortlessly from inconsequentiality to passion (or pain). As they lie idly discussing the man in the moon and his relationship with the first two astronauts, Ferdinand and Marianne reach their moment of closest intimacy, with Marianne's tenderly murmured words, 'fuck me' (oddly translated as 'Stop it. Stop it' in the English published version).

The first forty-two minutes of *Pierrot le fou*, what I see as the first act of its unfolding drama as the couple cross France 'like ghosts, through a mirror', represents the early narrative style of Jean-Luc Godard at its finest, showing his ability to create a compelling line of progression through constant digression and to illuminate the passion that unites his characters while continually showing or talking about other things: books, paintings, landscapes. Godard has admitted that the latter part of his film was 'invented on the spot, unlike the beginning which was planned' (Milne, 1972: 218). Certainly, from this point on, the film becomes increasingly more of a sketch, though the director is doubtless exaggerating when he says that *Pierrot le fou* is 'not really a film. It is rather an attempt at cinema' (ibid: 215). Though it lacks the overall structural symmetry of *L'année dernière à Marienbad*, its latter sections do frequently allude to, echo or develop earlier ideas, as if beginning the story all over again, from scratch.

The central part of the film, depicting 'the last romantic couple', begins at the high point of the pair's passion but over its eleven scenes and thirty-four minutes becomes increasingly a study of irreconcilable differences, with the characters constantly expressing their doubts direct to camera. The beginning is bright enough, with Ferdinand beginning the writing of his diary and Marianne happy fishing on the shore, but the idyll, with its tame parrot and domesticated fox, is never wholly convincing. A first quarrel – about books – ends with Karina/Marianne looking questioningly direct to camera as she reassures Ferdinand that she will never leave him. A second quarrel, again about books, is more violent and results in Marianne again addressing him as Pierrot and urging that they must make some money from the tourists. Between these two quarrels, a key moment is the brief (four shot) scene on the beach which begins and ends with Marianne kicking her way through the edge of the sea, muttering 'What am I to do? I don't know what to do!'. Marianne finds a way of defining their differences – 'You talk to me with words and I look at you with feelings' – and they prove her right when they each define what they love and desire. For Marianne the list is, 'Flowers. . . animals. . . the blue of the sky. . . music. . . I don't really know. . . everything'. For Ferdinand it is, 'Ambition. . . hope. . . the movement of things. . . accidents. . . and what else?. . . I don't know. . . everything'.

On the way to meet the tourists, Marianne again talks of the need to find her brother Fred and calls Ferdinand a coward. The mimicry of incidents in the Vietnam war, involving Belmondo playing a US officer and Karina made up as a Vietnamese, is one of the least convincing moments of the film, though it looks forward to Godard's later political film making and is well-received by the audience within the film. At the end Marianne again talks directly to camera about her difficulties with Ferdinand and her need to be alive. Yet before the couple's problems arise again, they sing and dance together in the woods in a beautifully shot sequence which captures their closeness as well as their incompatibility, with Marianne singing of her chance line, while Ferdinand replies with praise of her hip line. At the centre point of this section of the film (scene 19) Ferdinand broods on life and dreams in the middle of a maize field, talking directly to camera in an unbroken shot lasting a minute and a half. He develops a theme first mentioned by Marianne in their first conversation together in the car: 'One no longer needs a mirror to speak to oneself. When Marianne says "it is a fine day" what is she really thinking? I have only this image of her, saying "it is a fine day". Nothing else. What is gained by trying to explain this?'

Ferdinand gets his answer – in part at least – in the very next scene. As they are boating on the river, Marianne's past reappears, in the person of the midget last seen outside Marianne's flat when she and Ferdinand were forced to flee. While Marianne goes off with him, Ferdinand goes to the bar, where the midget's girl friend dances to the music from the jukebox, perhaps in a homage to Sam Jaffe as the doomed Dr Riedenschneider in John Huston's *The Asphalt Jungle*. Marianne meanwhile phones from an apartment, seeking Ferdinand's help in her confrontation with the midget. Distorted shots show him brandishing a pistol and Marianne waving a pair of scissors. But when Ferdinand arrives, Marianne has vanished, the midget is dead (stabbed through the neck with scissors), and he himself is tortured by two heavies, keen to get their hands on the $50,000 lost in the burnt-out car. Alone, and at his lowest point here at the end of the second act of the film, Ferdinand contemplates suicide on the railway track, while we hear his voice-over recitation of a Lorca poem, *Lament for Ignacio Sánchez Mejías*, 'Ah! what a dreadful five in the afternoon. . .'.

From this point, slowly at first but with eventual increasing pace, the film moves towards its final resolution in its last thirty minutes. Unlike in a conventional Hollywood movie, we do not see Ferdinand actually making an effort to find Marianne. Instead it is she who finds him. Ferdinand is in Toulon, where we first see him watching newsreel footage of the Vietnam war and a short film by Godard himself which alludes, again indirectly, to the film's theme. *Le grand escroc* features Jean Seberg as a film journalist who is investigating an eccentric crook who prints fake banknotes to give to the poor. Confronted, he turns on the journalist, asserting that her work – photographing people and passing off the result as truth – is just the same as his. In *Pierrot le fou* we have just a fragment of Seberg's voice-over: 'We are looking for that moment when one abandons the fictional character in order to discover the true one, if such a thing exists'.

Marianne finds Ferdinand, whom she of course addresses as Pierrot, on the quayside in Toulon, where he is working for Princess Aicha Abadie. She has been looking for him, she says, and has found her brother and even been back to the cottage to pick up Ferdinand's diary, in which she has written a poem, addressed, of course, to 'Pierrot le fou'. Despite all that has happened, he goes off with her again. As she later tells her 'brother' Fred, 'Pierrot' will do anything for her. Ferdinand is drawn into the robbery devised by Fred, which is handled with the same deliberately confusing, seemingly random order of events as the escape from Marianne's flat at the beginning of the film. But this time there is a welter of literary allusions – to Conrad, Stevenson, Faulkner and Jack London, as well as a mass of murders and double-crossings. In a penultimate act of betrayal – introduced as 'Next Chapter. . . Despair. . . Next Chapter. . . Liberty. . . Bitterness' – Marianne takes the proceeds of the robbery and abandons Ferdinand at a bowling alley. When he attempts to follow her, he sees her sailing off with her 'brother'. After one final further delay – a chance meeting with Raymond Devos, obsessed by a song which has haunted him all his life, though no-one else can hear it – Ferdinand is on his way in pursuit.

Even when Ferdinand lands on the island, still humming Devos's tune, the final outcome is still in doubt. But in a swift, unexpected burst of violent action, there is shooting, and Ferdinand responds by killing first Fred and then Marianne. He carries Marianne into the house, where she dies asking the forgiveness of 'Pierrot'. After attempting vainly to phone his wife, Ferdinand makes almost a first, and certainly a final, decision. He wraps dynamite around his head, lights the fuse. . . and then – too late – changes his mind. As the camera swings away from the explosion, we hear the voices of Marianne and Ferdinand in a quotation from Rimbaud's poem, *L'Eternité*:

> She's found again. . .
> What?
> Eternity
> It is the sea. . . run away. . .
> With the sun. . .

Even this brief analysis of *Pierrot le fou* points to the difference between the two main characters. From beginning to end Marianne has a clearly defined and openly expressed goal – to enjoy herself, to have a good time – and also an awareness of how this can be obtained: by joining up with Fred. When Ferdinand asks a little girl outside the bowling alley, 'Tell me, have you seen a young woman, looking like a Hollywood film star', there is a logic in his question, since Marianne certainly has the approach to life and temperament of a character in a Hollywood movie. But, from the their first moment alone together until they are separated by death, Ferdinand is hesitant, his lack of real identity constantly emphasised by Marianne's refusal to call him anything but Pierrot. It is the resultant passivity which causes Marianne to taunt him with being a coward, a fool who can only keep driving down a straight line, and, ultimately, it drives her away from him. His suspicion of Marianne may partly be based on the conviction that appearances tell us nothing, which is expressed three times in the film: by Marianne in their first car scene, in the film clip from *Le grand escroc*, and by Ferdinand himself in his meditation in the maize field. Whereas Hollywood narrative has been aptly characterised as 'a moralistic form of storytelling that has the basic premise that good motives triumph, and the world is understandable, consistent, manageable, and responsive to goodness and truth' (Dancyger and Rush, 1991: 32), Ferdinand's own vision is very different, as his diary records: 'In the end, the only interesting thing is that path which human beings take. The tragedy is that once one knows what one wants, where to go, what one is, everything still remains a mystery'.

Despite the vivacity of Anna Karina's performance, Godard's approach to the character of Marianne has much of the paranoia displayed by the authors of the classic Hollywood *film noir*, for whom 'women are central to the intrigue of the films. . . . Defined by their sexuality, which is presented as desirable but dangerous to men, the women function as the obstacle to the male quest. The hero's success or not depends on the degree to which he can extricate himself from the woman's manipulations' (Kaplan, 1978: 2–3). But Ferdinand has no male quest and lacks a true goal throughout the film. This is crucial since – as the scriptwriting manuals tell us – 'The main character is heading somewhere. There is something s/he wants. Just as motivation pushes the character forward in a specific direction, the goal pulls the character towards the climax. The goal is an essential part of drama' (Seger, 1987: 117–8). In the absence of a goal, plot and protagonist become separated. *Pierrot le fou* may have a definable three-act structure and each act may have its particular tone and setting, but a fundamental inner pattern of transgression, recognition and redemption is missing from Ferdinand's progression through the narrative. He never confronts his own responsibility for participation in crime and murder, and his recognition of Marianne's betrayal leaves him passive, unable to prevent himself being caught up again in her machinations with Fred. His final killings cannot therefore offer redemption. They remain gratuitous, offering no retrospective meaning to the couple's love. Marianne's death is unmourned and Ferdinand's own a mere bungled travesty.

Shot breakdown

PIERROT LE FOU
(Overall: credits + 327 shots: 106 minutes)

ONE [credits + 122 shots: 42 minutes]

Credits

1 *Ferdinand's Apartment* (1–10)	10 shots
Marianne arrives to babysit	
2 *The Party* (11–20)	10 shots
Ferdinand meets Sam Fuller and leaves the party early	
3 *The Car* (21–6)	6 shots
Ferdinand picks up Marianne from the flat and takes her home	
4 *Marianne's Flat* (27–37)	11 shots
Marianne's song	
5 *The Escape* (38–56)	19 shots
The couple escape from Frank at the flat, revealed as the scene of a murder	
6 *The Garage* (57–65)	9 shots
The couple steal petrol for the car	
7 *The Car* (66–71)	6 shots
They stop and kiss during their drive through the night	

 8 *The Cafe* (72–88)   17 shots
   They try to make money by telling stories
 9 *The Fake Crash* (89–93)   5 shots
   They burn the car,but without salvaging
   the stolen money
10 *The Garage* (94–104)   11 shots
   They steal a Ford Galaxie
11 *The Car* (105–14)   10 shots
   The couple address each other and the
   spectators
12 *The Beach* (115–22)   8 shots
   They discuss the moon and make love

TWO [88 shots: 34 minutes]
13 *By the Sea* (123–33)   11 shots
   Ferdinand begins his diary
14 *The Woods and the Cottage* (134–9)   6 shots
   The couple quarrel
15 *The Beach* (140–3)   4 shots
   Marianne is bored
16 *The Cottage* (144–52)   9 shots
   A fresh argument
17 *The Jetty* (153–74)   22 shots
   They entertain some American tourists
   and Marianne proclaims that she wants
   to be alive
18 *The Woods* (175–7)   3 shots
   The couple sing and dance together
19 *The Maize Field* (178)   1 shot
   Ferdinand broods on love and dreams
20 *The River* (179–85)   7 shots
   Marianne's past reappears: the midget
21 *The Apartment* (186–95)   10 shots
   Marianne phones for help
22 *The Apartment* (196–208)   13 shots
   Ferdinand finds the midget dead and
   is caught and tortured
23 *The Train Line* (209)   1 shot
   Ferdinand contemplates suicide

THREE [118 shots + end credit: 30 minutes]
24 *Toulon* (210–34)   25 shots
       Ferdinand alone, goes to the cinema
25 *The Docks* (235–64)   30 shots
       Ferdinand meets up with Marianne again
26 *The Motorboat* (265–71)   7 shots
       They travel out to the island
27 *The Beach* (272–5)   4 shots
       Marianne reunited with her 'brother', Fred
28 *The Raid* (276–98)   23 shots
       The robbery occurs with a mass of double-crossing
29 *The Bowling Alley* (299–305)   7 shots
       Marianne takes the money and abandons Ferdinand
30 *The Jetty* (306–13)   8 shots
       Ferdinand, in pursuit of Marianne,
       meets Raymond Devos
31 *The Island* (314–20)   7 shots
       Ferdinand kills Fred and Marianne
32 *The House* (321–7)   7 shots
       Ferdinand kills himself with dynamite
       End Title

Bibliography

Anderson, Joseph L., and Donald Richie (1959), *The Japanese Film: Art and Industry*, Rutland and Tokyo: Charles E. Tuttle.

Andrew, Dudley (1984), *Concepts in Film Theory*, Oxford and New York: Oxford University Press.

Antonioni, Michelangelo (1963), *Screenplays*, New York: Orion Press.

Antonioni, Michelangelo (1969), *L'avventura*, New York: Grove Press.

Antonioni, Michelangelo (1989), *L'avventura*, New Brunswick and London: Rutgers University Press.

Aristotle, *On the Art of Poetry*, in T. S. Dorsch (ed.) (1965), *Classical Literary Criticism*, Harmondsworth: Penguin Books.

Armes, Roy (1971), *Patterns of Realism: A Study of Italian Neo-Realist Cinema*, South Brunswick: A. S. Barnes and London: Tantivy Press.

Armes, Roy (1981), *The Films of Alain Robbe-Grillet*, Amsterdam: John Benjamins.

Arnheim, Rudolf (1969, new edition), *Film as Art*, London: Faber & Faber.

Aston, Elaine, and George Savona (1991), *Theatre as Sign-System: A Semiotics of Text and Performance*, London: Routledge.

Auerbach, Erich (1957, second edition), *Mimesis: The Representation of Reality in Western Literature*, New York: Doubleday.

Aumont, Jacques, and Michel Marie (1989), *L'analyse des films*, Paris: Nathan.

Baker, George Pierce (1976 [1919]), *Dramatic Technique*, New York: Da Capo.

Barthes, Roland (1977), *Image-Music-Text*, London: Fontana.

Barthes, Roland (1985), *The Grain of the Voice*, London: Jonathan Cape.

Baskaran, S. Theodore (1981), *The Message Bearers: The Nationalist Politics and Entertainment Media in South India, 1880–1945*, Madras: Cre-A.

Bazin, André (volume one: 1967, volume two: 1971), *What is Cinema?*, Berkeley: University of California Press.

Bellour, Raymond, 'The Obvious and the Code', *Screen*, 15, 4, Winter 1974–5, 7–17.

Bellour, Raymond, 'Segmenting/Analysing', *Quarterly Review of Film Studies* 1, 3, August 1976, 331–53.

Bennett, Benjamin (1990), *Theater as Problem: Modern Drama and its Place in Literature*, Ithaca and London: Cornell University Press.

Bennett, S. (1990), *Theatre Audiences: A Theory of Production and Reception*, London and New York: Routledge.

Bettelheim, Bruno (1978), *The Uses of Enchantment: The Meaning and Importance of Fairy Tales*, Harmondsworth: Penguin Books.

Birch, David (1991), *The Language of Drama*, London: Macmillan.

Blacker, Irwin R. (1988), *The Elements of Screenwriting*, New York: Macmillan.

Bordwell, David (1985), *Narration in the Fiction Film*, London: Methuen.

Bordwell, David (1989), *Making Meaning: Inference and Rhetoric in the Interpretation of Cinema*, Cambridge, Mass.: Harvard University Press.

Borges, Jorge Luis (1962), *Ficciones*, London: Weidenfeld and Nicolson.

Booth, Wayne C. (1983, second edition), *The Rhetoric of Fiction*, Chicago and London: University of Chicago Press.

Bradley, A. C. (1961 [1904]), *Shakespeare's Tragedy*, London: Macmillan.

Brady, Ben, and Lance Lee (1988), *The Understructure of Writing for Film and Television*, Austin: University of Texas Press.

Braudy, Leo (1977), *The World in a Frame: What We See in Films*, New York: Anchor Books.

Brecht, Bertolt (1964), *Brecht on Theatre: The Development of an Aesthetic*, London: Methuen.

Bresson, Robert, 'Cannes Press Conference, 14th May 1957', *Cahiers du cinéma*, 75, October 1957, 3–9.

Bresson, Robert (1977), *Notes on Cinematography*, New York: Urizen Books.

Brook, Peter (1972), *The Empty Stage*, Harmondsworth: Penguin Books.

Brook, Peter (1988), *The Shifting Point*, London: Methuen.

Browne, Nick, 'The Spectator-in-the-Text: The Rhetoric of *Stagecoach*, *Film Quarterly* XXIX, 2, Winter 1975–6, 26–38.

Burch, Noël (1979), *To the Distant Observer: Form and Meaning in the Japanese Cinema*, London: Scholar Press.

Campbell, Joseph (1975), *The Hero with a Thousand Faces*, London: Sphere Books.

Carrière, Jean-Claude and Pascal Bonitzer (1990), *Exercice du scénario*, Paris: Femis.

Carroll, Noël (1988a), *Philosophical Problems of Classical Film Theory*, Princeton: Princeton University Press.

Carroll, Noël (1988b), *Mystifying Movies: Fads and Fallacies in Contemporary Film Theory*, New York: Columbia University Press.

Casetti, Francesco (1990), *D'un regard l'autre; le film et son spectateur*, Lyon: Presses Universitaires de Lyon.

Casetti, Francesco, and Federico di Chio (1990), *Analisi del film*, Milan: Bompiani.

Cavell, Stanley (1971), *The World Viewed: Reflections on the Ontology of Film*, New York: The Viking Press.

Chateau, Dominique (1986), *Le cinéma comme langage*, Paris: AISS-IASPA.

Chatman, Seymour (1978), *Story and Discourse: Narrative Structure in Fiction and Film*, Ithaca and London: Cornell University Press.

Chatman, Seymour (1985), *Antonioni, or The Surface of the World*, Berkeley: University of California Press.

Chatman, Seymour (1990), *Coming to Terms: The Rhetoric of Narrative in Fiction and Film*, Ithaca: Cornell University Press.

Collet, Jean, Michel Marie, Daniel Percheron, Jean-Paul Simon, and Marc Vernet (1977), *Lectures du film*, Paris: Editions Albatros.

Copans, Jean, 'Contrepoint: *Ceddo*, entre l'Histoire et les mythes' in Daniel Serceau (ed.), *Sembène Ousmane*, Paris: CinémAction, 34, 1985.

Cucca, Antoine (1988), *L'écriture du scénario*, Paris: Editions Dujarric.

Dancyger, Ken and Jeff Rush (1991), *Alternative Scriptwriting: Writing Beyond the Rules*, Boston and London: Focal Press.

Dmytryk, Edward (1985), *On Screen Writing*, Boston and London: Focal Press.

Dorsch, T.S. (ed.) (1965), *Classical Literary Criticism*, Harmondsworth: Penguin Books.

Douin, Jean-Luc (1989), *Jean-Luc Godard*, Paris: Editions Rivages.

Durgnat, Raymond (1974), *The Strange Case of Alfred Hitchcock*, London: Faber & Faber.

Dyer, Richard (1979), *Stars*, London: British Film Institute.

Dyer, Richard (1987), *Heavenly Bodies: Film Stars and Society*, London: British Film Institute and Macmillan.

Eagleton, Terry (1976), *Criticism and Ideology*, London: NLB.

Eco, Umberto (1981), *The Role of the Reader*, London: Hutchinson.

Eco, Umberto (1985), *Reflections on 'The Name of the Rose'*, London: Secker & Warburg.

Eco, Umberto (1989), *The Open Work*, London: Hutchinson.

Egri, Lajos (1960, revised edition), *The Art of Dramatic Writing*, New York: Simon & Schuster.

Eisenstein, Sergei M. (1984), *On the Composition of the Short Fiction Scenario*, Calcutta: Seagull Books.

Elam, Keir (1980), *The Semiotics of Theatre and Drama*, London and New York: Routledge.

Ellis, John (1982), *Visible Fictions*, London: Routledge, Chapman & Hall.

Esslin, Martin (1968, revised edition), *The Theatre of the Absurd*, Harmondsworth: Penguin.

Esslin, Martin (1976), *An Anatomy of Drama*, London: Temple Smith.

Esslin, Martin (1983), *Mediations: Essays on Brecht, Beckett, and the Media*, London: Sphere Books.

Esslin, Martin (1987), *The Field of Drama*, London and New York: Methuen.

Etherton, Michael (1982), *The Development of African Drama*, London: Hutchinson.

Faulstich, Werner, and Ingeborg Faulstich (1977), *Modelle der Filmanalyse*, Munich: Wilhelm Fink Verlag.

Faulstich, Werner, and Helmut Korte (ed.) (volume two (1925–44), 1991: volume three (1945–60), 1990: volume four (1961–76), 1992), *Fischer Filmgeschichte*, Frankfurt am Main: Fischer Taschenbuch Verlag.

Feldmann, Susan (ed.) (1963), *African Myths and Folktales*, New York: Dell.

Fergusson, Francis (1968), *The Idea of a Theatre*, Princeton: Princeton University Press.

Field, Syd (1982, expanded edition), *Screenplay: The Foundations of Screenwriting*, New York: Dell.

Field, Syd (1984), *The Screenwriter's Workbook*, New York: Dell.

Finnegan, Ruth (1976, second edition), *Oral Literature in Africa*, Nairobi: Oxford University Press.

Finnegan, Ruth (1977), *Oral Poetry: Its Nature, Significance and Social Context*, Cambridge: Cambridge University Press.

Fleishman, Avrom (1992), *Narrated Films: Storytelling Situations in Cinema History*, Baltimore and London: The Johns Hopkins University Press.

Forster, E. M. (1962), *Aspects of the Novel*, Harmondsworth: Penguin.

Gardies, André (1989), *Cinéma d'Afrique noire francophone*, Paris: L'Harmattan.

Gakwandi, Shatto Arthur (1977), *The Novel and Contemporary Experience in Africa*, London: Heinemann.

Gaudreault, André, *Du littéraire au filmique*, Paris: Méridiens Klinksieck.

Gaudreault, André, and François Jost (1990), *Le récit cinématographique*, Paris: Nathan.

Giddings, Robert, Keith Selby and Chris Wensley (1990), *Screening the Novel: The Theory and Practice of Literary Dramatisation*, London: Macmillan.

Gilman, Richard (1987, new edition), *The Making of Modern Drama*, New York: Da Capo Press.

Girard, Gilles, Réal Ouellet and Claude Rigault (1978), *L'univers du théâtre*, Paris: Presses Universitaires de Paris.

Godard, Jean-Luc (1969), *Pierrot le fou*, London: Lorrimer Publishing.

Godard, Jean-Luc, *Spécial Godard* (*Les carabiniers, Pierrot le fou et films 'invisibles'*), Paris: L'Avant-Scène du Cinéma, 171–2, July/September 1976.

Goldman, William (1984), *Adventures in the Screen Trade*, New York: Warner Books.

Gorbman, Claudia (1987), *Unheard Melodies: Narrative Film Music*, London: British Film Institute and Bloomington: Indiana University Press.

Graham-White, Anthony (1974), *The Drama of Black Africa*, New York and Hollywood: Samuel French.

Hanlon, Lindley (1986), *Fragments: Bresson's Film Style*, Rutherford: Associated University Presses.

Hauge, Michael (1989), *Writing Screenplays That Sell*, London: Elm Tree Books.

Hawks, Howard, *Le grand sommeil*, Paris: L'Avant-Scène du Cinéma, 329–30, June 1984.

Heath, Stephen, 'Film and System: Terms of Analysis', *Screen* **16**, 1, Spring 1975, 7–77, and 2, Summer 1975, 91–113.

Heath, Stephen, 'Narrative Space, *Screen* **17**, 3, Autumn 1976, 68–112.

Heath, Stephen (1982), *Questions of Cinema*, London: Macmillan.

Hornby, R. (1977), *Script into Performance: A Structuralist View of Play Production*, Austin and London: University of Texas Press.

Ionesco, Eugène (1962), *Notes et contre-notes*, Paris, Gallimard.

Izod, John (1984), *Reading the Screen*, Harlow and Beirut: Longman and York Press.

Jarvie, Ian (1987), *Philosophy of the Film*, New York and London: Routledge, Chapmen & Hall.

Jeyifo, Biodun (1985), *The Truthful Lie: Essays in a Sociology of African Drama*, London: New Beacon Books.

Jolayemi, Solanke (1982), 'Traditional Society and Political Institutions', in Richard Olaniyan (ed.), *African History and Culture*, Lagos: Longman.

Kael, Pauline (1971), *The Citizen Kane Book*, London: Secker and Warburg.

Kaplan, E. Ann (ed.) (1978), *Women in Film Noir*, London: British Film Institute.

Kermode, Frank (1967), *The Sense of an Ending: Studies in the Theory of*

Fiction, New York: Oxford University Press.

Knight, Everett (1969), *A Theory of the Classical Novel*, London: Routledge, Chapman & Hall.

Kozloff, Sarah (1988), *Invisible Storytellers: Voice-Over Narration in American Fiction Film*, Berkeley and London: University of California Press.

Kuhn, Annette (1985), *The Power of the Image*, London: Routledge, Chapman & Hall.

Kundera, Milan (1988), *The Art of the Novel*, London: Faber & Faber.

Kurosawa, Akira (1969), *Rashomon*, New York: Grove Press.

Laffay, Albert (1964), *Logique du cinéma: Création et spectacle*, Paris: Masson et cie.

Lehman, Ernest (1972), *North by Northwest*, New York: The Viking Press.

Licart, Albert (n.d.), *Théâtre et cinéma: psychologie du spectateur*, Brussels: Editions de la Revue Nationale.

Lindgren, Ernest (1963, second edition), *The Art of the Film*, London: George Allen & Unwin.

Lotman, Jurij (1976), *Semiotics of Cinema*, Ann Arbor: University of Michigan Press.

Lubbock, Percy (1957), *The Craft of Fiction*, New York: Viking Press.

MacCabe, Colin, 'Realism and the Cinema: Notes on Some Brechtian Theses', *Screen* 15, 2, 1974, 7–27.

MacCabe, Colin, 'Principles of Realism and Pleasure', *Screen* 17, 3, 1976, 7–27.

Maclean, Marie (1988), *Narrative qs Performance: The Baudelairean Experiment*, London: Routledge.

Maillot, Pierre (1989), *L'écriture cinématographique*, Paris: Méridiens Klincksieck.

Malkmus, Lisbeth, and Roy Armes (1991), *Arab and African Filmmaking*, London: Zed Books.

Mamet, David (1992), *On Directing Film*, London: Faber & Faber.

Marion, Frances (1937), *How to Write and Sell Film Stories*, New York: Covici and Friede.

Martin, Wallace (1968), *Recent Theories of Narrative*, Ithaca and London: Cornell University Press.

Mast, Gerald (1982), *Howard Hawks, Storyteller*, New York: Oxford University Press.

McBride, Joseph (1972), *Focus on Howard Hawks*, Englewood Cliffs, N.J.: Prentice-Hall.

Metz, Christian (1974a), *Film Language: A Semiotics of the Cinema*, New York: Oxford University Press.

Metz, Christian (1974b), *Language and Cinema*, The Hague and Paris: Mouton.

Metz, Christian (1982), *The Imaginary Signifier*, Bloomington: Indiana University Press.

Miller, William (1988), *Screenwriting for Narrative Film and Television*, London: Columbus Books.

Milne, Tom (ed.) (1972), *Godard on Godard*, London: Secker & Warburg.

Monaco, James (1977), *How to Read a Film*, New York: Oxford University Press.

Morgan, M. (1987), *Drama: Plays, Theatre and Performance*, Harlow

Beirut: Longman and York Press.

Morrissette, Bruce (1985), *Novel and Film: Essays in Two Genres*, Chicago: Chicago University Press.

Mulvey, Laura (1989), *Visual and Other Pleasures*, London: Macmillan.

Nicoll, Allardyce (1936), *Film and Theatre*, New York: Thomas Y. Crowell.

Nichols, Bill (ed.) (volume one: 1976; volume two: 1985), *Movies and Methods: An Anthology*, Berkeley and London: University of California Press.

Okpewho, Isidore (ed.) (1985), *The Heritage of African Poetry*, Harlow: Longman.

Olaniyan, Richard (ed.) (1982), *African History and Culture*, Lagos: Longman.

Page, Adrian (ed.) (1991), *The Death of the Playwright?: Modern British Drama and Literary Theory*, London: Macmillan.

Palmer, Jerry (1987), *The Logic of the Absurd: On Film and Television Comedy*, London: British Film Institute.

Pavis, Patrice (1987), *Dictionnaire du théâtre*, Paris: Messidor/Editions Sociales.

Pavis, Patrice (1992), *Theatre at the Crossroads of Culture*, London: Routledge.

Perkins, V. F.(1972), *Film as Film*, Harmondsworth: Penguin Books.

Peter, John (1987), *Vladimir's Carrot: Modern Drama and the Modern Imagination*, London: André Deutsch.

Pfaff, Françoise (1984), *The Cinema of Ousmane Sembene: A Pioneer of African Film*, Westport: Greenwood Press.

Pfister, Manfred (1988), *The Theory and Analysis of Drama*, Cambridge: Cambridge University Press.

Potter, Cherry (1990), *Image, Sound and Story: The Art of Telling in Film*, London: Secker & Warburg.

Prédal, René (1991), *Michelangelo Antonioni, ou la vigilance du désir*, Paris: Editions du Cerf.

Prédal, René, *Robert Bresson: L'aventure intérieure*, Paris: L'avant-scène du cinéma, no. 408–9, January–February 1992.

Prince, Gerald (1973), *A Grammar of Stories*, The Hague: Mouton.

Pronko, Leonard C. (1967), *Theatre East and West: Perspectives Toward a Total Theatre*, Berkeley: University of California Press.

Quigley, Austin E. (1985), *The Modern Stage and Other Worlds*, New York and London: Methuen.

Ranger, Terence, 'The Invention of Tradition in Colonial Africa', in Eric Hobsbawm and Terence Ranger (ed.) (1983), *The Invention of Tradition*, Cambridge: Cambridge Univesity Press.

Ricardou, Jean (1973), *Le nouveau roman*, Paris: Editions du Seuil.

Richie, Donald (1965), *The Films of Akira Kurosawa*, Berkeley: University of California Press.

Richie, Donald (ed.) (1972), *Focus on Rashomon*, Englewood Cliffs: Prentice-Hall.

Rimmon-Kenan, Shlomith (1983), *Narrative Fiction: Contemporary Poetics*, London and New York: Methuen.

Robbe-Grillet, Alain (1962), *Last Year at Marienbad*, London: Calder Publications.

Robbe-Grillet, Alain (1965), *Snapshots and Towards a New Novel*, London:

Marion Boyars.

Robbe-Grillet, Alain, 'Brèves réflexions sur le fait de décrire une scène de cinéma', *La Revue d'Esthétique*, 20, 2–3, April–September 1967, 131–8.

Rohdie, Sam (1990), *Antonioni*, London: British Film Institute.

Root, Wells (1979), *Writing the Script: A Practical Guide for Films and Television*, New York: Henry Holt and Company.

Rosen, Philip (ed.) (1986), *Narrative, Apparatus, Ideology: A Film Theory Reader*, New York: Columbia University Press.

Rothman, William (1988), *The 'I' of the Camera*, Cambridge: Cambridge University Press.

Saussure, Ferdinand de (1974, new edition), *Course in General Linguistics*, London: Fontana.

Schechner, Richard (1988, revised edition), *Performance Theory*, London and New York: Routledge.

Schechner, Richard, and Willa Appel (ed.) (1990), *By Means of Performance: Intercultural Studies of Theatre and Ritual*, Cambridge: Cambridge University Press.

Scholes, Robert (1974), *Structuralism in Literature: An Introduction*, New Haven and London: Yale University Press.

Scholes, Robert (1982), *Semiotics and Interpretation*, New Haven and London: Yale University Press.

Scholes, Robert, and Robert Kellogg (1966), *The Nature of Narrative*, London and New York: Oxford University Press.

Seger, Linda (1987), *Making a Good Script Great*, Hollywood: Samuel French.

Sémolué, Jean (1959), *Bresson*, Paris: Editions Universitaires.

Serceau, Daniel (ed.), *Sembène Ousmane*, Paris: CinémAction, 34, 1985.

Solanke, Jolayemi (1982), 'Traditional Social and Political Institutions', in Richard Olaniyan (ed.), *African History and Culture*, Lagos: Longman.

Sontag, Susan (1978), *On Photography*, London: Allen Lane.

Soyinka, Wole (1976), *Myth, Literature and the African World*, Cambridge: Cambridge University Press.

Steiner, George (1975), *After Babel: Aspects of Language and Translation*, Oxford: Oxford University Press.

Styan, J. L. (1975), *Drama, Stage and Audience*, Cambridge: Cambridge University Press.

Szondi, Peter (1987), *Theory of the Modern Drama*, Cambridge: Polity Press.

Thompson, Kristin (1988), *Breaking the Glass Armor: Neoformalist Film Analysis*, Princeton: Princeton University Press.

Todorov, Tzvetan (1969), *Grammaire du Décaméron*, The Hague: Mouton.

Todorov, Tzvetan (1977), *The Poetics of Prose*, Oxford: Basil Blackwell.

Toliver, Harold (1974), *Animate Illusions: Explorations of Narrative Structure*, Lincoln: University of Nebraska Press.

Törnqvist, Egil (1991), *Transposing Drama*, London: Macmillan.

Torok, Jean Paul (1988), *Le scénario: histoire, théorie, pratique*, Paris: Editions Henri Veyrier.

Truffaut, François, *Hitchcock*, London: Secker & Warburg.

Turim, Maureen (1989), *Flashbacks in Film: Memory and History*, New York and London: Routledge.

Ubersfeld, Anne (1982, second edition), *Lire le théâtre*, Paris: Editions Sociales.

Vanoye, Francis (1989), *Récit écrit - récit filmique*, Paris: Editions Nathan.

Vanoye, Francis (1991), *Scénarios modèles, modèles de scénarios*, Paris: Editions Nathan.

Waugh, Patricia (1984), *Metafiction: The Theory and Practice of Self-Conscious Fiction*, London and New York: Methuen.

Williams, Raymond (1991, new edition), *Drama in Performance*, Milton Keynes and Philadelphia: Open University Press.

Willis, E. E., and C. D'Arienzo (1981), *Writing Scripts for Television, Radio, and Film*, New York: Holt, Rinehart & Winston.

Wilson, George M. (1986), *Narration in Light: Studies in Cinematic Point of View*, Baltimore and London: Johns Hopkins University Press.

Winston, Douglas Garrett (1973), *The Screenplay as Literature*, Rutherford: Fairleigh Dickinson University Press and London: Tantivy Press.

Wood, Robin (1968), *Howard Hawks*, London: Secker & Warburg.

Wood, Robin (1984), 'Rashomon', in Christopher Lyon (ed.), *The International Dictionary of Films and Filmmakers, Volume 1: Films*, Chicago: St James Press.

Yeger, Sheila (1990), *The Sound of One Hand Clapping: A Guide to Writing for the Theatre*, Oxford: Amber Lane Press.

Index of names and film titles

Film titles beginning with definite or indefinite articles are indexed under the first significant word